To Adrien,
A gift from Ryan Tanaka
Courage is a choice!

Rusty Komori

superior

CREATING A SUPERIOR CULTURE OF EXCELLENCE

RUSTY KOMORI

MADE FOR
SUCCESS

Made for Success Publishing
P.O. Box 1775 Issaquah, WA 98027
www.MadeForSuccess.com

Distributed by Made for Success Publishing

First Printing

Library of Congress Cataloging-in-Publication data

Rusty Komori
    Creating a Superior Culture of Excellence

        p. cm.

LCCN: 2024933019
ISBN: 978-1-64146-838-1 *(Special Hardcover Edition)*
ISBN: 978-1-64146-839-8 *(eBook)*
ISBN: 978-1-64146-840-4 *(Audiobook)*

Printed in the United States of America

For further information contact Made for Success Publishing
+1(425) 526-6480 or email service@madeforsuccess.net

TABLE OF CONTENTS

INTRODUCTION

I FEEL FORTUNATE to have had a perfect streak when I coached 22 varsity tennis teams, leading them to win 22 consecutive State Championships. During this process, I developed a repeatable system for superior performance. *Superior* is a playbook with a proven system for you and your team to go *beyond good to great* and *become superior leaders*. It's a guideline with powerful concepts to help you attain phenomenal results in business, sports, and life. Let's take a quick preview of the five sections in this book.

First, having the right mindset is the most critical step in setting you on the correct path toward accomplishing your goals. It gives you the opportunity to reach anything and everything you focus on in life. You'll discover how to fully Master Your Mindset to put yourself on a trajectory to achieve extraordinary results.

Second, leadership can seem complicated and oftentimes complex. A clear and simple method to manage the complexity is to identify the 3 C's of Leadership. When you make better choices, have clear and effective communication, and create a superior culture of excellence, you will make a huge positive impact. You will be a leader that others will want to follow. In fact, they will feel compelled to follow you because they know you have empathy for them and you care deeply about their well-being. In addition, you will inspire and build other superior leaders to continue your legacy.

Third, we will explore the 4 P's for Achieving Success as a framework. The 4 P's will enable you to focus clearly on your objectives and accomplish your goals. When you take care of your people, define a clear purpose, determine the correct process, and exhibit consistent performance, you will continually be in a position to succeed.

Fourth, maximizing the 6 Keys for Peak Performance will always put you in a position to win by giving you and your team the ability to constantly perform at an elite level. All six of these keys are absolutely necessary to possess in order to perform optimally. When you perform to your potential in these six categories, consistent peak performance happens, which greatly increases the probability of success.

Fifth, mastering the 8 Keys for Sustaining Success will allow you to have continued accomplishments. It's definitely a challenge to make it to the top of the mountain and even more to stay there while everyone else is striving to be where you are. It's difficult to win a championship and be number one. And it's fulfilling to orchestrate a championship streak, especially by winning the right way. These eight keys will also further define you as a leader, as a person, and as a legacy.

Finally, *I want to inspire you to be superior.* I want to challenge you to be superior as a parent, a son or daughter, a coach or player, a leader or a team member. It's a mindset. It's discipline. It's superior thinking that leads to superior actions, which leads to superior results. It's your character. It's your identity. It's winning with humility and losing with grace. It's words and actions of honor, integrity, and respect. It's a lifestyle that develops your ultimate potential in everything you do in life. It's not a switch that you turn on and off. It's a switch that's on all the time. This is when you surpass being great and enter into the highest realm of superior excellence. This is when you can turn your success into long-lasting significance.

Be Superior!

MASTER YOUR MINDSET

section 1

MANY PEOPLE BELIEVE it's hard to coach adults, it's harder to coach college students, and it's even more difficult to coach teenagers. It's also difficult to win one championship. Winning a repeat or a three-peat is extra hard. I was the head coach of the Punahou School Boys' Varsity Tennis Team for twenty-two years, and we were fortunate to win twenty-two consecutive State Championships. The media shared with me that it's the longest state championship streak in all sports in the United States. Yes, a perfect twenty-two out of twenty-two.

I've learned an important lesson from this experience: There's a tremendous difference between a culture of excellence versus building your *superior* culture of excellence, and there's a gigantic difference between paying attention to details versus *superior* disciplined details. Before striving to build your superior culture of excellence, you must first begin with mindset. Having the right mindset is essential for achieving success in any area of life. Simply, your mindset is *the collection of thoughts and beliefs that shape your behavior, reactions, and responses to different situations.* A positive mindset allows you to approach challenges with optimism and resilience, seeing them as opportunities for growth rather than insurmountable obstacles. It will help you stay focused and motivated even when you experience setbacks and failures. The right mindset plays a crucial role in determining the level of success you can achieve in your personal and professional life and will help you develop the skills and habits necessary to achieve your goals and reach your full potential.

Conversely, a negative mindset can be a major obstacle, leading to self-doubt, fear, and a lack of confidence. It can also leave you feeling hopeless, demotivated, and unable to see the good in any situation. People with this negative mindset may often shy away from challenges, give up easily when things get tough, and believe that their abilities are predetermined and unchangeable. It also leads to stress and anxiety, which results in self-sabotage because they're focusing on their shortcomings and thereby missing out on opportunities.

I've seen research about how having a positive mindset directly impacts your overall well-being. These studies have shown that having the right mindset can reduce stress, improve mental fitness, and increase life satisfaction. By cultivating a mindset that focuses on gratitude, optimism, and self-belief, you will cope with challenges more effectively and build stronger relationships, which will lead to a more fulfilling journey through life. What do you think is the mindset of champions?

Chapter 1

VICTIM VS. VICTOR MINDSET

"If you can build a muscle,
you can build a mindset."

—Jay Shetty

A VICTIM MINDSET is characterized by feelings of helplessness, hopelessness, and powerlessness. It's a belief that outside forces are responsible for one's problems and that there is little that can be done to change the situation. People with a victim mindset tend to focus on what is wrong, dwell on past mistakes or failures, and see themselves as helpless victims of circumstances beyond their control. They may also blame others for their problems and feel sorry for themselves, which often leads to a sense of feeling stuck and unable to move forward from their situation.

In contrast, a victor mindset is characterized by feelings of empowerment and resilience. Victors take responsibility for their actions and outcomes, and they are committed to finding solutions and taking proactive steps to overcome all challenges. People with a victor mindset view setbacks and failures as opportunities for growth and learning, and they always exhibit a positive attitude, even in the face of adversity. They also have the ability to be laser-focused on one positive among twenty negatives.

All of us experience adversity and challenges in our lives, and some people experience deeper levels than others. Hitting rock bottom in your life may or may not happen to you, but if it did, how would you deal with it? What if the unimaginable occurred? Could you rise up and keep a positive perspective? What if you had not one but two major accidents that changed your life forever? You might know someone who lived through something inconceivable, and you observed how they responded, either in a good way or a bad one.

W Mitchell is someone who truly inspires me, and I know he will inspire you as well. W was a good-looking young man, and on July 19, 1971, something happened that changed his life forever. He was riding his newly purchased motorcycle at sixty-five miles per hour when he was distracted for a split second and crashed into a laundry truck that had turned in front of him. He suffered only minor injuries, but then the motorcycle's gas cap popped off, and W Mitchell was turned into a human fireball. Two-thirds of his skin burned off. He lost most of his fingers and thumbs because they were burned to the knuckles, and his face was completely disfigured.

I would have to say that most people in his condition would have given up on life, but not W Mitchell. He was determined to focus on the good in his life and made a decision to start his own business. Within three years, he became a millionaire. He also learned how to fly airplanes and completed his first solo aircraft flight. Then, one clear, chilly Colorado morning on November 11, 1975, he took three passengers on a flight, not realizing there was a thin layer of ice on the wings. The plane crashed soon after takeoff, and only three people walked away. He wasn't one of them. He had injured his spinal cord, leaving him paralyzed from the waist down with zero hope for recovery. Because he no longer needed his toes, the doctors cut them off and sewed them onto his hands. In addition, his wife left him, commenting that she couldn't be with a "fried cripple." After all of this, W Mitchell still refused to give up and was subsequently elected mayor of Crested Butte, Colorado. Soon after, he found the woman of his dreams whom he married.

Because of his experiences, W Mitchell has been a compelling motivational speaker for many years, inspiring hope in countless others who have their own challenges and difficulties to overcome in life. He famously said, "Before I was paralyzed, there were ten thousand things I could do. Now there are nine thousand. I can either dwell on the one thousand I've lost or focus on the nine thousand I have left." He also said, "It's not what happens to you; it's what you do about it." His story always reminds me to see the light in the darkest of situations. How many times can you get knocked down and keep choosing to get up? Life is definitely not easy and often not fair, but life is life, and each of us has the choice to take control of our lives and live.

When bad things happen, most people blame the situation for happening and feel sorry for themselves. But if you view life from that perspective, you can't truly welcome adversities and life's challenges correctly. Life doesn't happen *to* you. Life happens *for* you. W Mitchell had two major adversities in his life, and because of those "unfortunate" accidents, he found his true purpose in life by inspiring millions of people to bounce back from every tragic situation or setback they might experience. Some people have the victim mindset and think, "It's not fair. I can never win. Why did this happen to me?" Remember, life happens. It's how we respond that matters. That's the difference between winning and losing in the biggest, most important game of all—life. Are you winning or losing in your game of life?

In order to win in the game of life, you need to change from a *victim* mindset into a *victor* mindset. We can't control things in life that are beyond our control. A devastating hurricane, a flood, or a fire might cause you to lose your house and all of your irreplaceable possessions. You might be involved in a serious car accident, resulting in a long rehabilitation process. You might receive word from your doctor that you have a cancerous tumor. You might be laid off because of financial cutbacks at your company. The normal response from most people in these situations is the victim mindset. But this is when you start to lose in the game of life. You need to flip it into the victor mindset by finding the good in what most would perceive as a bad situation. When you can live your life thinking that life happens for you, this attitude becomes contagious for everyone close to you, and you'll inspire others to be victors in their own lives.

It reminds me of a quote from the great Bruce Lee, who said, "When you find yourself in a room surrounded by your enemies, you should tell yourself, 'I am not locked in here with you; you are locked in here with me.'" This is the kind of mindset you should have if you want to succeed in life. Get rid of that victim mentality.

I also like to look at that quote from a slightly different perspective by changing "your enemies" to "unfortunate situations." Whether you are dealing with unfortunate situations in your life or helping someone deal with theirs, the victor mindset is paramount. We can inspire hope in others if we have built trust with them. If they believe in us, we can believe in them and help them believe in themselves. Belief is extremely powerful, but so is doubt. Choose to be around people with positive energy who consistently lift you up to see the possibilities instead of negative people who bring you down and make you feel hopeless.

When faced with an unfortunate situation, a victor mindset allows individuals to focus on solutions rather than dwelling on the problem itself. It enables them to approach setbacks as temporary obstacles and look for ways to overcome those barriers. There are three ways you can actively change your mindset by consciously reshaping your thoughts, beliefs, and perspectives. One way is to have awareness and self-reflection. Start by becoming aware of your current mindset and identifying any negative or limiting beliefs. Then, reflect on how these beliefs affect your thoughts and actions. A second way is to use positive affirmations. Use positive affirmations to counteract negative self-talk. Then, repeat empowering statements about yourself and your abilities to reinforce a positive mindset. A third way is by surrounding yourself with positivity. Surround yourself with positive people, books, podcasts, and other resources that inspire and motivate you. The environment you expose yourself to will significantly influence your mindset. Inspiring others to see the positives in their lives, feeling valued, and living with dignity is very impactful. By reinforcing the victor mindset, you can make a priceless difference in others because they trust you and know that you have empathy for them.

THE ROBBIE LIM STORY

My players always looked forward to my world-famous quote of the day. After every practice, I'd give the team an inspirational quote to build their mindset. I wanted them to leave practice thinking about motivational and important life lessons beyond the tennis court. I know my quotes inspired Robbie Lim to become a great player, leader, and teammate. In fact, Robbie began using his own inspirational quotes from movies to inspire and motivate his teammates. I loved it, not only because it was entertaining watching him imitate Al Pacino in *Any Given Sunday*, for instance, but also because it was meaningful to his teammates.

Robbie Lim went from being a follower to a leader right before my eyes. Sharing those quotes, having discipline, and fostering the victor mindset, along with a good foundation of character traits he already had to build on, made Robbie one of the best team captains we ever had. One thing you need to know about him: He had average talent in tennis and was an average athlete as well. His younger brother and sister, who both played in Punahou's tennis program, had much more natural talent than he did. But what made Robbie special was his character, mental toughness, and smart play. As a sophomore in 2002, Robbie won the state singles championship in Wailea, Maui. He was seeded fourth in the tournament but still went on to be a young singles champion for all those reasons.

The following year, when he was a junior and our team captain, Robbie created some memorable stories that I shared with my teams for years to come. He went undefeated during our regular season, won the league championship in singles, and was the number-one seed at the state championship tournament held on Oahu. In the quarterfinals, he faced Iolani School's number one player on the stadium court. It was an unusually hot, humid, and windless day, and what's more, the stadium court was sunken, which made it the hottest court in the entire facility. Robbie's opponent was a tall, talented player who was a very tough competitor. Each athlete wanted to beat the other very badly and was willing to endure these extreme conditions.

The match started with both players hitting extremely hard, heavy shots. Both of them were exhibiting exceptional footwork. But then, things began to change for the worse. Robbie had won the first set and his opponent the second. At the start of the third set, they both began suffering from painfully debilitating cramps almost simultaneously. What had looked like a high-level championship contest soon took on the appearance of a ten-and-under match. Robbie and his opponent moaned and groaned with every step they took to get to the ball. When they did hit the ball, it was a soft lob shot traveling no faster than two miles an hour. They were both giving it all they had, and neither player would give up and retire the match. They continued playing in this way, and the match passed the three-hour mark. For those of us on the sidelines, it was almost as painful to watch. Finally, Robbie won the set, limped up to the net to shake hands, and then immediately sought out the trainers. Both players were lying side by side on the trainers' tables, receiving fluids and ice treatments. Soon after, Robbie's parents took him to the hospital for an IV.

That evening, Robbie called. When I asked how he was feeling, he said, "Not so good, Coach. I think I might have to default my semifinal tomorrow." For a skinny kid, Robbie was also very tough, so the possibility of a default showed me just how much pain he was feeling. He didn't think his body could recover in time, even after the IV. But I told him to get a good night's sleep and see how he felt in the morning and to mentally plan to be ready to play his 8 a.m. semifinal. Robbie could have easily slipped into the victim mindset, but he didn't.

When Robbie arrived the next day, things didn't look good. He appeared weak and wasn't his normal, upbeat self. Even walking looked difficult, and I could only imagine how he'd feel playing tennis in this condition. He asked what I thought he should do. I told him that since he was here, he might as well try to play. "If it gets too bad," I said, "you can retire from the match." He agreed and took the court without even warming up.

Robbie's opponent was strong and talented—the number one player for Kahuku High School. From the start, the match wasn't pretty to watch. Robbie could barely move six feet in any direction and had problems hitting more than two or three shots per point. His opponent was serving and returning serves very well and was clearly dictating play. It was as if Robbie had his hands tied behind his back and was taking punches one after another. His opponent won the first set 6–1, and I went on the court to talk with Robbie during the two-minute coaching break. We actually shared a laugh that he was able to win one game. I asked him if he wanted to retire from the match, but he said he wanted to stay out there and show his opponent some respect, even though he was being outplayed and felt extremely weak.

As I started to leave the court, I asked Robbie, "Who's the champ?"

"I'm the champ," he said in a soft whisper.

"Who's the champ?"

"I'm the champ," he said again, sounding a little more convinced this time.

"Yes, you are the champ," I answered, "and champs give everything they've got, with no excuses. You need to stay out here as long as you can. You never know—you might begin to feel better. Now, who's the champ?"

"I'm the champ!"

"All right, champ," I said as I walked off the court. "Go!" I hoped that Robbie might somehow find a way to turn things around, but as they started the second set, he still looked bad. I mean, really bad. Hope faded quickly as the Kahuku player executed shot after shot and point after point while Robbie, though still standing, almost seemed to be losing his pulse. Down 2–5 in the second set, Robbie got up from a water break to switch ends of the court. He was now one game away from losing after winning the state championship the previous year.

Standing by the fence, I yelled, "Who's the champ?"

Robbie walked closer, and all of a sudden said, "I'm the champ!" with a look on his face that I hadn't seen the whole match.

"Who's the champ?" I asked again.

"Coach," he said, "I'm the champ!"

And then—wow! Did he start to come alive! He began bouncing on his feet, moving faster and increasing pace with each shot. After being close to losing his pulse, Robbie was finally showing some real life. But was it too little too late? After holding off three match points, Robbie tied the second set at 5–5, and his opponent began making unforced errors. Now Robbie was looking like his normal self again, and he won the second set, 7–5.

You can only imagine what the spectators were thinking. I walked back onto the court during the ten-minute coaching break that follows split sets. I congratulated him on his comeback and on his will to find a way to win. He hadn't won yet, but

I could see the determined fight in him. He'd been on the ropes with both hands tied behind his back, almost ready for a knockout, but now here he was at even sets and just a couple of minutes away from starting the third.

"Who's the champ?" I asked as we stood facing each other, bouncing on our feet in unison.

"I'm the champ!" he answered with tenacity. We shook hands and hugged, and I walked off the court.

The third and deciding set was sure to be a battle. The spectators became more vocal, applauding the brilliant shots and the effort and will to win by both players. Loud cheers erupted for both players after every point.

Robbie won the third set, 6–0. It was remarkable. It was inspiring to his teammates and everyone who witnessed it. You hear people say never give up. But actually seeing those words in action makes them so much more meaningful. In tennis, time cannot run out. You need to win a certain number of points to win. There is no stalling. There are no time-outs. There are no substitutions. (Although, believe me, I wish we were allowed substitutions; I could have used them many times over the years.) Robbie's performance was truly remarkable. Most players in his situation would have retired from the match after losing that first set. But not Robbie—understanding his place as the defending champion, wanting to honor and respect his opponent by staying on the court even if he was going to lose, speaks volumes about his character. And remember, this was only the semifinal. He had only a one-hour rest break before he played in the state championship final.

During that break, Robbie experienced both intense focus and great excitement about playing in the final match. But his opponent, a Farrington High School player who was seeded number two, was also looking extremely confident. He was a strong, talented lefty who hit heavy topspin shots and moved extremely well. It was definitely shaping up to be an epic contest, especially because the Farrington kid had dominated his semifinal match and had had much more time to relax and recover while Robbie made his dramatic comeback.

This worried me. How would Robbie perform after expending so much physical, mental, and emotional energy? Would he have enough drive and determination to defend and earn a second state singles championship? Would our months of preparation and discipline be the little variable that made a big difference in the final outcome?

As he and his opponent began their five-minute warm-up with each other, spectators crowded into every open space, filling in row after row around the court. Once the match started, both players were looking really good. It actually seemed that each was playing his best tennis of the tournament. That's always a great thing to see, and it doesn't happen as often as we'd like. Robbie and the Farrington player had very similar styles of play: They were aggressive baseliners with consistent serves and return of serves, and they were each trying to attack the other's backhand.

But from the start, Robbie dominated and won the match, 6–0, 6–0. Midway through the contest, a sports writer for *The Honolulu Advertiser* found me and told me she couldn't believe what she was witnessing. She said it was incredible watching Robbie compete and win his second state singles championship. I told her that what was most incredible was that he'd been one game away from losing in the semifinals and then went on to win twenty-three straight games to take the championship. Robbie earned the respect of everyone there that day. He respected his opponents and competed with class, whether he was winning, losing, or tied. It had been an amazing display of character and heart. As his coach, I would have felt proud of Robbie regardless of the outcome. But he reinforced himself as a leader among his peers and gave me yet another memorable story to share with our future teams and players.

ROBBIE LIM

Heart is something that can be very difficult to see and measure. It often manifests itself only in times of extreme stress and adversity. You never know how strong a person really is until his back is against a wall. And it's a beautiful thing to see when it shows itself in players during competition. All great leaders have heart. It was evident that Robbie had heart and a victor mindset.

Chapter 2

TURN OBSTACLES INTO OPPORTUNITIES

"Obstacles are not roadblocks;
they are detours to something greater."

—Robin Sharma

OBSTACLES ARE A PART OF LIFE, and they appear in many forms, such as challenges, setbacks, or limitations. However, these obstacles can be an opportunity for you to learn, grow, and develop new skills. By reframing obstacles as opportunities, you're able to turn adversity into a source of motivation and inspiration. Instead of feeling defeated by a problem, you can focus on finding creative solutions to achieve personal and professional growth. It's a mindset that helps you build the resilience to bounce back from setbacks, overcome challenges, and adapt to change.

Dealing with roadblocks can also lead to new and unexpected paths in life. When you face an obstacle, you need to adjust and pivot to find a different way to succeed. These pivots can lead to new paths in life that you might not have otherwise considered. Airbnb, the popular lodging service, was born out of an obstacle in 2007. The company's founders, Brian Chesky and Joe Gebbia, were struggling to pay the rent for their apartment in the San Francisco area. At the same time, the surrounding hotels became fully booked due to the Industrial Design Conference. Chesky and Gebbia came up with the idea of renting out an air mattress in their living room and turning it into a bed and breakfast for conference attendees. They saw an opportunity to turn their obstacle into a business idea. Since 2008, Airbnb has become one of the most successful start-ups in the world, making a significant impact in the hospitality industry. Airbnb currently has over seven million listings in two hundred twenty countries and is valued at over $100 billion.

Many successful entrepreneurs have faced obstacles such as limited financial resources, lack of experience, or market competition. However, instead of being discouraged by these obstacles, they use them as a chance to innovate and differentiate themselves from their competitors. Uber, the popular ride-sharing service founded by Travis Kalanick and Garrett Camp, was born when they were attending a technology conference in Paris in 2008 and became frustrated finding a taxi. They immediately realized that there was a need for a more efficient and convenient way to get a ride in urban areas. In 2010, Uber was officially launched in San Francisco. It quickly gained popularity, especially because of the simplicity of the Uber app. With a simple tap of a button, a user could order a ride, GPS would pinpoint their location, and the fare would be charged to the credit card listed on the user account. In addition, Uber drivers can earn income by having the freedom and flexibility to choose their own driving hours. Currently, Uber has expanded to over nine hundred metropolitan areas worldwide and diversified its services to include different types of rides, such as UberX, UberPOOL, and UberBLACK.

Another obstacle that commonly happens is in the realm of career development. Sometimes, you might face challenges by being passed over for a promotion, losing a job, or not having the required qualifications for a desired position. Instead of letting these obstacles hold them back, successful people will use them as an opportunity to develop new skills, gain experience in a new industry, or pursue a different career path. Apple co-founder Steve Jobs turned an obstacle into an opportunity when he was fired from Apple in 1985. This was a major setback for him, especially because he helped build Apple into a technology powerhouse. Instead of letting this setback defeat him, he started a new company called NeXT Computer, which focused on developing innovative workstations for the education and business markets. Although NeXT struggled initially, its technology and design caught the attention of Apple, which later acquired the company and brought Jobs back on board as CEO. This gave Jobs the opportunity to return to Apple with a renewed sense of purpose and vision, and he led the company to unprecedented success with products such as the iPod, iPhone, and iPad.

A person who experiences a major health setback may use that experience as an opportunity to adopt a healthier lifestyle and become an advocate for others who are facing similar challenges. Another obstacle Steve Jobs faced was being diagnosed with pancreatic cancer in 2004. Rather than giving up, he used his experience with cancer as a catalyst to innovate in the healthcare industry. Jobs researched and inspired health-related products such as the Apple Watch, which can monitor a user's heart rate and detect irregularities, and the Health app, which tracks a user's physical activity and health data. His drive and determination in the face of adversity inspired countless people around the world and cemented his place in history as one of the greatest innovators of our time.

Turning obstacles into opportunities can also be applied to personal growth. Personal obstacles such as health issues, relationship problems, or financial difficulties can be challenging to overcome. However, by reframing these obstacles as opportunities for personal development, you can emerge stronger and more resilient. Helen Keller lost her sight and her hearing when she was nineteen months old, which led many people to believe that she was incapable of learning or communicating with others. However, with the help of her teacher, Anne Sullivan, Keller learned how to communicate through touch and eventually went on to attend college, becoming the first deaf and blind person to earn a Bachelor of Arts degree in the United States. She also became a prolific author and wrote fourteen books. She was named one of Time magazine's 100 Most Important People of the 20th Century. Despite the immense challenges she faced, Keller refused to accept that her disabilities made her incapable of learning and achieving her goals. She used her experiences and unique perspective to advocate for the rights of people with disabilities, becoming a prominent figure in the women's suffrage movement and fighting for social justice. Her determination and perseverance in the face of adversity transformed her disabilities into opportunities to create lasting change.

Oprah Winfrey is one of the most influential media personalities of our time. Coming from a disadvantaged background, she was born to a single teenage mother on welfare in rural Mississippi. When she was nine to thirteen years old, Winfrey suffered sexual abuse from her cousin, other relatives, and her mother's boyfriend. At fourteen, she ran away from home and moved in with her father in Tennessee. Winfrey overcame years of poverty, abuse, and discrimination throughout her early life. However, she refused to let these circumstances define her future. She focused on education, was hired by a local radio station to do the news part-time, and received a full scholarship to Tennessee State University. If we fast-forward in time, she built a media empire, including her talk show, *The Oprah Winfrey Show*, founded her own production company Harpo Productions, and launched her cable network OWN. She turned her difficult past into a source of strength and empathy by using her platform to connect with millions of people and address important social issues. TIME magazine named her "one of the most influential people," and she became the world's first Black female billionaire. She said, "Challenges are gifts that force us to search for a new center of gravity. Don't fight them. Just find a new way to stand." Winfrey's ability to transform adversity into opportunities for personal growth and to uplift others has made her a role model for countless people around the world.

Michael Bennett

In the realm of life, it is all too effortless to find solace in the familiarity of our habits and selves, even when they fail to align with our true desires. We often find ourselves trapped in the grip of fear, paralyzed by the thought of relinquishing our former selves and undergoing the profound transformation necessary to become something new. However, it is within the realm of obstacles and challenges that we discover the extraordinary power of turning adversity into opportunity. Transition, defined as the process of moving from one state or condition to another, lies at the core of our existence. It is during these transitional periods that we are presented with the remarkable opportunity to redefine ourselves, liberate ourselves from the shackles of our comfort zones, and embrace the vast unknown. However, we must acknowledge that the path ahead is fraught with obstacles.

Reflecting on my personal journey in the year 2020, after retiring from a successful career in the NFL, I found myself yearning for new horizons. Despite being a Super Bowl champion, I hesitated to explore uncharted territories such as tennis. The fear of not excelling and the daunting prospect of starting from scratch in a new sport gripped me tightly. Nevertheless, it was during this transformative journey that I came to understand the true essence of humility and the unwavering courage required to confront the unknown.

As I delved into the study of architecture, a profound realization unfolded before me: the true worth of an object lies not in its entirety but in the harmonious integration of its individual parts. Similarly, obstacles and opportunities are interconnected components of a greater process.

They demand sacrifice, resilience, and an unwavering commitment to attain a state of righteousness.

To truly transform obstacles into opportunities, we must undergo a paradigm shift. Instead of perceiving hurdles as insurmountable walls, we must view them as bridges that lead us toward the realization of our future selves. It is through these challenges that we cultivate wisdom, foster personal growth, and unlock the boundless potential that resides within us. Let us embrace the profound power of turning obstacles into opportunities and embark on a journey of self-discovery and limitless evolution.

Michael Bennett
Super Bowl Champion, 2013 Seattle Seahawks
Pro Bowl selection (2015, 2016, 2017)

Chapter 3

DIFFICULT VS. IMPOSSIBLE

"What is now proved was once only imagined."

—William Blake

WHEN WE FACE A SIGNIFICANT CHALLENGE, it's easy to feel overwhelmed and think it's impossible. But is it really impossible? Or just difficult? The greatest leaders always find a way to succeed regardless of the level of difficulty they're facing. These successful people are willing to push the limits of what may be possible. They know that the impossible is what nobody can do until somebody does it. This is how records get broken. Plus, there are many things in life that have yet to be discovered or invented. I know that you will agree with me when I say that all of us are capable of doing more and achieving more than we think we are capable of.

Let's look at the Wright Brothers and their first flight. For centuries, humans dreamed of flying. But for most of that time, it seemed like an impossible dream. Even as technology advanced in the late 19th century, many people believed that heavier-than-air flight was simply beyond the capabilities of human beings. But two brothers from Ohio, named Orville and Wilbur Wright, believed that it was possible. They spent years studying the principles of flight and designing their own aircraft. They obviously faced numerous setbacks and failures along the way, but they persisted. On December 17, 1903, the Wright Brothers achieved the impossible. They flew their aircraft, the Wright Flyer, for a distance of one hundred twenty feet and a duration of twelve seconds. It was officially the first powered, sustained, and controlled flight in history. Their achievement changed the world, ushering in a new era of transportation and exploration. It was a powerful reminder that even the most impossible-seeming dreams can be achieved with hard work, determination, and persistence.

Temple Grandin is a professor of animal science and a leading advocate for the humane treatment of livestock. But her journey to this position was far from easy. Grandin has autism, which made social interactions and communication difficult for her as a child. Despite her challenges, Grandin was determined to pursue her passion for working with animals. She found that her unique perspective allowed her to see things that others couldn't. For example, she noticed that cattle in slaughterhouses were often frightened and stressed, which made them more difficult to handle and, ultimately, reduced the quality of their meat. Grandin developed a series of innovative designs for livestock facilities that reduced stress and improved animal welfare.

Although her views were initially met with skepticism and resistance from the livestock industry, Grandin persisted, advocating for her ideas and working with industry leaders to implement her designs. For example, she studied the behavior of cattle by observing how they react to ranchers, objects, movement, and light. Grandin then designed curved corrals with the intention of reducing stress, panic, and injury in animals being led to slaughter. Today, her designs are widely used in the livestock industry, improving the lives of millions of animals every year. Grandin's story is a powerful reminder that even when something seems impossible, it is possible to find a way forward with determination and perseverance.

Elon Musk is a visionary entrepreneur and technology innovator who has set his sights on some of the most audacious goals of our time. One of his most ambitious and far-reaching goals is to make humanity a multi-planetary species by establishing a human colony on Mars. Musk sees this as a necessary step for the survival and long-term future of the human race, as well as an opportunity for exploration, discovery, and scientific advancement. His company, SpaceX, has been working on the development of a range of technologies and capabilities needed to make a human mission to Mars possible. These include the Starship spacecraft, a fully reusable rocket system that is designed to carry humans and cargo to Mars and back. SpaceX has also been conducting test flights and other missions to demonstrate the capabilities of its rockets and spacecraft, and to gather data and insights that will help inform the design and operation of future missions. Despite the many difficulties that remain, the possibility of humans going to Mars is becoming increasingly realistic and tangible. Because of Elon Musk, it's possible that we could see the first human missions to Mars within our lifetime.

Can you imagine being a drummer in a rock band and losing one of your arms? Would you be able to overcome this devastating experience and emerge even stronger? Or would you give up because how can a drummer with only one arm continue playing the drums? Rick Allen is the drummer in the world-famous rock band Def Leppard (which happens to be my favorite band!). On New Year's Eve in 1984, one of the worst things that you could ever imagine happening to a band happened to Def Leppard.

Rick Allen and his girlfriend at the time were in his Corvette driving on a winding country road near Sheffield, England. Allen said, "This Alfa Romeo came round a corner and went blazing past. As I continued on, I realized this Alfa had slowed, so I would catch up. For three or four miles, every time I tried to pass, he would speed up. This kept going on, and finally, I kind of lost my cool and put my foot down. Suddenly, this long corner revealed itself, and it was too late. I lost control, and as the car rolled, the seat belt came undone and took my left arm. The arm stayed in the car, and I disappeared through the sunroof, banging my head really badly going out, and ended up probably one hundred fifty yards away in a field, literally just lying there. What saved my life was that I tensed up so I didn't bleed out. I wasn't unconscious. There was an off-duty cop and a nurse who helped fix me up. About forty-five minutes later, an ambulance arrived and took me to the hospital. It wasn't until then that I actually bled out when they put me under anesthetic."

Allen was in a coma for two weeks, and during that time, the doctors reattached the arm. Allen said, "Everything seemed to be going okay until I ended up getting a really bad infection. That's when they decided to take the arm completely, which obviously I didn't know about because I was in a coma. It wasn't until a couple of weeks after the accident that I realized what had happened. I didn't want to do this anymore. I felt defeated, self-conscious, and wanted to just disappear. But my family, friends, and hundreds of thousands of letters from all over the planet put me in a different head-space. I discovered the power of the human spirit, and that was a springboard into where I am now."

Allen made rapid progress in his physical rehabilitation. When he made his first attempt at standing up, he was unbalanced and fell to the floor. A week later, he'd learned how to walk again by shifting his weight to steady himself. He also learned basic skills of how to eat and tie his shoes with one hand. When the band's producer, Mutt Lange, visited Allen in the hospital, they talked at length about the accident, his projected recovery, and how he could rebuild his life. They also talked about playing drums. Allen demonstrated how he could play complex rhythms with his feet, and Lange explained how modern technology and an electronic drum kit could help him. This would allow him to replicate patterns using his right hand and left foot that he would previously have played with two hands. Shortly after, they developed four electronic pedals for his left foot to play the pieces he used to play with his left arm. At no point in time did the band members even consider moving on without Allen. I love this so much! Lead singer Joe Elliott simply said, "Rick was in the band until he said he wasn't."

Bassist Rick Savage said, "When he told us how he could play the drums again, we thought even if he can't do it completely on his own, if it means we have another drummer as well as Rick, at least he's still in the band and still with us."

I loved Def Leppard even more because of how the bandmates rallied around and supported Rick Allen. Their connection and respect for each other beyond the band exemplify why they are one of the most successful rock bands in history. Allen reflected back, saying, "It was obviously an awful time losing my arm, especially being a drummer. But honestly, it's really become a blessing. It's something that I've been able to share with others, especially some of our wounded warriors, and just being able to share my life experience and inspire others. What a great deal. You know, it's really become something very special and very healing to myself as well. Not only to the men and women that I work with, but to me."

Another one of the most inspiring stories of someone achieving the impossible is the story of Arunima Sinha, a former national-level volleyball player from India. In 2011, she was traveling on a train and was attacked by robbers who attempted to snatch her gold chain. When she resisted and fought back, the robbers grabbed all four limbs and threw her out of the moving train. As she was lying on the tracks, another train coming from the opposite direction ran over her left leg. While she was screaming in pain, rodents came to feast on her bleeding, oozing wounds until she finally passed out. She didn't think she would survive that night, and soon after, the doctors amputated her leg below the knee. She said, "Imagine a normal girl who did all her work using her hands and legs, and suddenly, one day, she loses one of her body parts. It is indeed very difficult to live the life of an amputee, but if you start looking through a different perspective, it all changes. Lying on the hospital bed, I decided to take the hardest leap in life and even thought to myself that there must be some reason why the Almighty has kept me alive even after such a traumatic incident, and it surely means that history is in the making."

After the incident, Arunima was devastated but determined to turn tragedy into triumph. She set her sights on climbing Mount Everest, the highest peak in the world, despite having no prior mountaineering experience. This was an incredibly challenging feat even for those with all their limbs, let alone for someone with a prosthetic leg, but she was determined to prove that disability could not hold her back. She said, "I felt bad, but I also knew that it was a part of life because when you start thinking big, no one really supports you or your decision, but once you achieve it, everything falls into place and people begin to appreciate you. When you start directing your thoughts in one direction and convince yourself that there is no other way out, that is when you will succeed."

Arunima trained rigorously for two years, and on May 21, 2013, she became the first female amputee to Climb Mount Everest. Arunima has since climbed the highest peaks on all seven continents, becoming a symbol of hope and inspiration for people around the world. She said, "Every mountain has its own set of challenges, but I believe the biggest challenge is your mental stability. There have been times in my journey toward Everest that my prosthetic leg came out, or my ankle twisted, heel came on toe, shortage of oxygen. On my journey to Mount Vinson, nobody showed confidence in me even though I had climbed so many mountains before. It's sad sometimes to see that people don't really trust your mental strength and start judging you with your physical capabilities."

Her achievements have not only inspired other amputees to pursue their dreams but have also challenged societal norms and beliefs about what is possible. Arunima said, "By conquering all seven summits, I will prove that physical disability can never be a hindrance in achieving your life's goal if you have mental strength, strong willpower, and firm determination."

Mastering your mindset is crucial for achieving success and fulfillment in life. A positive mindset puts you on the path to accomplishing anything you set your mind to because the way you think directly impacts your behavior, decision-making, and overall well-being. The right mindset influences your attitude, which impacts your experiences and outcomes in life. By taking it to the highest level of mastery, you will not only able to achieve success, but you'll be able to sustain success, lead a purposeful life, and be in a position to achieve greatness.

Chapter 4

MENTAL FITNESS

"Act as if it was, and it will be."

—Lailah Gifty Akita

MANY PEOPLE THAT YOU KNOW might be suffering in silence and bleeding in places you can't see. Mental fitness can be defined as *a state of well-being and optimal functioning of the mind.* It encompasses various aspects, including emotional resilience, cognitive abilities, and psychological well-being. Just as physical fitness is crucial for maintaining a healthy body, mental fitness is essential for nurturing a healthy mind. It involves developing and practicing skills to enhance mental strength by maintaining a positive mindset, managing stress effectively, and building emotional intelligence. Mental fitness encompasses self-awareness, self-care, and the ability to adapt to challenges and setbacks. It also includes engaging in activities that promote mental stimulation and growth, such as learning new skills and practicing mindfulness or meditation. Mental fitness needs to be a lifelong journey of self-discovery and self-improvement as you strive to cultivate a healthy and resilient mind capable of navigating life's ups and downs.

Let's delve into the vital role of mental fitness in addressing and combating the challenges posed by depression and suicide. Depression is a complex mental health condition that affects millions of people worldwide. It manifests as persistent sadness, lack of interest or pleasure, feelings of worthlessness, and a loss of energy or motivation. The burden of depression can be overwhelming, often leading individuals to contemplate suicide as a means of escape from their pain. However, by recognizing the significance of mental fitness in tackling these issues head-on, we can pave the way for a brighter future. When it comes to depression and suicide, mental fitness plays a critical role in providing individuals with the necessary tools to cope, recover, and prevent further distress.

Resilience is *the ability to bounce back from adversity and adapt to challenging circumstances.* By fostering mental fitness, individuals can enhance their resilience, enabling them to withstand the trials and tribulations associated with depression. Cultivating positive coping mechanisms, such as maintaining healthy relationships, engaging in regular exercise, and practicing mindfulness, helps develop emotional strength and provides a buffer against the negative effects of depression.

Depression often hijacks emotional well-being, leaving individuals feeling trapped in a cycle of negative thoughts and emotions. By prioritizing mental fitness, individuals can learn to regulate their emotions effectively. This involves recognizing and acknowledging their feelings, seeking support from trusted individuals, and engaging in activities that promote joy and fulfillment. By developing emotional intelligence and strengthening emotional well-being, individuals can navigate their way out of the depths of depression. Depression can also erode a person's sense of self-worth and purpose, making it challenging to find the motivation to seek help. However, mental fitness empowers individuals to cultivate psychological strength and challenge these negative thoughts and beliefs. By engaging in cognitive-behavioral techniques such as reframing negative self-talk and practicing self-compassion, individuals can develop a more positive and resilient mindset. Psychological strength serves as a powerful tool in combating the feelings of hopelessness that often accompany depression.

Mental fitness not only benefits individuals directly but also fosters a supportive environment for those struggling with depression and suicidal thoughts. By promoting mental well-being and providing resources for mental health education and awareness, communities can break the stigma surrounding these issues. Support networks, both online and offline, can be established to encourage open conversations, share experiences, and provide assistance to those in need. Creating an environment that prioritizes mental fitness paves the way for improved mental health outcomes for everyone. Because depression and suicide pose significant challenges, it requires a multi-faceted approach for effective prevention and recovery. Through building resilience, nurturing emotional well-being, developing psychological strength, and creating supportive environments, mental fitness will be a powerful shield against the darkness of depression, ultimately bringing hope and healing to everyone.

Having the right perspective in looking forward to challenges and welcoming adversity is absolutely necessary. It's a mindset. How much adversity do you think championship teams can tolerate? How much can you tolerate? These teams always look forward to adversity and rise to all challenges. If you're doing a long-distance run with a friend and you begin to feel tired and a bit exhausted, do you stop or do you keep going? If you're weight lifting in the gym and feel fatigued, do you quit or keep pushing through it? We've all had these thoughts and experiences because we're human. But if every day matters, we need to keep improving ourselves and overcome these daily challenges all the time. Not just sometimes. All the time! This needs to become a habit. In order for it to become a habit, you need to look forward to your next challenging experience and view it as an opportunity to improve yourself. Use your new and improved mental fitness, and you'll have a great sense of accomplishment when you get through it.

One way to guarantee success is to have the mindset that success is never owned—it is rented, and the rent is due every day. If you earn a number-one ranking in business, you have achieved success. But how do you sustain success? You can win a championship today, but it doesn't guarantee that you will win a championship again in the future. It's what you do every day that assures success for you and your team. It's a mindset that you need to have to keep moving your team forward in the right direction. After winning or achieving something significant, ask your team, "How can we outdo what we've done? What can we do to be better today than we were yesterday?" Professional sports teams study films of games they've played to review things that worked and what didn't work. They also study films of their next opponent to learn as much as they can in order to be as prepared as possible. They're willing to take time and focus on the details to make success more likely.

Mastering your mindset will give you the confidence to achieve anything you're aiming for. It's conditioning your mind to know that you can accomplish anything you set your mind to, ignore the doubters, and disregard people who are pessimistic and negative. It's you consistently focusing on encouraging yourself and being optimistic. It's your inner voice saying, "I can do it, and I will."

Sergeant Chris Kim

In 2016, I was a Homicide Detective with the Honolulu Police Department. My wife and I had recently moved into our dream home, and we had been married for ten years. We had two daughters in private school, and my wife was a flight attendant. Life was great. We looked like the ideal family.

But later that year, I started to notice that my wife was acting differently. She started flying a lot more and not coming home as often. I noticed that she was always on the phone. I tried to overlook it, but as time progressed, I started to watch her more, and the changes became more obvious. I ended up going through her phone and discovered that she was having an affair with a pilot from work.

I was shocked, hurt, and sad. I felt like we had a good marriage. I could not understand what drove her to have an affair.

I asked her why she did this. At first, she just denied everything. But eventually, she admitted she was unhappy with our marriage and agreed to go to marriage counseling. For two months, I hoped and prayed that things would get better. I asked her to stop seeing the pilot, but she continued to see him. She would treat me like a stranger, and it was obvious that she was in love with her pilot.

After a long two months, I woke up one morning and told myself that I couldn't live like this, and I didn't want to work on our marriage anymore. So, I met with an attorney, and in November 2016, we started our year-long divorce process.

As the process went on, I started getting more and more distraught and disheartened. Attorney bills were mounting up. I felt like every time we would go to court, nothing would go in my favor. I felt like everything was going against me. And I just couldn't handle that pressure.

I started showing classic signs of someone contemplating suicide. I found myself calling up friends and giving away valuables. I felt like I didn't need them anymore. I was no longer going to be on this earth, and I just wanted to give things away to the people I cared about. I even planned where and how I would die.

One of my former beat partners, Carlos Ocasio, knew that I was going through some hard times. In early 2017, he called me about a book his friend had written and offered me a copy. He felt like this book could help me. I thought he was crazy, but I picked up the book anyway. I sat on my sofa and looked at the back of the book. The book, titled *Beyond the Lines*, was about Rusty Komori, a tennis coach who holds the national record of twenty-two consecutive state championships. My immediate thought was, "I don't even like tennis. Why would I want to read this?" But as I sat there, something told me to read it. Rusty had my attention from the very first chapter.

Rusty Komori writes about welcoming adversity, being resilient, and having a victor mindset. He focuses on the power of choosing positive thoughts, even after a challenge. The more I read, the more I could tell that my mind was slowly changing. I felt like God put this book in my hands for a reason. I was in such a deep and dark place, and this book gave me hope. Reading *Beyond the Lines* truly changed my mindset and saved my life.

Inspired, I found myself wanting to take on a new challenge. I submitted an application for a coordinator position at a program called Crime Stoppers, and I was selected for the position in October 2017. I put my heart and soul into this new job. I had renewed energy and renewed focus, and I wanted to accept that challenge.

In 2019, I attended the Crime Stoppers USA National Conference in Tempe, Arizona. On one of the evenings, we were in a large ballroom for dinner and an awards ceremony. There are approximately three hundred fifty programs registered with Crime Stoppers USA. Every year at this awards ceremony, they select one coordinator from all the programs as the Coordinator of the Year.

I was shocked when I was selected for the award. When I got to the podium, I looked out into the crowd, and I just started crying. I told the attendees that if they only knew what I had gone through two years ago if they only knew the amount of grief and heartache that I had endured. And now, receiving the award for being number one in the nation for the first time in Crime Stoppers Honolulu's thirty-eight-year history it was just overwhelming.

I returned to Honolulu, and I received so much attention. There was news coverage of my award. I was invited to Honolulu City Council and the Hawaii State Capitol, where I received awards from the Mayor and City Council.

I knew that it was because of reading *Beyond the Lines*. It had changed my mindset. As soon as I'd started to change my mindset, doors started opening for me. I'm on the cover of *Mid-Week* newspaper. I'm in magazines and the *Star-Advertiser* paper. I'm in regular news segments. I was cast in numerous speaking roles on *Hawaii Five-O*, *NCIS Hawaii*, and *Magnum PI*. It was all due to changing my mindset, ceasing to put out negative energy into the world, and starting to try to be positive.

So, here I am today, in my sixth year as the coordinator. I'm very appreciative, humbled, and blessed. To all those reading this, I want you to know that although there are times when you feel like you can't go on, you have to believe you can persevere. No matter what you're going through, just know that things will get better. I'm living proof of that. I'm a survivor.

Chris Kim
Sergeant, Honolulu Police Department
CrimeStoppers Honolulu Coordinator

Section 1: Master Your Mindset

Now that you've completed Mastering Your Mindset, please take ten minutes to honestly rank yourself and answer the subsequent questions. The purpose of the assessment is to help you identify action items that will enable you to move forward with your leadership journey to becoming a superior leader. Below, you will find questions with corresponding gray boxes. Please use these boxes to rate yourself on a scale of 1-10 (1 being "needs improvement" and 10 being "superior") on your ability to do the specified task. Then, answer the corresponding free-response question.

Rate how consistently you have a victor mindset.

Describe a situation recently that challenged your victor mindset.

_____

_____

_____

How would you rate your ability to focus on one positive among twenty negatives?

In the past, personally or professionally, what situation has put you in the victim mindset?

_____

_____

_____

Rate your skill level at turning obstacles into opportunities.

Describe a problem that you are currently facing. How can you re-frame this problem into an opportunity?

_____

_____

_____

How would you rate your mindset when dealing with roadblocks?

In the past, what was a roadblock you dealt with and overcame?

_____

_____

_____

How would you rate your ability to find the possibilities in what most people would call an impossible situation?

What have you previously considered impossible but now recognize as just "difficult?"

_____

_____

_____

How would you rate your mindset when pursuing a seemingly impossible goal?

If you were to challenge yourself today, what is one area in your life where you can excel to "superior" status?

_____

_____

_____

How would you rate yourself regarding your current mental fitness?

What are some areas in your life that challenge your mental fitness?

_____

_____

_____

How would you rate your ability to consistently demonstrate resilience?

Specifically, what are some situations that test your tolerance level and your ability to be resilient?

_____

_____

_____

Add up your total score for this assessment and enter your score here.

THE 3 C'S OF LEADERSHIP

section 2

Chapter 5

CHOICES

"Getting knocked down in life is a given.
Getting up and moving forward is a choice."

—Zig Ziglar

SUCCESS IS NOT EASY. If it were, everyone would be successful. It takes sacrifice, commitment, and relentless perseverance. Not everybody is willing to pay the price of success. It takes hard work, but more importantly, it takes smart work in order to achieve anything of significance. It goes without saying that life is very challenging. Let me make a prediction right now: You will have countless challenges in your own life. You've had many of them already, and there are definitely more on the way. The question is, do you deal with your challenges in a positive way? What's more, can you help others deal with their challenges in a positive way? Before you can help others, you need to help yourself.

This is not being selfish. When you're in an airplane, and there's a change in cabin pressure, the flight attendants always advise passengers to put on their own oxygen masks before helping others with theirs. The principle is simple. You need to help yourself before you can effectively help others.

Do you know why there are so many bad leaders in the world? It's because nobody taught them how to be good ones. You can go to school to learn to be a good engineer or a good doctor. You can take golf lessons to become a good golfer. You can go to soccer practice and become a good soccer player. But most schools sadly don't offer classes in leadership, which would be extremely useful considering the number of people in leadership positions. Just think about how many team members are adversely affected by people who don't really know how to lead. Fortunately, you can make the choice right now to learn how to be a good, effective leader—and possibly a great one.

KNOWLEDGE IS POWER

There are many different types of people in the world. There are positive people, and there are negative people. There are people who are confident and people with low self-esteem. There are people who are ambitious and people who are complacent. There are people who are disciplined and people who are undisciplined. There are people who react before thinking and people who think before reacting. There are people who care about others and people who only care about themselves. There are people who care about winning with integrity and people who want to win at all costs. What kind of leader would you want to follow? What kind of leader do you want to be? What kind of leader produces the best, consistent results for a team in business or sports?

Everyone has the power to make choices. You will either make good choices or bad ones, but they are your choices to make. And all of these choices have certain effects you need to be aware of. These effects cause your team to have good experiences or bad experiences. These effects cause your team to have good productivity or low productivity. These effects can be healthy or unhealthy. These effects can cause you to win or lose. These effects can deepen the team bond or cause the team to deteriorate. And all of these effects happen because of a single choice. Your choice. Knowledge is powerful, and the more you learn, the better choices you can make. These better choices can help you become a better leader in helping your team achieve its goals.

We have all been on a team at some point in time. We have observed the team leader, whether an employer or an athletic coach, and we can usually recall whether that leader was good, mediocre, or just plain bad. What did he do that was good? What could she have done better? Did the leader generate enthusiasm for you and the rest of the team? It's always interesting to reflect back on these experiences as a team member and imagine how things might have been different if you were the team leader. Likewise, it's important for a leader to always put him or herself into team members' shoes to understand what they're thinking and feeling. If you're a team leader now, how do you think your current team members would grade and evaluate you?

Have you had a friend who had a bad experience in the workplace because the boss or manager treated her unfairly? Do you have a son or daughter or know of a child who was playing a sport and stopped playing because the coach led their team with questionable decision-making or other actions that made for a bad experience? Or perhaps you have experienced these unfortunate situations in the workplace or in athletics? Whatever the scenario, it probably involved an unsuitable leader and his or her effects on others. Making decisions and choices is a part of life and something we do every day. We have all made decisions in our lives, both good and bad, and we learn from them. Great leaders are constantly learning, which helps make them even greater.

START VS. FINISH

It's easy to choose to start something, but it's just as easy to stop doing it. Anyone can choose to go running or work out in the gym. Anyone can choose to eat healthier and go on a diet. Having the right intentions is good, but having the follow-through to do it every day is what counts. The concept is simple. Without commitment, you will never start, but more importantly, without consistency, you will never finish. We're all guilty of having started something without finishing it. If something is really important to you, you will find a way. If it's not important enough, you will find an excuse.

Let's explore this concept a bit further. The act of starting something is often accompanied by enthusiasm, curiosity, and a sense of anticipation. We like starting something because it represents the birth of an idea, a goal, or a project. Starting is the spark that ignites the fire of possibility, propelling us into action and setting the wheels in motion. However, while starting is important, it's the act of finishing that brings a sense of accomplishment and fulfillment. Finishing requires self-discipline, perseverance, and the ability to overcome obstacles. It signifies the culmination of effort, the attainment of a goal, and the realization of one's potential.

Many of us want to be physically fit, and we have a clear idea about the fitness level we'd like to achieve. But do we have the dedication to work on it every day? Starting a new workout regimen is often fueled by the desire for self-improvement, increased strength, or enhanced well-being. It begins with setting goals, developing a training plan, and taking the first steps toward physical transformation. However, it's the consistency of completing the workouts, sticking to the schedule, and persevering through the inevitable challenges that lead to tangible results. We can't do things only when it's convenient or only when we feel like it. Whether it's lifting heavier weights, achieving a desired level of fitness, or running a marathon, the sense of achievement comes from finishing what was started.

Speaking of self-discipline, we are all presented with the same choice in decision-making every single morning. That choice is whether or not to get out of bed when the alarm goes off. Some of us choose to get up and out of bed immediately, while others choose to hit snooze and stay in bed a while longer. Having the self-discipline to wake up after hearing the alarm is the right choice and needs to become a habit. The next choice we have is whether or not to make the bed. Some of us will, and some of us will choose to leave it unmade. Those of us who make that bed have just completed the first task of the day. This might not seem like much, but it really is. By completing the first task of the day, you're more likely to want to accomplish a second task, then a third, and so on. You will have a tendency to be more productive and put yourself in more favorable positions to accomplish things that day. And if you do have a bad day, you'll at least come home to a bed that's already made. So, wake up and make your bed!

RISK PROMOTES GROWTH

Taking risks can be scary. It requires courage. And it's a choice you make. If you're complacent and play it safe, you will never grow. As babies, we begin crawling and then take the risk to try and stand up on our own. Failure is falling. But we get up and try to stand again and again. Soon after we master standing on our own, we take the risk of walking. And then we take the risk of running. And then sprinting. We've all taken these risks; otherwise, we'd all still be crawling.

But when do we actually stop taking risks or become too scared to take them? Is it when we weigh the risk of succeeding versus failing? Sometimes people are complacent and resist change because they focus on what they have to give up instead of what they have to gain. In order to grow, you need to take risks. The legendary investor Warren Buffet said, "Risk comes from not knowing what you're doing." Great leaders take calculated risks. They are educated and have the knowledge and courage to take calculated risks at the right times.

Amazon's Jeff Bezos said, "Nine times out of ten, you're going to fail. But every once in a while, you'll hit a home run that, in business terms, is more like one thousand runs. Given a ten percent chance of a one hundred times payoff, you should take that bet every time." Bezos also said, "Failure and invention are inseparable twins. To invent, you have to experiment, and if you know in advance that it's going to work, it's not an experiment. If you're not stubborn, you'll give up on experiments soon. If you are not flexible, you will pound your head against the wall, and you will not see a different solution to a problem you are trying to solve."

I've spoken with countless people who feel stuck in their lives, whether it's a job where they dislike their manager or a sports team with a bad coach. Sometimes, we become so consumed in our daily routines that we forget that we have the power of choice. We can make a change. We don't have to be stuck in that situation every day for the rest of our lives. And yes, it's often scary and frightening to make a change and do something different to possibly make your life better. Think of the alternative if we do nothing. We will continue to add misery to our lives, and probably the lives of others, because of that unfair manager or coach.

Everything you do, every choice and decision you make, involves some level of risk. But remember, risk promotes growth, and growth determines destiny. You can choose complacency, or you can choose to try something different. What do you think successful people do? What do you think champions do? They're never complacent and always have the courage to make proper choices that align with the goals they want to achieve. When you make these better and new choices, you give yourself an opportunity for new experiences and new feelings. These new experiences and feelings lead to bigger and better things you wouldn't have discovered had you chosen the status quo.

There are three main categories of choices you can make that will keep you on the right path in life: mindset, health, and personal growth. You only get one mind and one body when you enter this world. It's not like trading in an old car for a new car. You can't trade in an old body for a new one. You need to take care of the body and mind you were given. Whenever you make these daily choices to improve your mindset, health, and personal growth, you will continue to head in the right direction in living a better life.

Let me identify some examples of choices you can make for yourself right now. You can choose to be positive and have a favorable outlook on life. You can choose to focus on finishing something that you started. You can choose to eat healthier, which will make you feel better about yourself. You can choose to exercise more, which will improve your health and fitness. You can choose to learn something new by reading a book (which you're obviously doing right now) or attending a seminar, which is an opportunity for learning and personal growth. You can choose to help somebody and do something nice for that person, which adds to your personal fulfillment. Think about the alternatives to these examples if you don't choose wisely.

Once you make these choices, you need to commit and do them consistently until they become a habit. A winning attitude is a habit, but so is a losing one. So, how do you build good habits? I believe that when you have a thought about doing something, you only have three to five seconds to do it, or your brain actually starts to talk you out of doing it. Think about how true this is. How many times have you thought about going for a run—but instead, we check Instagram? Or we think about going to the gym, and instead, we turn on the television. Once you have a thought about doing something productive, train yourself to do it immediately. It's as simple as that.

The greatest coaches are constantly finding ways to be better, and they take calculated risks to improve themselves and their teams. They take nothing for granted and outdo what they have done. Trying different things to see what works and what doesn't work is a good thing. What's costly is doing nothing new and being idle. These great coaches also know that there are consequences for every choice they make. There's a cause and effect, and effects from effects. You need to look at the big picture, as well as the smaller segments, and then connect the dots to stay on the right path.

What do you want to achieve, and what do you need to do to achieve it? If you want to improve, you can't continue doing the same thing over and over again. You don't achieve greater success by being complacent, and you can't sustain it either by doing the same thing. Once you achieve success or win a championship, other teams will try to emulate you. You just created a blueprint of success for others to follow. Every successful person and championship team has taken risks—calculated risks—to improve on their success.

Think about it. A basketball player who has never attempted a potentially game-winning shot is definitely taking a risk. If the player misses, the team loses; if he makes it, they win. When LeBron James experienced this situation for the first time many years ago, I'll bet even he felt uncomfortable and nervous. Since then, he's been in this same situation time and time again, but now, he is turning uncomfortable into comfortable and nervousness into excitement. It becomes exciting to him because he thrives under pressure and looks forward to it. Obviously, he's made many game-winning shots, and he's also missed many. But how do you want to live your life? What do you want to accomplish? LeBron became LeBron because he took risks to achieve his success. He makes a positive impact, which inspires and encourages people around him to do the same.

Think about when you were in your youth on a basketball court by yourself shooting hoops, imagining there were three seconds left in the game, and it was up to you to take the game-winning shot. You count three, two, one, and shoot the ball. Whether it goes through the hoop or not, it's the action of trying that matters. Obviously, we know there's a big difference in practice and in a game when it really counts. But having the imagination to do it in practice often leads you to have the courage to take a risk in a game. When you keep putting yourself in that position a second, third, and fourth time, you deal with the situation better each time, which leads to success. Can you imagine if you never tried? Then you'd have zero chance of improvement and no chance for success.

In an interview, Apple co-founder Steve Jobs talked about how taking risks affected his company when he started it with his business partner, Steve Wozniak. "There's no risk," he said. "That's why you need to do it young, and that's why we started Apple. We said, you know, we have absolutely nothing to lose. I was twenty years old, and Woz was twenty-four. We have no families, no children, no houses—Woz had an old car; I had a Volkswagen van. I mean, all we were going to lose was our cars and the shirts off our backs. We had nothing to lose, and we had everything to gain. And we figured even if we crash and burn and lose everything, the experience will have been worth ten times the cost. So there was no risk. I think that's a healthy way to look at it. The only thing you have in your life is time, and if you invest that time in yourself—to have great experiences that are going to enrich you—then you can't possibly lose. So I always advise people, 'Don't wait.' Do something when you're young when you have nothing to lose and don't have the responsibilities to other people that you will acquire later on in your life."

LOOK AHEAD

Not long ago, I had dinner with my friend Jennifer, who complained about a client who was extremely rude and mean to her on a phone call. She shared with me that while she continued to be professional and positive, internally, she was feeling upset and disrespected. She also shared with me that her phone call with that client lasted only four minutes but ruined the rest of her day. My response to her was, "Why would you let a bad four minutes affect the rest of your day?" There were another twenty-three hours and fifty-six minutes that she allowed those four minutes to affect. And she was probably affecting other clients, coworkers, and family members because of how those four minutes bothered her. Obviously, she still wasn't over it because she was now venting to me, and this incident had happened weeks before.

Once I asked her that question, everything started to make sense. She reflected on how that one incident was affecting various parts of her life. She could clearly see how she was revisiting that incident daily. I told her she had a choice to make. She needed to choose to let it go and move on, and that's exactly what she did. I told her the lesson here is never to let a bad four minutes ruin your day. We all have had and will continue to have similar unfortunate interactions with people that might make us feel how Jennifer felt. The great thing is that we have a choice in how we respond.

As a coach, it's imperative to always look ahead to what you want to accomplish in life and to train your team members to do the same. It's like driving a car. There's a reason why the front windshield is so large and the rearview mirror is small. In fact, it's often tempting to look behind you into the past because there are three rearview mirrors. But your focus always has to be on what's ahead of you. Be aware of who's around you—behind and to the side—but the focus always has to be looking through that big front windshield. That's how you accomplish goals in life. Learn from your past and train yourself and others to always choose to focus on what's ahead of you.

Speaking of cars, I recently parked my own in a shopping mall garage, and when I returned an hour later, I noticed something different just above the right rear tire. Upon closer inspection, it was clear that somebody had banged my car, leaving a sizable dent and scratch as they were trying to park next to me. There was no note, and of course, I felt sick. I don't know about you, but my car is a part of me, and I felt as though I had been dented and scratched myself.

The next day, I took my car to a body shop for an estimate and found that the repair job would cost $2,500. I then learned from my insurance company that I have a $1,000 deductible in such situations. The sick feeling of the day before instantly became much worse. I began to think about the value of $1,000 and all the things I could buy instead of paying an auto repair company for something that wasn't my fault. I had a choice to make. I could focus on the past, look in the rearview mirror, and continue to let this bother me, or I could move on and look through my big front windshield at all the opportunities ahead of me. What choice did I make? Well, because I talk the talk, I must also walk the walk and choose to move on with a positive mindset.

Training yourself and your team to make a conscious choice in controlling what you think, say, and do keeps you on the path toward peak performance. This type of self-control was an important discipline and habit I consistently worked on with my team, practically on a daily basis. I would tell them, "If we can control our thoughts, mouths, and hands, we have a great chance of controlling the tennis ball and our destiny."

Think about how this simple concept affects us in life. This was a big part of our success because I wanted us to think properly, speak intelligently, and only do things that would help us achieve our goals. Many teams do things to hinder their performance by shooting themselves in the foot unnecessarily. Bad choices help teams lose, so shouldn't we choose only those things that help us win? It seems logical, and it needs to become a habit of self-discipline and self-control. Having this awareness and always choosing the high road regardless of the circumstances is a valuable habit to develop.

BE RESOURCEFUL

Punahou School is known as a private school with a public purpose. We welcome teachers and coaches from other schools to come and see what we do to help our students. It's not just about bettering our own students; it's about helping improve our community—which could lead to improving our country and potentially the world. While I was at Punahou, this was a common occurrence for us at our tennis facility. We were very open and willing to help other schools in the US and abroad. Outside teachers and coaches would come to observe and learn why our tennis programs were very successful and then add what they'd seen to their own programs. I always remember the quote, "Helping one person might not change the world, but it could change the world for one person." I strongly believe that helping one person can be like a drop of water splashing in the ocean, causing a ripple effect to potentially help many others.

Through the years, I've been asked by coaches from other schools to participate in tennis clinics for their teams, and I've always accepted the invitation. Many of these teams are at public schools with very limited resources. Maybe their tennis balls are old, flat, and dirty, or their tennis courts are cracked and in need of resurfacing. Perhaps their players have worn-out shoes and old tennis rackets and can't afford private or group tennis lessons. And yet, it's not about having the nicest courts or fanciest uniforms or newest equipment. It's about how well you can play the game. Everyone has the same rules to abide by and the same-sized tennis court with a net in between. When I share this with these teams, it makes complete sense to them. I tell them that it really comes down to your desire for greatness. If you really want to be good or even great at something, you can. Nobody can deny you the opportunity to be great or achieve a number-one ranking. It all depends on you and how badly you want it.

I would also share with these teams that no matter how little you have or how bad things appear, there are always others who have less and worse situations than you. I've seen videos of little kids learning and practicing tennis in the Philippines on tennis courts with surfaces of dirt. Many of these kids are playing tennis in flip-flops because they can't afford shoes and are using old donated tennis rackets. And yet, they have passion and a strong desire for excellence. These kids are having fun learning and improving in their sport. They have limited resources, and their coaches are teaching them to be very resourceful and to keep the correct perspective. When I watch these videos on YouTube and see their incredible progress in developing their fundamentals, I am extremely impressed with their perseverance and commitment to being better than they were yesterday. The reason I love tennis is that it all depends on you and your passion for achieving greatness. The great Andre Agassi said, "It's no accident that tennis uses the language of life: advantage, service, fault, break, love, the basic elements of everyday existence, because every match is life in miniature."

DEAN SHIMADA

Coach Dean Shimada is the counselor for Waianae High School and was also the former head coach for their boys' and girls' varsity tennis teams. He's been a friend of mine for many years and is a man of outstanding character. A few years ago, he asked me to be a guest speaker during one of his team practices, and I gladly agreed. When I arrived at his practice, it was clear to me that all of his players were excited to be there with him and eager to get onto the courts to work on improving their tennis game.

Although Waianae High School does not have its own tennis courts on campus and needs to reserve public tennis courts for its practices, it's obvious to me that the boys and girls feel privileged to be there and greatly respect their coach. They also have limited resources, but luckily, Dean is very resourceful. He truly cares about the well-being of each team member and wants to help them make better choices, not only in school and on the court but also in life. He has their best interests at heart and empathy for them, and they know it.

As I was speaking and interacting with Dean and his team, it was clear to me that he had created a positive, safe learning environment for them. He has established a culture of excellence for his players in learning life lessons through tennis. Although tennis is an individual sport, he has created a special team where everyone plays a role and contributes to the success of the team. Success might not really be as much about winning (and trust me, they all obviously want to win) as it is about helping and encouraging each other to have fun and enjoy their experience together.

At the conclusion of their season, Dean invited me to the team party at Dave & Buster's and bought a copy of my first book for every boy and girl at his own expense. They were all so appreciative of this coach, who many of them looked up to as a second father. It was reciprocal because I could see that he cared for them as if they were his own sons and daughters. The highlight of the evening was when Dean asked his seniors to speak into a microphone, one by one.

Not one of those seniors talked about tennis. They talked about how they felt they were part of a special family and looked forward to being with their brothers and sisters at tennis practice.

They told next year's returning players that being on the team was the best choice they'd ever made in their lives, and they advised them to appreciate every day they had together. They thanked Dean's wife, Jo, and son, Alec, for allowing Dean to be their coach, acknowledging that it's time away from his family, and they thanked Dean for his commitment, time, and sacrifice to help them make better choices and improve their lives. Many of the seniors began to cry as they spoke, which caused many of us in the audience to cry as well. It was powerful. It was impactful. I was so proud of Dean and for the opportunity to witness and be a part of this priceless experience. The Waianae High School varsity tennis team might not have won the state championship, but they are definitely champions in life.

Chapter 6

COMMUNICATION

"Words are free. It's how you use
them that will cost you."

—Joshua Miller

DO YOU EVER NOTICE when someone speaks, either how meaningful or meaningless their communication can be? Think about someone who speaks briefly, and you listen intently to every single word. Now think about someone who speaks for thirty minutes, yet you can't remember a thing they said. Words are powerful. Silence is also powerful. What you say and how you say it makes a world of difference.

When I'm coaching my doubles teams in tennis, I want them to communicate effectively with each other. I want everything they say to each other in competition to be meaningful. For example, if Austin is serving and double-faults, Jacob might say, "Good try, Austin." Do you think this is a good response from Jacob as a doubles partner? Maybe, but it seems like a generic response to me—one that, repeated often enough, could soon become meaningless. What if, instead, Jacob says, "It's OK, Austin—on this next serve, hit your slice and aim for the middle of the service box." Now, this is quality communication. It's always better to focus on what to do (what you want to achieve) versus just saying "Good try" and hoping things will improve.

Now, the worst response from Jacob is no response. If Austin double-faults and Jacob says nothing, Austin might begin to feel bad, like he's letting Jacob down. In reality, Austin serving a double fault might not bother Jacob at all, but Jacob's silence might lead Austin to believe that he is making Jacob mad or irritated, which might ultimately lead to Austin playing worse. And this is all because of the power of communication, or lack thereof.

As the coach, I constantly strove to say only meaningful, important things to my team members. I chose my words carefully, and I found that they listened better because they knew if I said something, it was important and would result in a positive impact. Of course, they knew I had empathy for them because I often asked them about how they were doing in school, about their personal goals, if everything was good in their lives, and how I could help them in those areas. Because of my open communication, they knew that I cared for them as much more than just tennis players. I wanted them to succeed in life, which, coincidentally, helped them succeed on the tennis court.

THE 4 MISSES

I've seen that most problems in life happen because of what I refer to as the "4 Misses"—Miscommunication, Misunderstanding, Misperception, and Misinformation. Think about your own life and how many times you've encountered problems and dysfunction because of these 4 Misses. Think about the many times you've seen this happen with people around you. Consequently, I became proactive with my team. I shared this with them, knowing that we would definitely encounter situations that could take us on different tangents instead of keeping us on track to achieve our goals. I could even predict the future, telling my team, "When Dan gets mad at Jimmy this season, it could easily be because of one of the 4 Misses. Maybe Dan misperceived what Jimmy said because he didn't have all the information or all the facts."

Oftentimes, when situations would arise among members of my team, the other players would recognize it and say, "They're getting mad at each other, and it's totally what Coach Rusty said about the 4 Misses." Because I was proactive in communicating to them that things can and will happen, this alone often saved us from going off on the wrong tangents and dealing with unnecessary situations (and wasting valuable time) and instead kept us on the yellow brick road toward getting closer to achieving our goals.

Let's take a closer look at why it's important to be proactive in minimizing and ultimately avoiding these 4 Misses. Miscommunication occurs when the intended message is not effectively conveyed or received. If there's a lack of clarity, it can lead to conflicts, confusion, and misunderstandings. This breakdown will oftentimes impede progress in achieving goals and take you off track. Delivering your messages accurately and actively seeking feedback ensures that the recipient fully understands and comprehends the communication.

Misunderstandings happen when the meaning behind a message is interpreted differently than intended and often arise due to differences in context, knowledge, and perspectives. These unfortunate gaps can lead to faulty assumptions and misinterpretations of information. This breakdown might even unnecessarily damage a relationship with a team member or client that may never be fully repaired. Asking questions and restating information in one's own words can help bridge these gaps in understanding and maintain alignment with your goals.

Misperceptions occur when we form inaccurate or incorrect beliefs about a concept, situation, or person. Sometimes, we might hear a partial communication or third-party conversation that will lead us to believe something that does not match reality or the correct intent. It could very well lead to a misperception of what we heard or observed, which leads us to form our own impression of that situation. It's important to be aware and not jump to conclusions that might be inaccurate.

Misinformation refers to misleading or false information that can lead to misguided actions or decisions. Some people might even share partial truths or take things out of context on purpose. Another factor to be aware of is the abundance of viral content and unverified sources in today's digital landscape. Because of this, it's crucial to do your own fact-checking. Taking time to get all the factual information will allow you to separate truth from fiction and keep your team moving forward.

In regards to the power of nonverbal communication, I once saw something fascinating when an elderly blind man sat down beside a busy walkway near a shopping mall. He had three things with him: a pen, a cardboard sign, and a coffee mug. The message on his cardboard sign read, "I'M BLIND—PLEASE HELP." I'd estimate that for every twenty people that walked by, one would stop and give him coins or maybe a dollar bill. After thirty minutes, one passerby stopped in front of the man, picked up his sign and pen, and wrote a different message on the other side. While he was writing, the blind man reached out to touch and feel this person's shoes. Though they hadn't spoken a word to one another, he now realized the passerby was a woman, who then put the sign down with its new message and continued on her way.

Now, for every twenty people that walked by, I'd estimate that nineteen of them stopped and gave the man coins and dollar bills. This continued until his coffee mug began to overflow. After an hour, someone stopped and stood in front of the man, who reached out and found that it was the same woman. "Ma'am, thank you so very much," he said with excitement and gratitude. "May I ask, what is the message that you wrote?"

She replied, "It's a beautiful day, and I can't see it."

We need to make certain that our message really resonates with whomever we're communicating with. Is there a better way to communicate and reach your team members? Are you communicating correctly to inspire them to do what needs to be done? Is there a more effective way for your team members to communicate with your clients? Whether we are speaking verbally or nonverbally, communication is truly an art, and we constantly need to be aware of what we say and how we say it.

Speaking of communication, I would share some wisdom with my team that they should never make fun of someone who speaks broken English because it just means that they're proficient in another language. And here's more wisdom for you by the educator Walter Barbe, who said, "If you've told a child a thousand times, and the child still has not learned, then it is not the child who is the slow learner." All of us can definitely use words of wisdom, and we need to remember that most problems happen because of the 4 Misses. So be proactive and avoid the 4 Misses.

Dr. Glenn Medeiros

I had the pleasure of reading Rusty's first two books, and since that time, I've been a very big fan of his coaching philosophies. We've gotten to know each other personally as I worked and collaborated with him in preparation for my teaching of various leadership courses at both high school and college levels. The reaction to his teaching by my students has impacted them in a very positive way. I am planning on Rusty working with me as my personal Executive Coach, given the great results I have seen with my students after reading his work.

I was blessed to take on the role of President & CEO of Saint Louis School in Hawaii at the age of forty-five. During my first five years, with the help of many others, I was able to help turn the school around financially by almost doubling its enrollment, endowment, and savings and raising millions of dollars for the creation of new facilities. Although those were challenging years, everyone worked together collaboratively to help us reach many of our goals and objectives successfully.

Unfortunately, even when leaders are effective in turning around organizations in the short-term, long-term success for them can be out of reach when the 4 Misses occur: misunderstanding, miscommunication, misinformation, and misperception. In my particular case, my intentions were to help the school move forward. My focus was to enhance academic excellence, provide a safe and secure environment, and strengthen other areas in need by utilizing creative methods, all while knowing that financial resources were limited at the time, providing the opportunity for the 4 Misses to occur without the proper tools of communication at my disposal.

Ironically, when the school began to achieve success, suddenly, a power struggle began that caused a small but loud faction of people to misperceive and misunderstand some of my actions that were meant to help our educational institution thrive. In today's world of "cancel culture" and "political correctness," the use of social media can easily be used as a tool to attack individuals. When certain people disagree or do not fully comprehend the view of others, one small action can be taken out of context and may be seen as an example of their leader doing something that is unethical or self-serving in nature even when that leader's intention is simply to help the organization thrive. Thus, the importance of truly understanding the need to avoid the 4 Misses makes it imperative that all leaders today constantly strive to communicate in a fashion that not only protects themselves, but the institutions they represent. Rusty clearly outlines these concepts in his teaching philosophy, and they are key to not only being a successful CEO but to also assisting others in building their capacity to lead.

I look forward to working closely with Rusty not only in the aforementioned areas, but also by utilizing the various leadership strategies he has developed for me to become a stronger, more effective leader.

Dr. Glenn Medeiros, Ed.D.
President & CEO, Saint Louis School

FIND A CONNECTION

Effective communication is about connecting with people. People like it when you understand their situation. They become more open to sharing their concerns and feelings with you because you can relate to them. It's often a great opportunity for the leader to share an insightful story first about something they experienced. Then, it becomes more likely for the other person to open up and share something they experienced. This sets the stage for a good back-and-forth interaction where you can get into the deeper issues of concern.

I remember being in a London café on a trip to Wimbledon many years ago when the woman behind me tapped me on the shoulder and asked if I was from the States. When I said, "I am," she became excited and said, "Me too!" A few years ago, I was at a winery in Napa Valley when another customer asked me if I was from Hawaii. I said yes, and his face lit up, and he said that he was from the Islands, too. And when I was on a snowboarding trip in Whistler, Canada, a hotel employee asked me if I played tennis. When I responded yes, he said that he was a tennis instructor at a nearby club, and we talked for a good fifteen minutes about tennis.

The point is this: People like having things in common with other people. It makes them feel connected. It's the same idea when you communicate with someone. You are trying to find things in common. Maybe you both are single parents, or maybe your parents are divorced, and that's what you have in common. Maybe you both are small business owners or have been in leadership positions, and that's what you have in common. Maybe you both played sports or worked in finance, and that's what you have in common. Finding a connection, any connection with the other, starts the formation of a common thread, which leads to a strong bond.

Social media is a huge part of how we communicate and connect with people in society nowadays. Let's think about why people post on social media. The best and clearest explanation I found is by Honolulu life coach Alice Inoue. She says, "Much of what you see posted on social media is a carefully curated stream that shows a one-sided reality of what we want others to see and think about us. Whether you are aware of it or not, we post for either narcissistic or altruistic reasons. If we are feeling narcissistic, we post things that show how 'good' we are in some way that we look good, are having a good time, are being a good parent or spouse, or that show we are in love. We hope posts like this will garner positive feedback, as we all love praise, and we all want to highlight our success. If we are in an altruistic mood, we post things to help others—words of encouragement or an inspiring story, video, or photo. We hope these posts will assist others in their life journeys and that people will be appreciative because giving and serving others makes us feel good, as well. When you are posting about the good aspects of yourself or your life, you are showing that you have value. When you are posting something to help others, you are showing others that they have value. Social media is both a projection and a reflection. The more conscious you are of what you project, the better your reflection. It's about the yin and the yang, the push and pull, the polarity of life."

CHANGE VS. IMPROVE

If something is not working, change is necessary. But I often hear some leaders misuse the word "change," which could lead to confusion among members of their team. When people hear "change," they usually think that something will be different. They think that whatever they have been working on might be a waste of time because the leader now wants change. The leader should instead use the word "improve" because that's exactly what they're trying to do—unless, of course, they really want to do something completely different that warrants the proper use of the word "change." The effect is this might actually be a miscommunication by the leader, which usually leads to misperceptions and misunderstandings by team members and often causes them to possibly reject this idea of change.

When I'm helping a tennis player with their tennis game, how I communicate is vital. For example, if I say, "Stacy, we need to change your serve." What do you think she's thinking? She's probably thinking that we are going to make her serve differently, and she might feel that time was wasted practicing things that I had her previously working on. She might even refuse to try something new because she feels good about her current serve.

Let's try this approach. I'll say, "Stacy, we need to improve your serve," how do you think she will respond? Will she be open to hearing more about how we can improve her serve? Of course! Change scares people, but everyone wants to improve. I'll often use the word "adjust" when making an improvement. For example, I'll say, "Stacy, if we adjust your grip 1/16 of an inch toward the left, it will give you more spin and power, which will allow you the opportunity to reach your full serving potential." People perceive words in different ways. Instead of using the word "adjust," what if I used the word "change?" Stacy would most likely feel uneasy about "changing" her grip for her serve. Other words that I have used similar to "adjust" are "modify," "enhance," "fine-tune," "alter," and "transform."

So, keep in mind what you are trying to accomplish. Are you really trying to *change* something, or are you striving to *improve* something?

A change in management is something that every team usually experiences at some point in time. If a business has a new general manager or a sports team has a new head coach, it often leads to team members feeling a bit uneasy because of the unknown. They don't know this new leader. Because of uncertainty, team members know that this change will lead to one of three situations for them: the team could get worse, stay the same, or it could improve. As their new leader, you need to know what they're probably thinking and feeling in order to communicate to them that this is a fantastic opportunity for improvement. In order to get them to buy into your philosophy, your words and actions are extremely vital because your team will be watching everything you say and do. Conveying that it's an opportunity for growth, efficiency, and deeper purpose, both individually and collectively, will get them thinking about improvement as well. Keeping the focus on what you're striving to achieve together by involving them in contributing their creative ideas and collaborating to make the team stronger often gets them excited for the future with you as their new leader.

When I became head coach in 1994, I knew that I had to earn the trust and respect of every player on the team, and it was obvious to me that they would be watching everything I said and did. I wanted to inspire them, get them excited about what we could accomplish together, and know that we are all a reflection of each other. I started by setting our standard of excellence and higher expectations that I had of them and that they could expect from me as well. The irony is my standards and expectations had nothing to do with winning. It was about our character, integrity, ethics, playing by the rules, and representing Punahou School with ultimate class. I shared with them that we had only two team rules: listening and lateness. I always like to keep things simple and clear. I shared, "I expect punctuality from you, and you can expect the same from me. And I need you to listen to me, and I will listen to you."

This communication with my team set a tone of excitement and potential possibilities of what we could accomplish together with me as their new leader. Of course, I was dealing with high school boys, and some of them tested me regarding the consequences of not listening or being late. But this is part of discipline, and discipline is necessary for success. Needless to say, any violation of our rules resulted in consequences that greatly enhanced the violator's strength and conditioning—whether he was number one or number twelve on our team, because the rules are for everyone. And trust me, because of these consequences, they did not want to violate our rules. Again, your words and actions matter, and this helped me build trust and respect with my team and became the foundation for our success.

THE TRAVIS ING STORY

My varsity team tryouts were very intense, and I would often have twenty-five-plus players trying out for twelve spots. When it came down to thirteen players, the "sudden death" singles match would be played with the winner making the team and the loser coming only so close to making the team. One year, Travis Ing was that player who was defeated in a super close three-set match. You can imagine how devastated Travis must have felt, coming up just a little short of making the team and then having to meet with me in my office after the match.

I always tried to put myself in my player's shoes to understand what he was thinking and feeling. Needless to say, Travis was extremely disappointed and feeling down, big time. I would be, too! When Travis walked into my office, he was naturally going to be feeling really bad. My goal was that when he left my office, he'd be feeling good. I want people leaving a meeting with me feeling much better about themselves and their situation than when they first walked in.

So, let me share with you what I talked about with Travis. I said, "Travis, take a seat. Analyze the match for me. Tell me what happened."

"Coach, I know I had my opportunities, and I missed some key shots on some big points. I felt really nervous and didn't feel like I played up to the level I'm capable of."

I jumped in. "Travis, you're right. But what if this was the state singles championship, and you didn't bring it today? You can't tell your opponent to come back tomorrow, and let's play it again. No, you have to wait one year, maybe, to be fortunate to be in that situation again. Do you agree?"

"Yes, I know it was fair, and I had my chance to win."

"Travis, every tennis player knows how it feels to lose a tough, big match. I know the feeling for sure. It's miserable! But what's done is done. It's in the past. My question for you is, what are you going to do now? Are you going to quit tennis, or are you going to work even harder?"

"Coach, I want to make the varsity team. It's been a huge goal of mine for many years."

"Travis, every year we have two players playing in the sudden death singles match. Do you know why?"

"Well," he said, "in the informational meeting a few weeks ago, you said it's the fairest way."

"That's right," I told him. "It's the fairest way because I don't want to make a judgment call on who makes the team. I always put myself in your shoes because if I were in your situation, I would want to control my own destiny on the tennis court. Every player who lost the sudden death match over the years immediately got on the court the next day to work on their game and practice harder than ever. They motivated themselves because they all had your same goal of wanting to make the team. And you know what? All of them came back to tryouts the following year better, stronger, and smarter, and they all made the team with no problem. It's a choice. It's your choice."

"Coach, what do I need to do to be better?" Travis asked.

"Two big things stand out to me. One is consistency. You need to have better shot tolerance and be more patient with all of your shots. You'll play a really solid point, and then you'll make an unforced error on the next point. When this happens, you're no better than even. You need to win clusters of points, and that's why your consistency needs to improve. Second, you need to have a stronger mindset. The brain controls the body, which will keep you in the right internal climate. The key thing here is to focus on what you want to achieve and tell yourself that you're excited instead of getting nervous thinking about things that you hope won't happen."

"That makes sense," he said. "I'll start working on those things tomorrow."

I jumped in again, saying, "Travis, what's great about this is it's completely under your control. If you want to be great, then you can be great. If you need to be more consistent, then go practice being more consistent. If you need to improve your mindset and focus, then do that too. I'm expecting you to work on these things every day, and I'm hoping you will earn your spot on our team and contribute in a big way next year." "Thanks, Coach. I appreciate you sharing those things with me."

Travis left the office feeling better than when he first walked in. The next thing I needed to do was to talk with his parents. I know they were feeling as disappointed and sad as Travis, if not more so, especially his dad, Richard.

The following year, Travis went through tryouts playing at a much higher level and made the team with no problem. The bottom line is I wanted everyone to feel proud and connected to Punahou boys' varsity tennis, whether they were on the team or not. It only takes a little time for the coach to acknowledge players or parents, speaking sincerely with them for just a few minutes, but that exchange can have priceless effects down the road.

TRAVIS ING

Chapter 7

CULTURE

"The strength of the team is each individual member.
The strength of each member is the team."

—Phil Jackson

WHEN YOU'RE THE COACH, it's your responsibility to
create the culture you want for your team. There's nothing
wrong with having high standards for yourself and your team.
In fact, it's definitely better to start off with a higher standard
instead of a lower one. It's a good thing to be striving for limits
just beyond your reach. That's what makes good people great
and great people extraordinary. It's constantly striving for
superior excellence. Think about times in your life when you
thought that you couldn't accomplish something, but then you
did it and had the satisfying feeling that your perseverance had

paid off. That's when life becomes more meaningful because you faced a challenge and you overcame it. Every person is capable of doing so much more than what they think they're capable of.

Because of our team's winning streak, we were definitely in the public eye. There were many people supporting us who were impressed with our culture of excellence and others who wanted to see us lose, mainly because of jealousy. It's a bit like the New England Patriots—people seem to have either loved them or hated them just because they had a dynasty and won a lot. But shouldn't everyone applaud them because of their high standard of excellence, consistently having great teams during those "Tom Brady years" and winning multiple Super Bowls? Sometimes, it seems people just want to see a successful team lose, so they cheer against them for no good reason.

Because of our team's high visibility, I often reminded my players that we could do ninety-nine things right, but if we did one wrong thing, everyone would only remember that one thing. That's just how it is. So, I told them we could never do that one wrong thing. It's a privilege to be on top, and everyone else wants to be where we are. That's why, after we won our first state championship together, I wanted my team to focus every day on striving toward two things: a superior culture of excellence and superior disciplined details.

SUPERIOR CULTURE OF EXCELLENCE

Let me explain the difference between a culture of excellence versus a *superior* culture of excellence. A culture of excellence focuses on fostering an environment where high standards and continuous improvement are valued. It involves a shared commitment to prioritize quality, innovation, and exceptional performance. In a culture of excellence, there is a focus on setting and achieving ambitious goals, fostering a supportive and empowering atmosphere, and promoting a growth mindset. This culture encourages collaboration, open communication, and a willingness to learn and adapt. Individuals are motivated to go above and beyond, strive for continuous improvement, and deliver outstanding results.

A *superior* culture of excellence encompasses these elements and goes a step further, taking it to the highest level. While both cultures represent distinct levels of commitment and ambition in striving for greatness, a superior culture emphasizes a competitive edge and a drive to surpass expectations. It is characterized by an unwavering commitment to surpassing industry standards and achieving unprecedented levels of performance. A superior culture of excellence involves consistently pushing the boundaries, setting new benchmarks, and constantly raising the bar for success. In this type of culture, there is a relentless pursuit of innovation, efficiency, and exceptional outcomes. Individuals with a superior culture of excellence continually strive for greatness, challenging themselves to outperform even their own best achievements. It also becomes a way of life and a source of pride for all who are part of it.

As I was building our team's superior culture, it was extremely important to me that everyone on my team showed empathy for each other, and I wanted to make certain that each person was valued and respected. Every person matters, and every person is part of our superior culture of excellence. Building relationships on trust, honesty, and honor is the foundation of the culture of our Punahou Boys' Varsity Tennis Team. The culture of your team can be whatever you want it to be. Being a true champion in life isn't necessarily all about winning. Yes, it's nice to win, but at the end of the day, what's more important is your character as the leader and the character of your team. I know of many business organizations and sports teams that might not be number one in their fields but whose culture of excellence is highly respected by others. They're definitely viewed as winners. Building champion athletes of character who exhibit integrity and ethics at all times was my top priority and is what I'm most proud of.

To dig deeper, what are the qualities of a champion and a championship team? What standard of excellence do you want your team to have? What qualities do you want your individual team members to possess? What do you want your team to be known for? These are vital questions you need to answer in order to create your own superior culture of excellence. Such qualities as courage, discipline, humility, cooperation, resiliency, adaptability, loyalty, dedication, positivity, compassion, and self-control are amazing for any team to possess, and it depends on you as the coach to help your team acquire them. It's your job because it's your team. They are a reflection of you! So you, as the coach, had better possess these same qualities as well. Be the example for your team members. Be their inspiration. Be their role model!

As Punahou School's boys' varsity tennis coach, I wanted to build the best team that I could build every single year. The way I actually did it was by focusing on the well-being of all my team members. I wanted to really understand what was important to them and assist them in accomplishing their personal goals.

By communicating and understanding *their* priorities in life, I could help them make better choices, which would keep them on track toward the pursuit of their goals. It also paid off in that each member knew that I cared first and foremost about him as a person and second as a tennis player. This became a culture of caring and cohesion in which each team member felt safe and empowered, and I encouraged them to go after anything and everything in life. If you can think it or imagine it, you can achieve it.

You can't have a superior culture of excellence without teamwork. Helping team members through adversity deepens the commitment and trust among them. Think about an adversity situation of your own and who helped you through it. You probably have deeper trust and commitment with that person who helped you and shared that experience with you. It's the same when you're on a team and you get through a major challenge together. That's why building relationships is powerful. That's why being on a team is powerful. That's why creating a superior culture of excellence is paramount if you want to accomplish anything of significance.

I also wanted to make sure that my team members felt like they could talk with me about any concerns they had. I would give them honest feedback and expect the same from them. In fact, I also advised them that if they came to me with a problem, they should also bring a potential solution to that problem. I wanted them to think about different options and alternatives to find the best solution possible. As an exercise in role reversal, I also wanted them to think like a head coach or a CEO. Putting themselves in my shoes to see the whole spectrum and view the bigger picture instead of just their part of it often helped them understand my situation in helping both them and the team. In this way, I felt my teams had a bigger appreciation of me as a leader. It really opened their eyes to look at things from a different perspective so we could have the correct mindset when dealing with challenges together.

After every practice and match competition, I gave my team what I called my "world-famous quote of the day." Having them think about meaningful quotes that would help them in tennis and in life helped reinforce the things that we were working on, and they often remembered these words of wisdom during times of adversity. To this day, my former players recite certain "quotes of the day" when we meet. For example, I often shared a quote from Confucius: "Our greatest glory is not in never falling, but in rising every time we fall." Here are some other quotes I shared with my teams:

"A man is a hero not because he is braver than anybody else, but because he is brave for five minutes longer."

"When you want something you've never had, you have to do something you've never done."

"You didn't come this far to come only this far."

"The grass is not always greener on the other side. It's greener where you water it."

"One small crack doesn't mean you're broken. It means you were put to the test and didn't fall apart."

If you come across a quote that resonates with you, I highly encourage you to write it down and share it with your team. You never know when words of wisdom and inspirational sayings will positively impact your team, but I can guarantee it will, sooner or later.

Father Daniel Hendrickson

In positions of leadership, I am reminded time and again that fostering a culture that prioritizes excellence cannot be a destination one seeks to arrive at. Rather, it is an ongoing journey rooted in a compelling vision that serves as a personal and organizational guiding light. If you will, it is a beginning point that brightens, and as it gains intensity, it ignites the flames of aspiration within the hearts of others.

Drawing inspiration from the Jesuit charism of Magis, meaning "more" in Latin, a culture of excellence burgeons in environments where a greater good is always sought. In this sense, going beyond the ordinary is fully engrained in service of a mission be that personal, professional, organizational, or otherwise. It is through this shared focus on Magis that Creighton University, for instance, has been able to excel academically, in research, in service, in faith, and in the personal achievements of our graduates, because to always seek more is to always be growing, learning, and striving.

Regardless of where one stands on one's own path, each day is driven by a commitment to do more to achieve more is an estimable endeavor and one that, in fact, requires transformational leadership. This is why one of the greatest risks to the journey of building a sustained culture of excellence is unquestionably complacency. To accept the status quo at the very moment success is found is to confuse a milestone with the finish line. Every end is a beginning, and the journey must continue.

It is only by fostering a mindset of continuous improvement, and really, of an ability and interest to keep responding to the world around us, that we find the necessary balance to celebrate successes while also recognizing there is still so much more left to accomplish. It is only when this mentality is not just understood, but truly embodied, that we find the momentum to keep propelling so that none of us are ever at risk of getting stuck, or worse, falling behind.

I have always admired the simple but powerful words of the Victorian-era British Jesuit priest and poet Gerard Manley Hopkins, who in *As Kingfisher's Catch Fire*, captures the good ambitions of our lives and loves as nothing shy of holy, saying quite definitively, and thereby untiringly, "I say móre."

Father Daniel Hendrickson, S.J., Ph.D.
President, Creighton University

SUPERIOR DISCIPLINED DETAILS

I often hear people say that we need to be on the *same page*. When I was coaching, being on the same page was not good enough for me—it was not at the level of my high standard of excellence. I wanted my team members and me to be in the *same sentence on the exact word on the precise letter of that word.* That's the reason why there's a tremendous difference between good details and superior disciplined details. Many successful businesses and teams incorporate good details, but truly elite organizations have superior disciplined details. They are very meticulous and never sacrifice quality; great leaders know it's the little things that can separate their team or organization from everyone else. You can have superior disciplined details because it's a choice you can make, it raises your level to the highest standard of excellence, and it's a critical part of your superior culture.

Let's consider Toyota versus Ferrari and compare these two very different but extremely successful automobile companies. Toyota is the number one selling car in the world—more than ten million a year—and the company boasts a market cap of more than $200 billion. The cars are well-made, dependable, safe, and reasonably priced. People who own Toyotas are generally very happy with them. Ferrari, on the other hand, produces only about eight thousand cars each year in order to maintain the exclusivity of the supercar brand. In the interests of exclusivity, Ferrari ideally wants to deliver one less car than the demand, and their supercars are often preordered a year or so in advance. Ferrari is consistently rated as one of the world's most powerful and recognizable brands.

Why is it that when we see a Ferrari on the road, we're captivated, and our attention is drawn to it? After all, it's just a car, right? It has four tires and gets you from one place to the next. If you had a choice between owning a Toyota or a Ferrari, which would you choose? This is not a trick question. If the insurance and service visits were completely paid for, which car would you choose? Well, I think you and I would choose the Ferrari in a heartbeat. Ferrari may be in the same automobile market as other successful car manufacturers, but it's in the highest class in a league of its own.

Competitor Lamborghini was founded in 1963 when its founder owned a Ferrari and wanted to build cars that would exceed the Ferrari's details and style. It is truly a compliment when you set a high standard, and others emulate and compete with you to try to surpass your achievements. So, what separates

Ferrari from all the other automobile companies? Why are these cars so famous and unique and among the most sought-after in the world? It's their superior disciplined details. In addition to their distinctive design and style, they use the finest leather in the world, with each leather seat hand-sewn, and the car's meticulous final inspections employ an X-ray machine to identify the smallest cracks or flaws.

The overarching goal is attaining the highest possible standards for quality. The pride and superior details that go into a Ferrari are generally seen as symbols of speed, wealth, and luxury. For other car companies, a new model often involves just a small redesign with some additional horsepower. For Ferrari, a new model is a new concept with new positioning and completely new technological features. Ferrari consistently pushes for the highest standards and strives for the highest levels of detailed excellence—both in their cars and from members of their team. There is absolutely nothing wrong with other successful car companies, but we should all be striving for a strong and unique identity like Ferrari's. Because of their superior disciplined details, the company consistently develops the greatest cars in the world and has ultimate pride in its product and its team's superior culture of excellence.

HIGH ACHIEVERS VS. SUPERIOR ACHIEVERS

I love working with people who are high achievers. But I want to coach and inspire them to become *superior* achievers. Both possess a drive for accomplishment and success, but there are distinct differences between the two. High achievers are disciplined and consistently perform at a level above average and excel in their endeavors. They are goal-oriented and work diligently to meet and exceed expectations and strive to continuously improve their skills and performance. High achievers tend to set ambitious goals and often achieve remarkable results in their respective fields.

On the other hand, superior achievers go beyond high achievement and consistently demonstrate exceptional performance and surpass the standards set by high achievers. They set themselves apart by their ability to lead, innovate, and make a significant impact in their chosen areas. Superior achievers possess a unique combination of qualities such as visionary thinking, creativity, work ethic, and the ability to inspire and influence others. They often challenge the status quo and seek groundbreaking solutions to complex problems. Superior achievers are also driven by intrinsic motivation and a deep passion for their work, and they consistently push boundaries and redefine what is possible.

Legendary NFL quarterback Tom Brady led his teams to ten Super Bowls—winning seven, and was named Super Bowl MVP five times. Many people believe he is the greatest football quarterback of all time. But why was he able to achieve this unprecedented level of success? Let's take a look back at how his NFL career began. When Tom Brady played college football at the University of Michigan, he was named the "Comeback Kid" for his ability to turn around losing situations. He even led his team to win the 1999 Citrus Bowl and 2000 Orange Bowl. After graduating from the University of Michigan, Brady entered the 2000 NFL draft. Many NFL coaches and scouts evaluated him and concluded the following:

- Slow foot speed and lacked mobility
- Average arm strength and doesn't throw a tight spiral
- Can't drive the ball downfield
- Skinny and lacks great physical stature
- Gets knocked down easily

Some coaches and scouts even said that his good statistics in college were a product of him playing on a great team rather than him being a great player. Because of these concerns, Brady's value would plummet. After watching six quarterbacks get drafted, he was finally selected in the sixth round, pick number one hundred ninety-nine by the New England Patriots.

Brady said, "You're drafted based on your talent or your potential, but the sustainable part about talent and potential is working hard. Guys who were ahead of me were always physically way more gifted than me. I had to make up a lot of ground physically in order to catch them." Once he joined the Patriots, he committed to putting in more work and dedication than any of his teammates. Brady said, "Working hard is a very sustainable trait and a part of your character. If you don't have that, at some point, the talent does wear off." When asked about his former Patriot teammate, Kliff Kingsbury, said, "The total commitment, lifestyle, sleep, eat, study, work that he's put into that, it's insane. When I got there, I thought I worked hard, then I watched what he did, and it was on a whole different level. There's a reason he's the best there ever was."

In just his second season as the starting quarterback in New England, Brady led the Patriots to their first-ever Super Bowl victory. He was named Super Bowl MVP and became the youngest in his position to win the championship. Besides his work ethic, I'm tremendously impressed with his willingness to be a team player. Despite winning multiple championships, Brady has never been the highest-paid player in the NFL. Because NFL teams operate under a salary cap, it's estimated that Brady has sacrificed at least $60M to help his team build rosters that can contend to win Super Bowls.

Years later, when asked to reflect back on Tom Brady being drafted as the one hundred ninety-ninth pick, former San Francisco 49ers Head Coach Steve Mariucci said, "We didn't open up his chest and look at his heart. We didn't look at that. I don't know if anybody did. What kind of spine he had—and resiliency, and all the things that make him really great."

Brady was a high achiever in college and transformed into a superior achiever once he entered the NFL. And he was likely extra motivated after feeling disappointed about being drafted so low. He had something to prove to himself (as well as to those coaches and scouts) and began building his superior culture of excellence. After studying numerous superior achievers in sports and business, I've found a common thread in all of them—heart!

THE ROBBIE LIM STORY (CONTINUED)

Earlier, I shared Robbie Lim's story, but only through his junior year in high school. Here's what happened the following year. In 2004, Robbie was the two-time state singles champion and captain of our Punahou boys' varsity team, and what an incredible captain he was. He continued to help and nurture his teammates, partly by reciting inspirational quotes from well-known movies, which would motivate everyone—including me. Robbie had a lot of fun and gave one thousand percent effort all the time. Practices and matches were all the same to him. That's how the mindset is with champions.

After going undefeated during the regular season, Robbie won our league tournament, earning him the number-one seed for the state championship on the Big Island. When Robbie won the state championship as a sophomore, two of his opponents had issues with cramping. In his junior year, Robbie and his opponent both suffered major cramping in the quarterfinals, but Robbie persevered through these unforgettable matches to win his second state singles championship. Now a senior and two-time state champion, Robbie was definitely favored to win again.

If you know anything about the weather in Hawaii, you know it can get extremely hot during the month of May. Having my team members properly hydrated was a definite priority. In fact, I had them drink extra water starting one full week before we left Oahu for the Big Island. As prepared as we were, it was still guaranteed to feel like an oven, and everyone would need to deal with it.

Our team clinched the state team championship on the second day, and we were all looking forward to the semifinals and finals on the third day. Robbie matched up against the top player from the Big Island, who had a very strong serve and a powerful all-court game. As for me, I was planning ahead, thinking of what Robbie needed to do in the semifinals under the extremely hot conditions. I expected he would win and then have a one-hour rest period before playing the championship final.

I wanted to make sure he would give it his best and earn a third singles title. In order for Robbie to have that opportunity, we focused on our strategy and how well he could execute it. I told Robbie that this semifinal was going to be a tough match, that there was a hard way of winning and a smart way of winning. The hard way would be for Robbie to play a three-hour match using his usual aggressive baseline game to wear down and ultimately break his opponent physically and mentally. The problem would be that he'd most likely win but then have no gas left in the tank for the championship final. The smart way would be for Robbie to play shorter points by taking advantage of midcourt balls and attacking the net as soon as possible. In this way, he would still likely win the semifinal match but would have more gas in that tank for the final.

I went over these two strategy options with Robbie and told him it was up to him to make a choice and live with the consequences. Robbie went out on the court and gave his usual one thousand percent effort and competed with class. I was so proud watching him. However, he was doing it the hard way. It was like a heavyweight boxing match, and both players exchanged major blows with their powerful groundstrokes. It was a grueling match for both players. Robbie won 7–6, 7–5, but the match lasted three hours. The other semifinal, meanwhile, lasted barely an hour. Robbie had one hour to rest and recover, while his opponent had three.

In matches, Robbie was always very prepared and better hydrated than most. Most players would have a water jug or a small cooler with water and Gatorade. Not Robbie. He had one of those big family-size coolers loaded with water, Gatorade, fruit, and enough drinks for an entire team. And the funny thing is, he would have two of the younger players on the team carry it out onto the court for him.

Despite the grueling heat and his short break, Robbie seemed to be recovering well before the championship match. I was still very concerned that he'd expended too much energy in the earlier match and might not have enough left to go the distance. After reviewing our strategy with him, I looked at Robbie and said, "Who's the champ?"

He looked at me with confidence and replied, "Coach, I'm the champ!"

I responded, "Go get 'em, champ!" We both smiled as he walked onto the court, knowing that this was the final tennis match of his high school career.

His opponent was a tough competitor and another very strong player from the Big Island. I knew there was nothing further I could do to prepare Robbie for this occasion. Now, it was all up to him to compete and execute. And compete and execute is what he did. Robbie was playing brilliant tennis. His serves were strong, his groundstrokes powerful, his strategy effective, and all this was performed with a determined mindset. Robbie dominated and won the first set 6-1.

I walked onto the court for our two-minute coaching break and told Robbie to keep his focus, play one point at a time, and stay committed to our strategy. Because of the heat and the amount of energy he had expended in the semifinal,

Robbie's only hope was to play shorter points and attack the net as soon as the opportunity presented itself. Yes, this was the "smart way"—very similar to how I'd wanted him to play in the semifinal. I felt good seeing that he'd also committed to this strategy in the final. As the umpire yelled out, "Time," I hugged Robbie, telling him how proud I was and that this was likely the last time I'd be coaching him.

Robbie responded, "Coach, you're the champ!"

Robbie began serving the second set with a strong, focused mindset and continued to execute our strategy flawlessly. He was controlling the points with his heavy topspin groundstrokes, taking advantage of every midcourt shot and finishing off the point with his volley or overhead. It was total dominance, and every spectator could see why Robbie was a champion. But with a 3–1 lead in the second set, Robbie took an unusual amount of extra time before serving the next game. He looked over at me, and I knew something was wrong. Immediately after giving me that look, Robbie fell to the ground with extremely painful cramps in both legs. The umpire called a medical time-out, and I ran onto the court, where Robbie was screaming in pain. I mean, he was screaming! The pain was so severe that we moved him into a shaded area next to the court. As we tried to keep the spectators away, Robbie began experiencing full-body cramps, and the screaming grew even louder. After five minutes of agony, the umpire said that Robbie needed to get back onto the court to continue playing or retire the match.

"Robbie," I said, "this is bad. I mean really bad. We need to retire from the match."

"Coach, I want to get back on the court and try," he told me.

"Robs, I know you can be stubborn in a good way, but this is being stubborn in a bad way. Let's retire the match. There's no way you'll be able to finish in this condition."

"Coach, please let me just try one more time."

"You know that I'm more concerned about you and your health rather than a tennis match, right?"

Robbie nodded and again said, "Let me try one more time."

I stepped aside, and Robbie grabbed his tennis racket and slowly hobbled back onto the court toward the baseline to serve. With a 3–1 lead in the set, he was only three games away and probably needed just ten more minutes to win the match. Still in obvious pain, Robbie hit the softest serve I've ever seen in my life and couldn't move two steps to play the next shot. The exact same thing happened on the next point. Before serving the third point, Robbie looked at me again and then fell to the ground. The cramps were back, along with the screaming.

I ran onto the court, and he hobbled his way toward the back fence to pick up his towel. He covered his head with the towel, crying. I started crying too. I lifted up one end of the towel, and then we were both under there crying together.

I said, "Champ, that's it. I told the umpire as I ran out here that you're done, that we retire."

"Coach, I don't want to give up. I never give up. I don't want to let my teammates down, and I don't want to let you down."

"Robs, the whole team and I are so proud of you. This is not giving up. You gave everything you had, and there's nothing left to give. We're calling an ambulance to take you to the hospital."

Then our entire team gathered around him, and everyone congratulated Robbie for giving everything he had. The paramedics came soon after to walk him slowly to the ambulance.

After I talked with his parents, Richard and Carin Lim, it was determined that Robbie wouldn't return on the flight with the team. He'd be treated with IVs at the hospital and would probably take an evening flight back to Oahu. I gathered my team together, and we left the tennis club and headed to Kona Airport.

Once we checked in and cleared security, we all sat down together in the restaurant and digested everything that had happened earlier. I listened to the guys talk about how impressed they were with their captain. They were inspired by watching how Robbie gave everything he had, and they were missing him because he wasn't going home with us. As I listened to these priceless comments, my phone rang.

The call was from a nurse back at the hospital. "Coach Rusty," she said, "your player Robbie is very stubborn. He wants to leave the hospital and get to the airport in time to travel back with the team."

"He's stubborn, all right," I answered, "but hopefully, he's recovering and feeling better there with you."

"He left ten minutes ago," she said. "He's coming to meet you there."

I shook my head and thought to myself, *That's Robbie!* I didn't tell any of the guys that their captain was on his way because I wanted to see their reaction. Twenty minutes later, Robbie walked into the restaurant with tears in his eyes. His teammates, also teary-eyed, were super excited to see him, and they all hugged him and told him how proud they were of him. It brought tears to my eyes, and it was clear to me that this was about much more than just playing tennis. This was the superior culture of excellence of our tennis team.

Section 2: The 3 C's of Leadership

Now that you've completed the 3 C's of Leadership, please take ten minutes to honestly rank yourself and answer the questions. The purpose of the assessment is to help you identify action items that will enable you to move forward with your leadership journey to becoming a superior leader. Below, you will find questions with corresponding gray boxes. Please use these boxes to rate yourself on a scale of 1-10 (1 being "needs improvement" and 10 being "superior") on your ability to do the specified task. Then, answer the corresponding free-response question.

How would you rate your ability to finish projects?

Name a project that you feel needs to be moved to completion.

_____

_____

_____

Successful people can become complacent, but to truly be superior, you must take risks. How do you rate yourself in taking calculated risks?

Risk promotes growth. What is a calculated risk you are contemplating to promote the growth of your objectives?

_____

_____

_____

How would you rate your overall ability to improve the three main categories of choices regarding mindset, health, and personal growth?

Specifically, what can you do today to improve in all three areas of mindset, health, and personal growth?

_____

_____

_____

How do you rate your ability to proactively avoid the 4 Misses (miscommunication, misunderstanding, misperception, misinformation)?

What specifically can you do this week to proactively avoid the 4 Misses?

_____

_____

_____

Rate your skill level at consistently preventing miscommunication.

What are some past examples of the 4 Misses affecting you?

_____

_____

_____

How would you rate your ability to find common connections with others?

What are examples of various ways you can communicate with someone to create powerful connections with them?

_____

_____

_____

Rate how aware you are of driving "improvement" versus misusing the word "change" when communicating.

What are two areas you can identify that you're focused on "improving" versus "changing"?

_____

_____

_____

How would you rate your ability to create a superior culture in your organization?

What are three big priorities you can focus on in order to build a superior culture within your organization?

_____

_____

_____

How would you rate your leadership in terms of striving for superior excellence?

What little details are you practicing today to support a culture of superior excellence within your organization?

_____

_____

_____

How would you rate your ability to raise your standards to superior disciplined details?

How can you adopt superior disciplined details to move your organization to Ferrari standards?

_____

_____

_____

How would you rate your ability to develop high achievers?

What can you do to transform and enhance your high achievers to become superior achievers?

_____

_____

_____

Add up your total score for this assessment and enter your score here.

THE 4 P'S FOR ACHIEVING SUCCESS

section 3

I WAS TWENTY-FOUR when I was asked by our athletic director and tennis director to be the head coach for the Punahou School boys' varsity tennis team. I felt honored, but I also felt a huge responsibility to help develop these impressionable high school players. I wanted to be the best coach for them, build the best team, and give them the best team experience. I wanted to positively enhance all their lives by helping them become champions on the tennis court and champions in life. I wanted to help them see the bigger picture in life and not worry about the petty things that often cause distractions and unnecessary stress. Basically, I wanted us to be the best in everything we did. Obviously, I set high expectations for myself and needed to create a system to achieve this. This was when I developed a framework I refer to as the 4 P's:

People + Purpose + Process + Performance = Success

People, purpose, process, and performance are crucial elements for a team to achieve success. Each of these components plays a unique role in contributing to the team's effectiveness and overall outcome. It ensures that the team has the right talent, a clear direction, efficient workflows, and a focus on continuous improvement. When these elements are effectively integrated, they create a strong foundation for success and enhance the team's ability to achieve their objectives, maximize potential, and deliver exceptional results.

Chapter 8

PEOPLE

"A bird sitting on a tree is never afraid
of the branch breaking, because her trust is not
on the branch but on her own wings."

—*Anonymous*

WHEN YOU'RE A LEADER, you deal with people. Great leaders are not dictators. Great leaders enjoy working with people and building a special team bond where everyone is important and everyone contributes equally. Great leaders genuinely care about them and will help them improve themselves in every possible way. Forming these bonds and connecting with people is imperative in order to build trust, respect, and loyalty. When you treat your people like family, the team begins to evolve into more than just a team—more like a second family. This is when the team members know their leader will do anything for them, and they, in turn, will want to do anything for the leader.

Empathy is defined as *the ability to understand and share the feelings of others*. All great leaders empathize with their team members, but, more importantly, every team member knows that their leader possesses this empathy. This connection between the team members and their leader should be a powerful one. It's also a necessary one—it's how they know their leader is concerned with their well-being.

Finding people with great character is of paramount importance when building a team, whether in business or sports. The character of team members influences not only the team's performance but also its culture and overall success. Building a team with individuals who possess integrity, honesty, and a strong moral compass fosters a culture of trust and collaboration. When team members have trust in one another, they can rely on each other's words and actions, leading to better communication, cooperation, and synergy. With this foundation of trust, team members can openly share ideas, give and receive honest feedback, and work toward common goals with shared dedication and respect.

During challenging situations, individuals with great character will often display resilience and ethical decision-making. These team members with strong values and principles can navigate complex scenarios while maintaining their integrity. They will make choices based on what is right even when faced with difficult circumstances. This framework helps build a team that can weather storms, learn from failures, and emerge stronger because they are guided by a shared commitment to doing the right thing. Team members with great character will also serve as role models and positively influence the team's culture and behavior. Their actions inspire others to uphold similar values and exhibit integrity, professionalism, and respect. This creates a virtuous cycle where the team's collective character strengthens over time. When everyone upholds high ethical standards and demonstrates strong character, it elevates the team's reputation, attracts like-minded people, and builds a foundation for long-term achievements.

MAKE AN IMPACT

You are a coach if you're in a position of influence. The question is, how good a coach are you? The best CEOs in business and the best head coaches in sports are always finding ways to better themselves and their teams. They're always searching for ways to be more effective and efficient. Complacency is never an issue with them. They're on a constant quest to go "beyond the lines" (you might recognize that as the title of my first book) in building deeper trust, respect, and purpose with their teams. Results, productivity, and winning become a by-product of going beyond the lines, and that's how you achieve success with your team. Ultimately, every coach should strive to further develop and enhance the character, self-discipline, and habits of every team member, giving them the tools to help others in turn.

Before you can coach people effectively, you need to coach yourself first. How can you build and train championship qualities in others if you yourself don't possess those qualities? Your talk would be meaningless to your team, and you'd be perceived as hypocritical and ineffective. Walking the walk is essential before talking the talk. Team members need to see you as someone with championship qualities and habits in order for you to help instill those same qualities and habits in them. This will make you real and relevant to them, which sets up the foundation for you to build a championship culture for peak performance with your team.

Are you making a difference in society? Do you have a positive impact on others every day? If you didn't show up at work today, would people miss you? If you're on a football team and you're not at the game with your team, would their odds of winning the game be a little lower because of your absence? Israelmore Ayivor said, "Everybody is standing, but you must stand out." You never truly know what your impact is on others until situations like these occur. If you believe in God, I'm sure He didn't create you just for you to be average. I'm sure He didn't create you to just take up space in this world. God wants you to make a positive impact, and the way you make a positive impact in this world is by making a positive impact on others.

If the coach leads with fairness and is someone the team respects, then every person on the team will have a deeper connection and commitment to the team because two things are happening: They're doing something they're good at, and they feel appreciated. Moreover, if they feel like they're making an impact by improving their lives and making other people's lives better, then they know they're doing something extremely meaningful. Think about it. This is something I strive for with my teams every single day. I let each individual know what their strengths are so that they know what they're good at and how they can help our team. I also let them know that it's imperative to keep building their strengths. Their mindset should never be complacent; I want them to always think about ways to make their strengths stronger. The strengths you have as a team allow you to be in a position to achieve success, which is why it's important to amplify these strengths.

Making someone feel appreciated is paramount. Everyone wants to feel like they matter. It's good to get a pat on the back. People need to feel that they're making a difference. A positive difference! I would do this by genuinely complimenting my players and telling them that I notice their effort and dedication, not only in improving themselves but also in encouraging and helping their teammates. You, as the leader, might notice these things, but you also need to articulate them. That's the key.

As head coach of the Punahou School boys' varsity tennis team for twenty-two years, I only missed one match. It was in April 2014, against Mid-Pacific Institute. The reason was my induction into Creighton University's Hall of Fame in Omaha, Nebraska. I didn't want to miss even a single match because my team was my priority as head coach. Honors and awards are nice but not a priority for me. I shared the news about the induction with my players, and it was they who convinced me to go. They reminded me that this was a special honor, that I needed to be at the induction, and that they would "take care of business" on the tennis court. They did, and we defeated Mid-Pacific 4–1. I was away from my team for three days, and when I returned to practice, they all told me how much they'd missed me. I knew I was making an impact. A positive impact!

PARENTS ARE COACHES

If you're a parent, you're a coach. You are coaching your sons and daughters through life. It's parents who first shape the fundamental character of their children. For me, as a tennis coach, I can enhance kids' lives by further developing their character and building championship habits in them. I can help build their superior culture of excellence and guide them in practices and matches. I can also coach the parents to reinforce what we are striving toward. We are all on the same team with the same ultimate goals—to give their sons or daughters a priceless, positive experience on the team and help them develop their full potential.

Through the years, I have encountered and worked with literally thousands of parents—all types of parents. Almost all of them have the right goals to provide for their kids and hope that they will find their passion and develop their full potential in life. But why do some kids behave inappropriately? Why do some kids fall far short of reaching their full potential? Why do some kids go off on the wrong tangents and get into trouble or do bad things to others? The answer is a variety of reasons. Yes, there are good and bad people in this world, and no doubt there always will be. A newborn baby is innocent and ready to be coached and trained by Mom and Dad. A newborn isn't born with prejudice or bad character. It's the parents' responsibility to coach their kids properly early on in life. But despite the best intentions, there are still bad parents in the world. If your kids go astray, go off on wrong tangents, and do bad things to others, don't blame them. Blame yourself.

Remember that no matter who you are or how good you think you are, you can always be replaced. A CEO of a failing business can be fired in hopes that a new leader will save the company and make it profitable. A sports team with multiple losing seasons will often fire the head coach in hopes that the new coach will turn things around by winning championships. Children, however, cannot fire their parents. Still, everyone can be accountable for his or her own actions.

As a coach, I take full responsibility for all of my players' actions on the team, good and bad. As a parent, you need to do the same. That goes for the CEO of a company too. Taking accountability for yourself and your team actually teaches others to take accountability for themselves. It's walking the walk. People see what you do and how you do it. The most impactful coaching often comes through your own actions. Think about a little boy or girl watching his or her parents treat others with kindness and respect. What message do you think that boy or girl learns from watching that action? Now, think about that little boy or girl watching their parents being disrespectful and mean to others. What do you think they learn from that action? Yes, kids do tend to emulate their parents, believing that their parents' actions are acceptable and appropriate. That's the power the leader has and why it's crucial to be aware of every action you take because of the message it sends to others.

I told my players that I would not protect them from a challenge. But instead, I was going to teach them how to face it. I would then share with the parents what I said to their sons so they could support and reinforce the lessons I was trying to instill in their children. Life is challenging, and they will definitely experience many adversities in their own lives. It's inevitable.

I've coached more than a thousand students over the past three decades. What helped my players and teams tremendously was keeping their parents engaged in what we did on the tennis court. I realized that this was most likely a new experience for them, which is why it was necessary for me to "coach" and clearly communicate what I was doing to train their sons and daughters. Obviously, this takes a little more time, but being proactive in this way is well worth avoiding the 4 Misses.

For example, I would advise parents that they should reward behavior and attitude, not the result. I've found that when you reward and value good sportsmanship, respect for your opponent, effort, resiliency, positivity, courage, fight, and toughness, this keeps everyone on the right track to do the things that are most important—to be genuinely good people. Incidentally, encouraging these great behaviors directly affects performance, which leads to better results and winning. I was always most proud when players of mine would win sportsmanship trophies (and I would make a big deal about it) because it was an acknowledgment that others recognized their amazing character.

Another example is parents shouldn't give their kids everything they want. They need to teach them the value of hard work and to appreciate things more. If everything is given to them, they will take things for granted and not truly appreciate working hard for something they really want. Having kids do household chores such as washing dishes, taking out the garbage, and doing laundry are simple yet important things that every child should be doing in every family. As a teenager, I did these things and also mowed lawns and washed cars for my neighbors to earn money. As a parent, saying the word "no" is often valuable in teaching and guiding kids. Why do some kids become spoiled and feel entitled? It's because the parents give them everything they want without having to work for it. The best kids are the ones who work hard for something they want because they'll appreciate the effort and time they put into it.

During my freshman through junior years in high school, I needed to ride our City & County's express bus to and from school, which took around an hour and a half each way. Once I got my driver's license, I must have asked my parents a hundred times to please let me drive to school instead of having to catch the bus. Their response consistently was, "No, you need to take the bus." At the start of my senior year, my parents finally allowed me to borrow my grandfather's old Dodge. It was brown and looked like an old man's car, which it was. But in my mind, I appreciated having a car and not having to ride the bus anymore, sleeping in a little bit longer, and being able to save time on my commute. The car's air-conditioning was broken, and I perspired a lot driving home from school in the Hawaiian afternoon sun. Because of this, I also appreciated cars with air-conditioning. I told myself that someday, when I could afford to buy my own car, it would be one with a functioning air-conditioning unit. Because of this experience, today, I definitely appreciate having the freedom to drive where I want, when I want—and with air-conditioning!

MAKE GOOD PEOPLE GREAT

Since retiring as head coach from Punahou School in 2015, I have been doing what I set out to do since I left—helping people in business, sports, and life. I like helping good people and making them great. I like coaching great people and making them extraordinary. And I want to inspire you to do the same. But how is it done?

After reading my first book, *Beyond the Lines: Creating a Leadership Culture to Achieve Extraordinary Results*, many CEOs began hiring me as a keynote speaker for their companies because they obviously care about making their teams better. They also purchased books for all of their team members, which is absolutely fantastic as it demonstrates that the CEO cares about them and their self-improvement. The CEO wants to help their organization by striving to improve each individual, which makes the entire team better collectively. They're on the right track, seeking more clarity and better alignment to achieve greater success for their organization.

There's a famous exchange between a CFO and a CEO where the CFO asks, "What happens if we invest in developing our people, and then they leave us?"

The CEO responds, "What if we don't and they stay?" Some relationships we have with people will last forever, and some have expiration dates. The best leaders and coaches will invest time and money in their people. You can't control whether a team member will stay on your team or leave. Obviously, if you had a choice, you would want them to stay. But *you always need to do things that are in the best interest of your people in order to help them.* Your impact will be positive, valuable, and long-lasting, and they will always remember and be grateful for the help that you gave them.

Another way of helping to improve your people and your organization is to hire a leadership/peak performance coach. Since my book became available, I have met with countless CEOs and business owners, head coaches of sports teams, and parents—all of whom have great principles, values, and discipline but don't know how best to use them to effectively help their team. They obviously are amazing people who care about bettering themselves and the people around them but *there's a gigantic difference between being a great person and a great leader.* Always remember this: If you think it's too expensive to hire an expert, just wait and see what happens if you enlist the services of an amateur or if you do nothing. You get what you pay for, and there's no substitute for quality and priceless guidance. The greatest leaders care deeply about their people and will always find ways to help them consistently improve.

When I meet with business leaders, I ask them what they feel are the top three things their company does that make their organization successful. Once they share their insights with me, I ask them to honestly rate those three areas on a scale of one to ten. I'm usually amazed that their ratings are sometimes only average to above average, often in the five to seven range—and yet these are the three things their company is known for! Every elite organization and team should have at least one area in which they can sincerely rate themselves in the nine to ten range.

Even moderately successful teams, who may only be average in a number of areas, should be outstanding in at least one area. Once they attain a high standard of excellence in that one area, it often becomes contagious to other areas in the organization. The potential for improvement in these companies is huge because they can visualize being much more effective and efficient with other team members and with clients. They can focus on superior disciplined details and strive to execute at the highest level. Once I highlight it in this way, it becomes very clear to these executives that they can choose to improve their organization in specific areas that allow them noticeably higher, more quantifiable levels of success.

A good example of this is Hawaiian Airlines, which at one point was becoming known as a second-rate airline, especially for its late departures and arrivals, and ultimately filed for bankruptcy in 2003. Two years later, Mark Dunkerley was appointed Hawaiian's CEO. Dunkerley's focus was on-time performance because, in his mind, there was no excuse for not being punctual in Hawaii, with its consistently good weather year-round. Under his leadership, Hawaiian Air soon became number one in the United States for on-time arrivals and a global leader for on-time performance. Achieving this rating was extremely significant, as he transformed what had been known as a second-rate airline into one that is now second to none. The company emerged from bankruptcy in 2005 and became hugely profitable, earning gross revenues of $2.64 billion during Dunkerley's fifteen-year tenure. I always say that everything starts with the head coach or CEO, and it's definitely true in this case. Mark Dunkerley is praised and credited for turning a failing airline into one that is achieving excellence in many categories, but it all started because they began to excel in one category first—on-time arrivals.

Speaking of successful business leaders, Sir Richard Branson is the founder of the Virgin Group, which encompasses more than four hundred companies. His businesses have impacted all of us at some point in our lives. In 2000, Branson was knighted at Buckingham Palace for his entrepreneurship in land, air, sea, and space travel. "When I started Virgin from a basement in West London," Branson once told an interviewer, "There was no great plan or strategy. I didn't set out to build a business empire. For me, building a business is all about doing something to be proud of, bringing talented people together, and creating something that's going to make a real difference to other people's lives."

The parallels between coaching sports teams and business teams are countless. Branson is also a firm believer in the correlation between sports and business. Branson said, "A lot of things learned through sport are transferable into other aspects of life. Skills acquired through tennis have been beneficial to business careers. Studies have shown that playing sports early in life is correlated with greater success in business, since competitive sports can teach discipline, teamwork, and leadership skills. One key lesson I've learned, which applies far beyond the tennis court, is to treat each point separately. It's critical to move on from the last mistake you made and focus on the next point, or in business, the next challenge. Tennis, like business, moves so quickly that if you dwell on the past for even a few minutes, an opportunity will have passed, and the moment will be lost. You have to get into the right frame of mind in order to perform your best, and need to be able to put setbacks behind you instantly."

Every team is a reflection of their leader. If there's dysfunction, low morale, and high turnover in a company, blame the CEO and the executives. They're the people responsible for their team. They're the coaches. A weak, ineffective leader will blame others when, in fact, it's the leader's fault for not finding a way to lead effectively. On the other hand, if a company has loyalty, high morale, and a culture of excellence, give all the credit in the world to the CEO and his or her executives. They're the leaders who know how to coach.

Dick Vermeil

My first and most fundamental principle is to *make sure your people know you care.* I have always believed great leaders have a way of making people feel like they like them, that they care about their well-being, and they show respect whenever it is appropriately earned. My coaching staff and I always worked within the simple concept that *players don't care how much you know until they know how much you care.*

Caring always leaves an ever-lasting impression. You need to make the commitment to be a leader who is sensitive to their needs and willing to say "I love you" when you truly and sincerely feel this kind of deep passion. It has happened to me on all the teams I have coached, including high school, junior college, Division I college, and in the NFL with three teams. We can all develop this caring, emotional attitude. Anyone can do it! All you have to do is instill a disciplined concept of caring into your daily mental preparation routine as a leader. When you do, you will find out as I did. Caring becomes the foundation of synchronizing attitudes while initiating a bonding process, and it pulls people together. Once they are together, they won't want to let the other guy down.

Let me ask you this, "Who do you put first, your people or your win-loss record?" When you put your people first, your win-loss record will take care of itself. Consequently, it ends up being a win-win situation for all involved, and your team becomes a very tough team to beat when you are tied together by this concept. Now, I'm not implying that you don't show some tough love along the way whenever needed. There are always times when you have to be compassionately tough on individuals because there are always people who can't drive themselves without a tough, sensitive, caring leader being their personal driver. You may often recognize there's more potential in a person than he may see in himself, which provides you an opportunity as his leader to help him recognize it and get better. When caring about your people is connected to getting better at something that really matters to them, it connects everyone to strive for excellence and for a larger purpose than personal gain. I constantly aimed to help our players move their commitment from their heads to their hearts, which led them to make contributions beyond the boundaries of their responsibilities and paychecks.

Dick Vermeil
Super Bowl Champion Head Coach
1999 St. Louis Rams

GREAT LEADERS ARE MADE

Great leaders are authentic and positive. They communicate well with people and inspire them to achieve both the task at hand and the broader goals that they set. Great leaders have high standards, strong principles, and values. They help others strive for those same standards, principles, and values. Great leaders listen and create a safe, fun environment. They understand the importance of teamwork and giving their team members opportunities for growth. They celebrate the success of others. A great leader generates enthusiasm and has a positive mindset. He or she creates a vision and then develops a detailed process to accomplish it. A great leader is always a mentor who genuinely cares about the feelings and well-being of team members. A great leader is strong and tough in a crisis situation, and they are dependable, trusted, and respected by the entire team. People don't want to be "managed," after all—they want to be guided. They know that no matter how challenging a situation might be, they can trust the leader to make the best decisions for the team.

In business, why is it that some assistant managers do not become good general managers? In football, why is it that some assistant coaches do not become good head coaches? There are numerous examples of successful offensive or defensive coordinators being promoted to head coach, expecting that their success as an assistant will carry over to their new role. But while there are some success stories, far too often, people struggle in their new positions and are terminated after just a year or two on the job.

The reason is clear. Anyone has the capacity to become a leader, but it doesn't mean that everyone wants to be or should be one. It's the same with parenting. Anyone can be a parent. But it doesn't mean that everyone wants to be or should be one. Some assistant managers are just good assistant managers—but will never be good general managers or CEOs. It's the same with an assistant football coach. An assistant coach might be an excellent offensive coordinator, but it doesn't guarantee that he'll be a good head coach. Promotions and advancement opportunities in business and sports are a good thing but only if you're prepared to lead in that new role. Are you educating yourself correctly to be prepared for an opportunity when it presents itself? Are you learning as much as you can to expand your skill set and help develop your leadership potential?

BOSS VS. LEADER

There is a tremendous difference between a boss and a leader. A boss cares about work. A leader cares about people. A boss often instills fear, while a leader generates enthusiasm. A boss dictates, and a leader asks. A boss often says "I," and a leader often says "we." A boss often blames others when a breakdown occurs; a leader corrects the problem and takes responsibility for it. A boss micromanages; a leader delegates. A boss has his own way of doing things, while a leader is interested in finding new and better ways of doing things. A boss takes credit, while a leader gives credit. A boss knows how things are done; a leader coaches people by showing them how things are done. Employees often say they work *for* a boss instead of saying they work *with* the leader. Employees often think of themselves as coworkers in their boss's environment instead of having the feeling they're part of a team with a strong leader. Which one are you? Which one do you want to be? If you're reading this book, it is clear to me that you care about people. You care enough to want to improve yourself as a leader in order to really help the people on your team.

Simply being in a leadership position doesn't make you a leader. A company's CEO might be the top executive, but they might not be a true leader. The general manager of a business might be in a leadership position, but they might not be a strong leader. The head coach of a sports team might run the program, but they might not be an effective leader. They all have the authority and the title, but their team members still don't have the desire to follow them. People must want to follow their leaders. People need to like and respect their leaders.

Great leaders are likable and have good relationships with people. Great leaders listen, are aware, and can take the collective pulse to consistently know what's happening with their teams. Great leaders make everyone around them better. They are creative and innovative and always find ways to keep things fresh. They are able to consistently inspire and motivate people on the team to give their best at all times. Team members want to follow leaders who know where they're going and who understand what goals they're striving to accomplish together. A great leader is fair and accountable for every action he or she takes, admitting when he or she has made a mistake and taking full responsibility for that decision. As a result, team members respect that leader even more, as no one needs to shoulder the blame but the leader himself. Great leaders have empathy and make people on their team feel like they belong. They *genuinely* want to help, support, and care for each team member—which in turn engenders further trust and loyalty.

Some leaders and coaches have their teams do things "above the line" instead of "below the line." My version of that is to focus on simply having high standards rather than low ones. But however you say it, it really comes down to what standards you and your team choose to live by. A great leader constantly strives for excellence and asks his or her team members to do the same. It's a matter of bettering yourself and having your team do the same—every single day. Focusing on performance goals definitely influences results. Everybody wants to win, get good results, and achieve certain goals. A great leader is never complacent. Instead, he or she seeks to outdo what was accomplished last year, a month ago, or even yesterday. Great leaders are always looking for ways to improve both themselves and their teams. This habit can almost become second nature if you have high standards.

Leadership is a skill that needs to be practiced. You cannot ask your team to do something that you aren't willing to do yourself. You must talk the talk and walk the walk. This is what great leaders do. It's how you will earn the respect of your team. You have heard it before, and it's true: You need to lead by example.

By definition, a good leader has followers. However, *a great leader builds other great leaders.* So many business owners and CEOs of successful companies have mentored others to follow their lead on the path to success. Think about the many great coaches whose assistant coaches or former players became head coaches or successful leaders of other sports teams or businesses. A great leader, ultimately, builds more great leaders.

POISE UNDER PRESSURE

When there's a crisis, people look toward their leader and closely observe their demeanor. The leader's words, actions, and physical presence will be under a microscope for everyone to see. If the leader shows weakness or uncertainty and appears unsettled, it does not instill confidence and belief in team members that the turbulent situation can be overcome. On the other hand, exceptional leaders always display remarkable composure in the face of adversity. Poise can be defined as *the ability to maintain calm and composure under intense pressure.* It is a characteristic that distinguishes exceptional leaders from the rest, and it's essential to exemplify this trait during times of crisis.

When leaders exhibit poise under pressure, it instills confidence in their team because it reassures them that the situation is manageable and that there's a path forward. During a crisis, leaders must make crucial decisions thoughtfully and swiftly. Poise allows leaders to evaluate options objectively, maintain focus, and choose the best course of action without succumbing to knee-jerk reactions. They are able to think rationally and make informed decisions even in the midst of chaos. Poised leaders will also convey information calmly and effectively because they know their team is looking for guidance and reassurance. This quality helps prevent panic, promotes teamwork, and facilitates coordinated efforts toward resolving the crisis. These exceptional leaders exhibiting poise under pressure radiate an aura of confidence, stability, and reliability, providing a sense of security to those under their leadership.

I think you'll agree with me that the President of the United States is under the biggest microscope in the world. When the September 11 attacks happened, I was watching television and closely observing President George W. Bush's response. His public demeanor conveyed a sense of strength, resolve, and unity, which resonated with many of us Americans. When he delivered a televised address to the nation, he expressed condolences for the victims, offered reassurance to the American people, and emphasized the need for unity. His measured and empathetic tone conveyed a sense of calm, providing solace and stability to a shocked and grieving nation.

President Bush exemplified poise whenever he spoke and worked to unify the nation and bridge political divides. He emphasized that our country would stand together in the face of adversity and that the attacks would not weaken America's resolve. His calls for national unity resonated with many citizens and helped foster a sense of togetherness during an unprecedented, difficult time.

When President Bush visited Ground Zero in New York City, the site of the World Trade Center attacks, just days after the event, the eyes of the world were on him. His physical presence there, expressing his support for the victims, rescue workers, and the city itself, was a powerful symbol of solidarity and leadership. It demonstrated his personal investment in the recovery efforts and provided comfort to those affected. I watched President Bush spend time with first responders, firefighters, police officers, and other individuals involved in the rescue and recovery efforts. His interactions with these heroes showcased his appreciation for their bravery and sacrifice. This engagement also helped boost morale and reinforced the nation's gratitude for their service. President Bush's poise and calm demeanor under pressure truly played a significant role in inspiring and rallying our country to remain resilient in the face of adversity.

COACHING VS. TEACHING

Legendary Dallas Cowboys Coach Tom Landry said, "A coach is someone who tells you what you don't want to hear, who has you see what you don't want to see, so you can be who you have always known you could be." I have great respect for teachers and their commitment to helping students in their classrooms. We have all learned from teachers in our past, and many of them have made positive, lasting impacts on us. I have stories about some great teachers I have had, and I'm sure you have similar stories as well. Some teachers help students learn specific subjects like math, science, and history, while other teachers help them learn specific skills such as violin, dance, golf, swimming, and yes, tennis.

The point is this: There's a significant difference between teaching and coaching. *A coach is a teacher who inspires a person or team through learning and guides them to be successful in life.* While teachers usually focus on helping students with specific subjects and skills, coaches help students with the whole person, not just the parts. For me as a tennis coach, I focus on training the entire player—physical skills, mental toughness, emotional awareness, strategy, and tactics, not to mention developing character, dealing with the environment, losing with grace, winning with humility, being a team player, and other important traits.

I can visualize a world where everyone becomes a coach; teachers become coaches in their classrooms, and business executives transform from managers into coaches for their team members, with the priority of helping the entire person, not just part of the person. I believe that, more often than not, coaches of sports teams have a much greater impact on their team members than teachers in the classroom. After all, an athlete typically spends significantly more time with his team and his coach than he does with his math teacher. A student might have a one-hour math class three days a week, but that same student might have football practice two hours a day, Monday through Friday, in addition to games on Saturday. Because of the time spent with the team, coaches' influence on the players and their development is extremely impactful. Ideally, this will have a positive, priceless effect.

Some teachers have a passion for teaching—they're great at doing what they do, and that's fine. An assistant manager might be fantastic doing what he does, and he doesn't want more responsibility—the general manager's job, for instance—and that's fine. An assistant coach might be valuable in that role and might not want to be a head coach, and that's fine, too. The point is this: These people have found their passion and have no interest in promotions, advancements, or more responsibilities. Not everyone aspires to become a CEO or head coach. But every role matters in your organization, and you can always enhance and improve the role you're in.

COACH THEM TO COACH THEMSELVES

As a tennis professional and coach, I obviously love tennis, but I also enjoy all sports. I love watching the different dynamics between coaches and athletes, especially when the pressure mounts in competition. For example, in football, when the game gets chaotic and hectic, what do you see the coach do? He calls a timeout to settle the team down. Well, in tennis, we have no timeouts. In basketball, the coach puts a team of five players on the court, but what does the coach do if one of his athletes is playing badly? He or she subs in a different player. In tennis, we have no substitutions. If I could have had timeouts and substitutions, I would have used them thousands of times.

Because of this, preparation was paramount for us. I needed to coach my players to coach themselves. Once I put my athlete on the tennis court for a competition, all I could really do was watch. At the state championship, coaching is not allowed during the match except between sets. On many occasions, I would be in agony watching my players because I felt like I was playing the match. I could almost feel an ulcer or a swollen appendix coming on because I'd feel the impact of every ball myself. I'd be squeezing internally, hoping that our shots would go in—but also hoping that my players would behave properly and play hard and smart from the first point until match point.

One of the most important things about preparation is controlling everything that you can control. Worrying about things beyond your control is completely useless and leads to mental and physical fatigue. Coaching and training your team members to focus only on things within their control is key. In business, a team member might feel unnecessary pressure because they're not hitting their projected sales numbers. Now, think about what this team member might begin to imagine. Because she isn't hitting the numbers, she might begin to think that her job is in jeopardy. You, as the leader, need to be aware of these thoughts, which will definitely inhibit performance. She may hit the numbers a week or two later, but you need to reassure her that you believe in her and that her job is secure. It's up to you as the coach to train good habits and make certain that your team members are focused on the right things. It sounds easy, but it's not. It takes awareness from the coach to consistently be in touch with the pulse and vibe of their team. I constantly told my players to "take care of business on our side of the net." Of course, we'd be aware of what our opponent was doing, but our primary focus was on what we did. If we can control everything within our control, it will lead to better execution, which leads to winning.

THE 3 CONS

People often talk about the pros and cons of a situation. Well, I assure you that these "3 Cons" are positive and absolutely necessary for coaches to help enhance each team member's commitment and experience with the team. When each team member practices these 3 Cons, trust and loyalty become deeper, and team excellence becomes higher. What are the 3 Cons? They're Contribute, Consistency, and Confidence. Every leader must instill these in each individual to help their team achieve success and potentially peak performance. Once this happens, it often becomes contagious because each team member will have a tendency to encourage and help other team members do what their leader did for them.

Contribute. People on a team want to feel that they're making a difference. They want to feel that what they're doing is important and impactful. Think about it. If every team member contributes to the purpose and goals of the team, it becomes meaningful to them because each person matters. Each person must contribute and do his or her part in helping the team achieve success. It's the coach's responsibility to share with each team member how important their role is in order for the team to achieve its goals.

As head coach, I would meet with each team member, asking them to tell me what they think their strengths are. I find it amazing at times how some people don't know what their strengths are. And sometimes, what they think is a strength might not actually be one. After listening to what they say, I share with them what I feel their strengths are and how they can contribute to our team's success. Once they know their strengths and how they can contribute, they feel more valued.

In a company, even the janitor plays an important role. Imagine if the workspace is dirty or messy. How would your company be perceived by your own employees and others?

It's necessary to acknowledge every person who plays a role and affects your team. A CEO and other team members who take five seconds to tell the janitor how appreciated he is for keeping things extra clean and orderly will make that person feel important. The janitor will feel valued because of that simple acknowledgment and will want to keep doing the best job possible.

It's crucial that the best CEOs always make time to spend time with their frontline team members. If you're a leader, you can always take a minimum of twenty minutes daily to be visible and talk with them. This needs to be a priority. You can show empathy by asking them meaningful questions: How's your family doing? Did your mom recover well from surgery? What can I do to help you perform your job better? It allows you to stay in touch with what's happening on the front lines. It shows that you care and value them. It shows them that what they do plays a key role in the success of your company. All of us leaders have demanding schedules and time constraints, and the key is to *minimize your time and maximize their feelings.*

Let me share with you what I did with my team regarding individual contributions. When we play a duel match against another school, we have 1st and 2nd singles and 1st, 2nd, and 3rd doubles (best of five wins). Well, oftentimes, my 2nd singles player wants to play 1st singles, and my 3rd doubles team wants to play 2nd doubles, and 2nd doubles wants to play 1st doubles. Remember how I want every player to feel important? How do I keep everyone happy to be playing in the position they need to play in?

First of all, at the beginning of our season, we would play singles challenge matches to establish a fair rank order on our team. This is important for integrity and fairness among my team and to provide an honest, correct roster for our opponents. Secondly, from this team ranking, I would select my singles and doubles players. I liked sharing with the team why I felt these players in these positions could help our team achieve our goal of winning a state championship. Because of my communication with them, they knew exactly what I was thinking, and there were no misunderstandings (avoiding one of the 4 Misses). Thirdly, connecting players together as doubles partners can be challenging. They need to buy into playing with and helping each other. Therefore, I'd weigh my options and look for the best fit among doubles teams. I always preferred to have a power player with a control player (instead of having two power players together or two control players together).

Once we got through these situations and competed in a duel match, my 3rd doubles team might feel like they were at the bottom of the lineup, even though we had four more players on our team who were not in the starting lineup that day. This is when I'd share with them how hugely important 3rd doubles is to the success of our team. I'd tell them that although the spotlight is usually on 1st singles and 1st doubles, it's actually 2nd singles, 2nd doubles, and 3rd doubles that I am depending on to bring us a victory. Those three positions are critical for us to win. I'd share with them that if we win in those three positions, then we win as a team regardless of what happens in 1st singles or 1st doubles. Sometimes, other teams have better players playing in those top positions, and they might beat us in those individual matches, but we will win as a team because we'll win the other three. When I explain it this way, every player understands the importance of every position. They all want to win—ideally, they want to win 5–0 because nobody really enjoys losing. Even the players not in the lineup that day will be cheering and supporting their teammates because everyone is valued and everyone contributes.

Think about the bigger picture and ask yourself, "How can I contribute to society? How can I make the world a better place?" We should all want to help other people and do things in a better way to ultimately leave a legacy for others to follow. When you think about it, it's really a privilege to be in this world and an even bigger privilege to be in the United States. If there's any doubt, just look at how many people from other countries want to emigrate to America.

Consistency. There are two types of consistency. The first is the consistency of performance of the coach and team members, which leads to higher productivity, better results, and winning. My team members expected consistency from me, and I expected the same from them. Being unpredictable with them would not have been good because they wanted to see consistency in my words and actions.

They wanted me to follow through and do the things that I said I would do. They wanted their leader to be reliable, honest, and trustworthy. In terms of developing my team members, I would focus on improving my players' fundamentals because that led to consistency in their performance, especially when the pressure was on. When there is pressure and a player has weak fundamentals, it is extremely visible. The same is true in business and in life.

The second is consistency in following up with your team members. A coach might schedule a meeting with a team member to focus on personal development to help that person make their strengths stronger and strive to improve on a weakness. This only helps if there are follow-up meetings to track improvement. Consistency is key! How many times have you had a meeting with someone and there was no follow-up? Things might improve briefly before the little progress that was made begins to quickly fade away.

You might be thinking that this will consume a lot of time. It doesn't. Oftentimes, I'll do a quick follow-up with my player that takes less than one minute, but the impact is huge. It doesn't have to be a scheduled half-hour meeting or anything of that sort. Sometimes, casual is better and more comfortable. For example, as I'm walking by, I would say, "Hey, Matt, how's that one thing coming along that we talked about?" Matt knows that because I'm following up with him, it must be important to me, which shows that it should be a priority for him. It also shows that I care about him and his development.

How many times have you heard someone say they are going to do something, and it doesn't get done? This drives me nuts! How do you think your team will respond to you? When you say you're going to do something, do it! Your words should mean something. The best coaches do what they say—always. This is part of consistency. As a coach, you need to be an example to your team. You are their role model. Words and actions matter. Little things matter. Little things lead to little victories. And little victories lead to big victories.

Consistency of words and actions builds trust and credibility, which makes it appealing for people to align themselves with a leader's values, vision, and mission. It establishes a track record of reliability, which helps to instill confidence in others for effective leadership, organizational success, and healthy relationships. Consistency between words and actions also ensures clear communication. When leaders consistently deliver messages that align with their behaviors, it reduces uncertainty, confusion, and ambiguity. This allows team members to understand expectations, goals, and values more clearly, which enables better coordination, decision-making, and collaboration. Always remember that people will be influenced by actions more than your words. After all, "love" is just a word until you give it meaning. And the same is true for these words: trust, respect, and honor.

Having consistency with your team members is absolutely necessary for moving your team in the right direction to accomplish the team's goals. The greatest leaders always have the best interests of their team members at heart and consistently know what they want and need. You are building other great leaders who may or may not be with you forever, and that's OK. You care about them and their improvement, and they know it.

Confidence. Once your team members know how they're contributing and you have established consistency, building their confidence leads to empowerment. People become confident when they know they're good at something and they know they're supported. Think about yourself and what gives you confidence. Now, think about doubt. Letting doubt enter your mind is a confidence killer. That's why your mindset is so important. You need to always focus on what you want to achieve and avoid unnecessary noise and distractions. Tunnel vision is good. Believe in yourself!

When Punahou School athletic director Chris McLachlin and tennis director Bernard Gusman asked me to be the head coach of our boys' varsity tennis team, I felt confident that they believed in me and that they knew I could do the job and do it well. They didn't micromanage me, and I felt one hundred percent supported with all of my decision-making. They are both great leaders who trusted me, and I felt empowered and did not want to disappoint them. I wanted to make them and Punahou School proud. I wanted to be the best version of myself that I could possibly be, and they gave me confidence through their words and actions.

This is why it's important for CEOs to give responsibility to their executives and for the executives to give responsibility to the directors, the managers, and the people on the front line. By doing this, you are showing that you have confidence in others to get the job done. They, in turn, should be the best they can be to not let their leader down. If and when a mistake happens, it's an opportunity for learning, and the leader must always be available for advice and support. However, with both championship teams and elite organizations, *it's unacceptable if the same mistake is made twice.* Team members should have the freedom to innovate and try new things to make the team better and not be afraid to make mistakes. They just need to learn from it so it doesn't happen again.

There are three reasons why establishing confidence in team members creates a positive cycle of empowerment that benefits both individuals and the overall team dynamic. Firstly, building confidence in your people cultivates a sense of belief in their abilities and strengths. When team members have confidence in their knowledge and skills, they feel empowered to take on challenges and tackle new opportunities. This self-assurance enables them to contribute more effectively to the team's goals and objectives. Secondly, establishing confidence in team members encourages them to take ownership and initiative. When individuals feel confident in their capabilities, they are more willing to step up and take responsibility for their work. This autonomy allows them to become proactive problem solvers, seeking out opportunities to contribute and make a difference. Lastly, confidence in your people nurtures a culture of collaboration and mutual support. When individuals feel confident, they are more likely to share ideas, provide constructive feedback, and engage in open and honest communication. This creates an environment where everyone's voices are valued and respected. As they recognize the impact of their contributions and feel supported by their colleagues, it leads to a virtuous cycle of empowerment within the team.

The word "encouragement" can be defined as *the act of instilling courage in another*. When you give encouragement to someone, you are showing that you believe they can do it because you have faith in them, and they should believe in themselves. It serves as a catalyst for personal growth, helping that person strive to develop their full potential with renewed determination. This simple act is extremely powerful and leads to building confidence in whatever they want to achieve, no matter how great the odds might be. If you think you can do it, you have a chance. If you think you can't, you have no chance. Giving thoughtful and genuine encouragement to each other will give your team opportunities to achieve greatness.

Ryan Tanaka

I first met Coach Rusty Komori in my junior year of high school, having played on Punahou's junior varsity tennis team that year. Nearly twenty-five years after graduating from Punahou School, Coach Rusty and I reconnected. I've read his books *Beyond the Lines* and *Beyond the Game* multiple times since then.

I've spent around two decades pursuing a career in business, and today, I operate a diversified group of companies in select industries with hundreds of employees. Our businesses strive to be best-in-class, client-focused, and community-driven. Over the years, I've been asked, "How is it possible to operate leading companies in varying industries?" I've consistently answered that it's because of our phenomenal people. We believe in Coach Rusty's concept of coaching rather than teaching, and within each company, we have strong managers who are dedicated to Coach Rusty's 3 Cons: contribute, consistency, and confidence.

Coach Rusty has been a keynote speaker for all of our companies many times. Our employees receive and read his books, and we continually discuss how to further incorporate Coach Rusty's evergreen concepts into how we operate and collaborate to cultivate an environment where ideas, experiences, and knowledge are readily exchanged. These principles help us to operate as a team with trust, honesty, and adherence to the highest standards of business and professional ethics. Coach Rusty's principles support our companies to be stewards of employee and community well-being and actively contribute to sustainable and long-term impact for the people of Hawaii.

Specifically, our employees are passionate about positively *contributing* to our client experiences and making an impact on our team culture. Our managers regularly spotlight when they see our employees demonstrate exceptional behavior toward our clients and toward each other, and this helps our employees turn obstacles into opportunities and understand how they can continue to make a difference.

We take pride in delivering the highest level of performance for our clients, and we regularly follow up with each other. We carefully examine client feedback, and our employees *consistently* innovate meaningful ways to delight our clients as well as support our team.

Sustaining record performance over the years for our companies includes empowering our employees and instilling our belief in them to be successful in their roles. Enabling our employees to improve their talents and strengthen their character builds their *confidence* in what they do.

Ryan Tanaka
CEO, Giovanni Pastrami Restaurant Group
CEO, KAI Hawaii
CEO, Underground Services Inc.

Chapter 9

PURPOSE

"One day you'll be just a memory for some people.
Do your best to be a good one."

—Anonymous

PEOPLE WANT TO WORK TOWARD SOMETHING.
More importantly, they want to work toward something
significant. They are willing to work through and overcome any
obstacle along the way to achieve it. Having a purpose in life gives
them direction. It puts them on a certain street, and hopefully,
they'll find the right way. Often, they must do this with a team.
But they need to know why it's important to have this mission and
accomplish this goal. Why is this goal meaningful? It's a leader's
job to identify a clear purpose with their team and show them the
right way. They must give them a vision for the mission.

For example, a basketball coach might show her team a video of players winning the basketball championship and climbing the ladder one by one to cut the net from the hoop. She'll have her team members visualize themselves cutting the nets after winning the championship this coming year. People need to have a vivid picture in their minds so they can see the end result. This is the vision and purpose you want your team to buy into, so they'll make the necessary sacrifices and commitment to begin the unwavering pursuit of this goal.

BUILDING RELATIONSHIPS

When someone's on his deathbed, what's the most important thing to him at that moment? Is it money? Is it his fancy cars? Is it his big, expensive house? It doesn't seem to be any of these, but instead, it's the relationships they've built with other people over the years. He wants to see his family and true friends. He wants to see the people he loves and cares about. Now, if that's the most important thing at the end of our lives, shouldn't we prioritize the importance of building meaningful relationships *during* our lives?

Think about the people in your life right now. If you desperately need someone's help, who would you call? Who would be there for you, without a doubt? Those are the people with whom you have built the deepest, most meaningful relationships. Those are the ones you can depend on, and they know you'd be there for them, too. I absolutely know the people in my life I can depend on if I need help.

Because of the importance of building relationships, I want to inspire and help as many people as I can in the world to live better, healthier, more meaningful lives. I want to inspire hope in everyone so that, in turn, they can inspire hope in others. People who feel hopeless also feel helpless. But it's often a mindset that can help someone who's living in darkness into seeing the light. It's showing that you care and taking time to encourage others to see that *one positive among twenty negatives.* It's inspiring them to focus on ways to get through their adversity. Life naturally has ups and downs for all of us, but we need to focus on the ups, not the downs. Tough times never last, but tough people do. Some people see the clouds and storms of a situation, but champions always see the sun peeking through. These champions have learned to dance in the rain, and I want to challenge you to do the same. Always look at it as an opportunity to turn what might appear hopeless into hope.

Also, think about this. If today were the last day of your life, would you still want to do what you're about to do today? And whom would you want to be doing it with? These are deep, meaningful questions that you need to periodically ask yourself to make sure you're living the life you want. You might be making others happy, but are you making yourself happy? I've seen some people live miserable lives, often disappointed because they're waiting for someone else to make them happy. Rather than waiting for someone to give you flowers, plant your own garden. Instead of relying on others to make you happy and do something nice for you, focus on making yourself happy. I mean truly happy. When you can ensure true happiness for yourself, you will have even better relationships with others. And happy people live longer, are healthier, and are more productive.

EXPLORE THE POSSIBILITIES

A man decided he was going to climb to the top of a very tall tree. He had never climbed a tree before, and a crowd of people had gathered, shouting at him, "It's impossible! You'll never be able to do it!" But the man persevered, climbed the tree, and reached the top. How did he do it? He was deaf and thought that everybody was simply encouraging him to reach his goal.

If we want to achieve something we've never achieved before, we need to try things we've never tried before. *The greatest people become even greater because they are always open to creative ideas, different solutions, and exploring new possibilities.* It doesn't matter what other people say (and sometimes they might say you're crazy), but it depends on you and what you believe you can do.

Great leaders expand their curiosity, which opens new doors of possibilities for themselves and their teams. Whether in sports or business, they inspire others to think beyond the status quo, emboldening them to explore uncharted territories and discover untapped potential. A leader's ability to expand their own curiosity is instrumental in driving growth and progress. When these great leaders remain curious, they engage in a lifelong process of learning and development, which sparks creativity and a hunger for knowledge, leading to the exploration of new ideas. By continuously seeking new insights and understanding, they're able to promote a culture of open-mindedness and intellectual curiosity within their organization.

Apple's Steve Jobs said, "Everything around you that you call life was made up by people that were no smarter than you. And you can change it. You can influence it. You can build your own things that other people can use. And the minute that you understand that you can poke life—if you push in and something will pop out on the other side—that you can change it and you can mold it. That may be the most important thing is to shake off this erroneous notion that life is there and you're just going to live in it versus embrace it, change it, improve it, and make your mark upon it. I think that's very important, and once you learn it, you will want to change life and make it better."

FIND YOUR GREATNESS

I love greatness. I love helping people on their quests to reach greatness. So, how does someone achieve greatness? You can't build the tallest, most beautiful skyscraper on a small foundation. You need a big foundation in order to build the best skyscraper in the world. And there's tremendous competition to see who can literally build the tallest, greatest, most unique skyscraper. But finding your own greatness isn't about competing against someone else. It's internal. It's feeling fulfilled. It's finding your purpose in life and making an impact by helping others be better. It's making a positive difference in the world.

Some people do great things, but all of us can do little things in a great way. And sometimes, average, ordinary people can inspire a movement, which will impact the world in an invaluable way. For example, when you're walking down the street and come across a piece of trash, do you pick it up or walk past it? If you pick up three pieces of trash every day, will it make a big impact in keeping your community cleaner? Can one person really make a difference? If you did this simple thing daily, you would have picked up 1,095 pieces of trash every year. If one thousand people did this, they'd pick up 1,095,000 pieces of trash. If you inspired one million people to do this, there would be 1,095,000,000 fewer pieces of trash in our world every year. So yes, average people can make a significant difference in society.

During our tennis season, my players and I volunteered at the Special Olympics on the University of Hawaii campus. Watching these athletes give their best effort in competition is truly inspiring to see. Even more inspiring is their support and encouragement for each other. They really have no limits. If they believe they can do it, they can. I like having my players watch these Special Olympic athletes because they are witnessing greatness in motion and because it helps keep them focused on the big picture in life. Whatever you do, give it your best and enjoy doing it. With the Special Olympics athletes, it's clear that the limits they have only exist in their own minds. If you haven't been to a Special Olympics event, I highly encourage you to go—and take your team with you.

Greatness is exemplified in a variety of ways and comes in all sizes and forms. My mom is an example—I know she loves me and would do anything for me. I greatly admire my sister Lori, a single mother, for raising her daughter Naia in the best possible way, showing her love, and, like our mom, doing anything for her. People often show their greatness for another person by donating a kidney, volunteering for a bone marrow transplant, or giving blood. Other people show their greatness by purchasing food for the homeless or donating their time working at a charity. Whatever the case, it comes down to doing something special for the benefit of someone who needs help.

I remember hearing a story about a blind girl who hated herself and her life. The only person she didn't hate was her boyfriend because he loved her and was always there to help her. One day, she told him that if she could somehow see the world, she would love to marry him. When she received an anonymous donation of a pair of eyes a few weeks later, she was, of course, absolutely ecstatic, now able to see everything and everyone in the world around her. Seeing her boyfriend for the first time, she was completely stunned to see that *he* was blind. "Now that you can see the world," he said, "will you marry me?" But to his great surprise, she didn't accept his proposal. He walked off, crushed and heartbroken. A few days later, she received a letter from him in the mail: "Please take good care of my eyes, dear."

Finding greatness is something we must first find in ourselves. Jennifer Lopez is a famous singer, dancer, actress, producer, and businesswoman, someone who has definitely found her greatness. "If I told you all the people who told me I wasn't going to act or sing or dance or I wasn't good at it or that I should stop or I should quit," she told an interviewer, "even after I became famous for doing these things! The truth is nobody knows what's inside of you. Only you know what's inside of you. Only you know what you can accomplish and what you're capable of and what your gut and your dreams and your desires and your wants and your ability. You only know. Nobody else knows. So whatever you feel in your heart and in your gut, you should follow that. Then, if that changes one day, that's fine too. Then you follow that. Everything I did there was no box for and there was no map for, and that was a good thing. You don't need so much to do something anybody's done before. You can blaze your own path."

We have a unique superpower within all of us—our greatness. We need to search for it, and once we find it, we'll be able to empower ourselves in helping countless others. It's exciting when we can explore the true potential in ourselves and our teams. When you build a solid foundation of strong values, principles, and disciplines, you give yourself the opportunity to achieve anything and everything you set your mind to. You, as a leader, will currently view yourself as average, good, or great. But I guarantee that all of us can be better. So, here's my challenge to you. I want you to closely examine your life right now to see how you can strive for the highest level of excellence in finding your greatness, and once you do, help others find theirs.

WHAT IS YOUR LEGACY?

I miss coaching my boys' varsity tennis team. It was a huge part of my life for twenty-two years. When a season ended, I always looked forward to the next one, excited to see which twelve boys would earn their spots on the team. Still, it was only twelve boys that I could help. It was only twelve boys that would be a part of a great team experience that year. I retired as head coach in 2015 because I felt compelled to do something bigger. I felt that, rather than coaching at just one school, helping just twelve boys each season, maybe there was a way I could help many more of them.

And then, a friend and former student urged me to find a way to help people, not just in sports but also in business. Having gone through my coaching, he believed that I was much more than a tennis coach. I was a leader, he said, who had developed a system that could unlock people's true potential. The same system that forged our unprecedented twenty-two-year championship streak. It's the same system he uses in his own company, with his own team. He knows it works because he has lived it himself, as have many of my other students and players. That's when and why I decided to write books.

ACHIEVEMENT VS. FULFILLMENT

Of course, a legacy doesn't happen when you're the only one who's affected. It happens when you help others by affecting them in a positive way. It happens when you help people grow and improve themselves. It happens when you guide them in following their dreams. That's why being on a team means more than accomplishing something on your own. You share the highs and lows. You share the struggles and victories. You help each other be better people.

Fulfillment happens when you do things for others without expecting anything in return. In our society, status, beauty, money, power, fame, and material things like big, beautiful houses and fancy cars are high on the wish list for most people. But do they ultimately bring happiness at the same time? Many of these people find that they're lonely and unhappy, that there's something missing on the inside. They have everything that you can possibly imagine externally, but they lack self-fulfillment internally.

So, if we identify character traits in detail and prioritize the ones that are most important in gaining self-fulfillment, I believe it is our moral traits that should top the list. Focusing on mental and emotional character traits is important, of course, but focusing on moral traits will help your team members feel most fulfilled.

- Examples of moral character include honesty, integrity, honor, loyalty, humility, respect for others, caring, courage, generosity, and compassion.

- Examples of mental character include self-discipline, focus, decisiveness, confidence, dedication, self-control, adaptability, patience, optimism, and self-awareness.
- Examples of emotional character include empathy, positivity, resiliency, openness, understanding, cooperation, forgiveness, and gratitude.

Certainly, all of these traits are important, but which of them should we ultimately strive for? Which of these should we instill in our team members? I strongly believe that having moral character brings the most fulfillment and happiness. I have seen it. As a coach, I am most proud of players who acquire many, if not all, of these character traits, whether or not they win or lose a competition. This is what I wanted to establish on my first day as head coach—helping my team realize that we develop great people first and great tennis players second. I had no idea when I began my coaching career that this is what I would accomplish. This would be my legacy. This is why, to this day, I refer to my old Creighton mentor as Coach Ed, and likewise, my players still call me Coach. It denotes the respect that team members have for their leader.

OWN NO TROPHIES

Hawaii's state championship trophy is big and absolutely beautiful. When we won the state championship during my first year as coach, I thought to myself, "How cool would it be if the coach were to give one of his players that state championship trophy to have, to own, to keep forever?" And that's what I did. Ross Inouye received that first trophy.

I've been presented with that big, beautiful, koa wood trophy twenty-two times, and today I own zero trophies. Every year since then, I gave the state championship trophy to the one player I felt significantly represented our team with the highest standards of superior excellence. Looking back, what would I do with all twenty-two trophies? It means so much to me that twenty-two of my players have them. I felt happy and fulfilled in giving the trophy to those twenty-two athletes as a symbol of the meaning of their teams' accomplishments. It's a constant reminder that commitment, sacrifice, teamwork, perseverance, resiliency, and discipline can help you achieve your goal. It's something special that they were a part of, and no one can take that away.

COACH RUSTY WITH
ROSS INOUYE

Sure, trophies are great to have. It's a symbol of victory. It's a symbol of being a winner. But it's also a symbol of something much deeper and greater. What did you have to do to get that victory? Why did you win? The trophy represents the countless hours and hard work involved in pursuing that goal. It is a symbol of sweat and pain. It is a symbol of sacrifice and commitment and never giving up even when your back is against the wall. It is a symbol of all the other people involved in giving you an opportunity to succeed—parents who drove you to practices and games, teammates who worked together and encouraged each other to give their best every day. It is so much more than just something you can look at and hold—it is something that's embedded deep in your soul.

THE JIMMY V. STORY

Jimmy Valvano, the legendary basketball coach and motivational speaker, left an indelible mark on the sports world and beyond. As the head coach of the North Carolina State University men's basketball team, Valvano led the Wolfpack to their historic NCAA Championship in 1983. The team's improbable run and Valvano's exuberant celebration, running around the court looking for someone to hug, have become iconic moments in sports history. Valvano's coaching ability to motivate his players is evident in their astonishing victory. It would be his only championship win, yet his legacy with his team members extended way beyond the basketball court. Valvano's charisma and larger-than-life personality made him a beloved figure in the sports world. His infectious enthusiasm and sense of humor endeared him to fans, players, and fellow coaches alike. Valvano also had an uncanny ability to captivate audiences with his wit and storytelling, making his speeches memorable and impactful.

Some years later, Jimmy V. was diagnosed with terminal cancer, and he refused to let it define him or dampen his spirits. He gave one of the most memorable speeches I've ever heard on the night he received the Arthur Ashe Award at the 1993 ESPY Awards. "Cancer can affect much of my physical body," he said that evening, "but it cannot touch my mind, it cannot touch my heart, and it cannot touch my soul." He also said, "Time is precious and you don't know how much time you have left." Jimmy V. passed away eight weeks later.

If you haven't seen his speech, I highly recommend that you find it on YouTube and watch it. Obviously, he was a great basketball coach, but he clearly had a passion for life that helped his players on the court and ultimately helped them in their lives off the court. His legacy was far-reaching, including the establishment of his V Foundation for Cancer Research. This one person, this one leader, impacted and helped improve the lives of so many people beyond basketball—including me!

THE MIKEY MACKINNON STORY

You never know when you will be a part of someone else's legacy. I started private tennis lessons with a seventh-grade student named Mikey MacKinnon. After our first two lessons, I observed him in a junior team tennis match. This was the longest tennis match I've ever seen. The format was just an eight-game pro set, but it lasted for three hours. Yes, three hours! Mikey moved very well and had very good shot consistency. His consistency was so good that it looked like he enjoyed extending tennis points by torturing his opponent with shots hit at no more than five miles per hour.

Mikey's opponent wasn't the only one being tortured; I endured having to watch identical points being played over and over again. Mikey won the match 8–2. At our next lesson, I told Mikey that we were going to work on turning him into an aggressive baseliner. It was imperative for him to learn power. Plus, he could thank me for saving him hours of time to do other things—like homework!

In 1998, Mikey was a senior on my varsity team. He was number one on the team and ranked number two in the state of Hawaii. He was a great team player and was well-liked by everyone. He listened well, worked extremely hard, and had lots of fun.

One day, during a varsity match against a smaller school, I played a weaker lineup and had Mikey practicing with three of his teammates on court two. During the match, I heard Mikey yelling, "Coach, come quick!" and saw him holding his right bicep. Fearing an injury, I ran over to court two to find out what happened. Mikey walked up to me, moaning slightly and still holding his arm. Then he rolled up his shirt sleeves and flexed his muscles. "Coach, my muscles—they're too big! They're breaking out of my skin!" I shook my head and laughed, relieved that he wasn't really injured.

Later that season, Mikey was playing in the state singles championship final against the number one ranked player in the state, a boy from Maui. Everyone was expecting an epic showdown from these top two seeds in the tournament. Throughout the first set, the level of tennis was extremely high, with both players hitting exceptional shots and giving every ounce of energy they had. But in what seemed to take only about fifteen minutes, Mikey lost the first set, 6–0. I walked onto the court to talk with him during the two-minute coaching break. I told Mikey that he was playing and competing very well and that his opponent couldn't keep playing in the zone like that for two whole sets. He had for one set, and maybe could for a set and a half, but unlikely for two.

I walked off the court, excited to see what would happen. Both players continued to make brilliant shots, but I'd been wrong. Mikey's opponent was still playing in the zone and beat him 6–0 in the second set. Then, after walking to the net to shake the winner's hand, Mikey stayed near the court, sitting in the shade. Everyone who'd watched the match was in complete shock—myself included. I could only imagine what Mikey was feeling after playing the last match of his high school career and having it end as it did. I sat down next to him, and the first thing he said was, "How are first doubles and the other guys doing?"

"They're doing good," I replied. "How are you, Mikey?"

"I'm OK," he said. "Wow, did my opponent play awesome or what?"

"Yes, he was awesome," I agreed. "He probably could have beaten anyone in the state today."

And that was it. Mikey picked up his bag and went over to cheer on his teammates, who were still competing. To do that after suffering this lopsided defeat shows you the kind of person he was. He was a leader and a role model, and he knew that the team was bigger than any one person.

After the season ended, I continued to train Mikey in private and group lessons to prepare him for college tennis. He was

excited to work on improving his tennis, as well as having fun
with his friends at the beach. But one Sunday that summer, he
didn't show up for our group training lesson. Now, you need
to understand that Mikey was always there for his lessons, even
when he was sick, so we all knew something unusual was going
on. When I finished our training and drove home, I called his
house. His dad answered the phone.

"Scott," I said, "Mikey never came to training today."

"Rusty, Mikey died today in a car accident."

No words came—I was in shock. "Coach," I finally heard
Scott ask, "are you OK?" His dad was trying to comfort *me*! I
could only try to imagine what he and his family were going
through.

Mikey's parents are incredible people, as are his older
brother, Rob, and younger sister, Heather. They asked me if
I'd speak at Mikey's memorial at the Punahou School chapel,
and I felt honored to do so. At the service, every seat was taken,
with an overflow of people spilling outside. I had prepared four
pages of memories about Mikey to share. But when I walked
to the podium, adjusted the microphone, and tried to speak,
I couldn't get out more than a word or two. My emotions
overwhelmed me, and I broke down in tears. Everyone in
the chapel began crying along with me. Rob came up to the
podium, put his hand on my shoulder, and said, "Coach, you
can do this." And I did. It was the hardest thing I ever had to
do. The MacKinnon family started a scholarship fund at the
school in Mikey's memory. The scholarship is awarded to three
students each year. One is a player on the boys' varsity tennis
team. Another is a tennis player, boy or girl, in the Punahou
academy (high school level). And a third is presented to a tennis

player, boy or girl, in middle school. In this way, Mikey's legacy is carried forward. Each year, the MacKinnon family, some of Mikey's teammates, and I gather at a luncheon with the three new Mike MacKinnon scholarship winners, where we're able to share with them the kind of person Mikey was. It is a most special legacy, and I'm honored to be part of it.

MIKEY MACKINNON

Chapter 10

PROCESS

"It is good to have an end to journey toward;
but it is the journey that matters in the end."

—Ernest Hemingway

ONCE YOU AND YOUR TEAM have a purpose, and they understand why it's important to work toward the goal together, you need a detailed process to achieve that goal. In order for the process to work, you need the discipline to execute it every single day. A day you waste is one you can never get back. You need to better yourself every day, and you need to get a little closer to achieving your goal every day. You need to make yourself take the right steps every single day, whether you "feel" like it or not. A thousand times, I've heard people say, "I don't feel like doing it today" or "I'm not in the mood today." My response is always, "You don't feel like it? You're not in the mood?—Well, you better get in the mood!" They need to understand that achieving this goal is something bigger than any one individual. This is something we must and need to do to help our team accomplish our goal. It's unacceptable for someone to be on a team and not do his or her part.

Every individual on a team needs to respect one another. And there will be respect if everyone contributes and does their part. The leader needs to make sure that this happens. You cannot have someone putting in the effort and doing their part when someone else isn't. This is when people lose respect for each other. This is when they will also lose respect for the leader if the leader doesn't address the problem and do something about it. Once there is respect, team members need to trust each other. They need to know that they have each other's back. They need to want to do something for you because you'd do the same thing for them. When every team member believes in the process and builds the correct daily habits to commit to the process, the team is well on its way to achieving its goals.

Process is an essential element in achieving success as it provides a roadmap for a structured and efficient approach to reaching desired outcomes. Without a process, it can be difficult to know what steps to take, when to take them, and how to measure progress. A detailed process breaks down complex tasks into manageable steps, making it easier to stay on track. By breaking down a task into smaller steps, it becomes more obvious to identify potential obstacles and develop strategies to overcome them. For example, if the goal is to launch a new product, a detailed process may include market research, product design, testing, and launch planning. By breaking down each of these steps, it becomes easier to identify potential challenges, such as market saturation or design flaws, and develop strategies to overcome them.

Another benefit of a detailed process is that it provides accountability. When goals are broken down into specific steps, it becomes easier to measure progress and hold individuals or teams accountable for meeting specific milestones. This can help to keep team members motivated as they can see the progress they are making toward the larger goal. A detailed process can also help to improve efficiency. When tasks are broken down into smaller steps, it becomes easier to identify areas where time or resources can be saved, and can help to streamline processes, reduce waste, and increase productivity. Whether it's a personal or professional goal, a well-defined process will provide structure and direction, keeping your team members focused on the desired outcome.

ONE PLAY AT A TIME

On January 2, 2016, the University of Oregon football team played Texas Christian University in the Alamo Bowl. In the week before the game, TCU's coach had suspended his starting quarterback for off-field issues. By halftime, Oregon was dominating, 31–0. But then Oregon's quarterback got injured and didn't play the rest of the game. Now, both teams were competing with their backup quarterbacks. In the second half, TCU—seemingly unfazed by the huge deficit—played the game one snap at a time, coming all the way back to tie the Ducks at 31–31. They then prevailed in triple overtime and won by a score of 47–41. It was an amazing comeback for TCU and a devastating loss for Oregon.

In sports, you're always in one of three situations—winning, losing, or tied. The effort and positive attitude to give it your best should always be there, regardless of the score. Too many teams play according to the score, which can easily bring their downfall. It can be a self-fulfilling prophecy. Obviously, you want to be aware of the score, but you don't want it to change your strategy if you're winning. If you're behind, you might need to alter or change your strategy. And if you're tied, your strategy might well be sound— you're in a position to win, but it will depend on your execution. Here's where having disciplined training in practice puts you and your team in a more favorable position to come out ahead.

Achieving success requires a mindset of performing one play at a time, or one point at a time, regardless of the score or any other circumstances. In tennis, I've seen many players win the first set but end up losing the match because they relaxed and lost focus. They think that because they've won that first set, they're well on their way to victory. A football team with a substantial lead at the end of the third quarter might relax and lose focus. A volleyball team leading the match two sets to none might relax and lose focus. As a tennis player, I've experienced both sides—jumping out ahead but losing the match, and falling behind but emerging victorious. Anyone who plays sports has had the same experience.

I constantly remind my players that it doesn't really matter who wins the first set. If we do, it only means we're ahead but haven't won. If we drop the first set, we're behind but still haven't lost. I want them to have the mindset of playing one point at a time. I want them to give it their best from the first point until match point. I want them to play the whole match. I want them to run the whole marathon. When you train your team to have this mindset, they become relentless competitors who control everything that they're able to control. And your opponent might have some mental lapses along the way, which of course, puts you in a more favorable position to win.

DOMINATE THE IN-BETWEEN

Achieving success also involves controlling your thoughts between plays or between points. A football game can last three hours or more, even though the actual playing time is just sixty minutes. In tennis, a match of two out of three sets might last for two hours, but the actual amount of time the ball is in play might be only fifteen or twenty minutes. The point is there's lots of time between plays or between points when our minds might wander and lose focus, which impacts how we play the next point. Controlling our thoughts between points is important. My teams worked on a routine to use between when the previous point ends and the next one begins. This is extremely critical in giving your best from the first point until match point. At high levels of play, just one mental lapse can cause you to lose the match. Controlling our thoughts, giving our best effort, having the right attitude, and keeping proper focus are disciplines we have total control over between points. This discipline, this habit, adds to our relentless competitive play in matches, which helps us attain success and sustain it, too.

I always emphasized to my teams that we must exhibit positivity, toughness, and fight regardless of whether we won or lost the last point. Obviously, you wouldn't have a negative response if you won the point, but it's very easy for average players to show negativity, frustration, and disappointment after losing one. It takes a lot of self-discipline to shake it off and to keep in mind that a negative response won't help you win the next point. In fact, it will help you lose it. This is all common sense, of course, but in the heat of the battle, anything can and will happen to undisciplined players. The disciplined ones will keep it together because their leader has trained them to do so. *Disciplined players have present focus.* They won't stress about what just happened (past focus), and they won't worry about what could happen (future focus). This is something the leader has trained his or her team members to control.

Players have a choice to show either strength or weakness between points. Players have a choice to show positivity or negativity. Players have a choice to show toughness or frustration. Players have a choice to show fight or give up. It's easy to lose a point and show weakness, negativity, and frustration, to make excuses and ultimately give up. It's very challenging to lose a point, have complete self-control, and show strength, positivity, toughness, and fight. But this is what great teams do. This is what great organizations do. In order to achieve success, the leader will analyze every little detail of every situation and guide their team into the best possible position to succeed.

THE ASHLEY ISHIMURA STORY

Years ago, I began coaching a seven-year-old girl named Ashley Ishimura in private tennis lessons. She had a passion for tennis, worked extremely hard, and listened well. Yes, three great ingredients to have in any student, for sure. But Ashley was not a gifted athlete, as many others are. I would consider her a blue-collar player with above-average talent for tennis. My main goal was to keep things fun for her. Nobody wants to do something that's not fun. I knew that if she continued to have fun with tennis, she would keep improving. My second goal was to work on developing her fundamentals and building an all-court game.

I trained Ashley one to two times a week, and after a few years, she was ready and eager to enter tournaments. The first tournament I watched her compete in was at the Hale Koa Hotel in Waikiki, playing in the age ten and under division. Although she was physically prepared, it was going to be a test to see where she was mentally and emotionally. She was excited for her first match, and I knew it was going to be a definite learning experience. She competed well, but her opponent had more tournament experience and made some questionable line calls on some key points, which affected Ashley. After losing the match, Ashley shook hands with her opponent, walked off the court, came directly to her parents and me, and began to cry. I feel that crying is actually a good thing because it shows me that she cares. After consoling her, I asked her if she wanted to play another tournament in a few weeks, and she said, "Yes!" I knew right then that this was going to be a long-lasting and memorable journey together.

Through the years—including many more tears after some tough defeats in matches—Ashley learned about life through tennis. She learned the value of hard work, perseverance, and sacrifice. She learned to be resilient, to never give up, and the importance of a positive attitude. She learned to win with humility and lose with grace. All of this because I was coaching all of her, not just teaching a part of her. She knew that I was honest and she could trust me. And she knew that I always had her best interests in mind. The touching thing to me was that she looked at me as more than a coach—and often conveyed that I was like a second father to her. Talk about making an impact!

⚡ COACH RUSTY WITH
ASHLEY ISHIMURA

If I fast-forward a few years, Ashley attended Punahou School, made the Punahou School girls' varsity tennis team as a freshman, and was number one on the varsity team all four years. After graduating from high school in 2015, Ashley earned a partial tennis scholarship to Creighton University in Omaha, Nebraska (Yes, that's where I went to college on a partial tennis scholarship as well). My former college roommate and current head coach at Creighton, Tom Lilly, recruited her. I told him that as good as Ashley was in tennis, she was an even better person with outstanding character. She was an amazing team player who was selfless and had a team-first mentality. Although she received full scholarship offers from other universities, she felt a great connection with Creighton, especially after meeting with Coach Tom and his wife, Jean, on a college visit. Since arriving at Creighton as a freshman, Ashley mirrored her experience in high school and was number one on the tennis team all four years. She graduated with a business degree in finance, and, needless to say, I'm so very proud of her and the person I helped her become by coaching her in tennis and in life.

ASHLEY ISHIMURA

Chapter 11

PERFORMANCE

"The difference between ordinary
and extraordinary is that little extra."

—Jimmy Johnson

AS A LEADER, when you focus on your people, identify a
clear purpose, and have a detailed process in place, you give
your team the best possible chance to perform to maximum
potential every time. Consistent performance achieves success.
Consistent performance allows you to sustain success. Whether
it's an athlete competing on the basketball court or an employee
selling cars at an auto dealership, consistency in performance
is paramount. Average or even good teams fluctuate in their
performance. They will win some and lose some. Great teams
seem to win all the time. When they don't, it's viewed as a

major upset because great teams build high expectations from everyone, including themselves, to win. These great teams expect to win every game. It's a standard. It's because they have a system in place for success. Players and employees come and go, for whatever reason, but the next person up fills in, and the team keeps on winning without missing a beat.

When I developed the 4 Ps, it made logical sense to me to have a system in place to do everything I set out to do, beginning on my first day at tennis practice as my team's head coach. Anything worthwhile that you want to achieve takes time. That's why every leader needs to have a plan for the team. That's why it's important to maximize every day. You get a little bit closer each day to accomplishing your goals.

PERFORMANCE GOALS VS. RESULTS GOALS

Everyone that I know wants to win at everything they are pursuing. I don't know anyone that likes losing. But what influences winning, making money, or achieving goals? It's your performance. It's what you do that determines whether or not you achieve your desired result. Let me share several reasons why your focus should be on performance goals instead of results goals.

Firstly, performance goals focus on the process of achieving success rather than just the outcome. This means that individuals who set performance goals are more likely to focus on the actions and behaviors that are necessary to achieve their goals rather than simply being fixated on the end result. It provides clarity so you can define specific outcomes that need to be achieved.

Secondly, performance goals are completely under your control. Results goals are sometimes influenced by external factors such as luck, timing, and the actions of others. In contrast, performance goals are typically related to your own efforts and actions. This means that you are more likely to feel a sense of ownership and responsibility for your success, which will increase your motivation and commitment to achieving your goals. Finally, performance goals are more flexible than results goals. Results goals are often very specific and rigid, which can lead to disappointment and frustration if the desired outcome is not achieved. In contrast, performance goals are focused on the process of achieving success, which allows for greater adaptability and the ability to adjust course as necessary. This can lead to greater resilience and the ability to bounce back from setbacks and obstacles. Let's look at three popular companies and their focus on performance goals, which led to them achieving incredible results.

Amazon, the e-commerce and technology giant, has demonstrated consistent performance through its relentless focus on customer satisfaction and continuous innovation. One example is its implementation of efficient supply chain management. The company invested heavily in building a vast distribution network, utilizing advanced logistics technologies, and optimizing warehouse operations. This allowed Amazon to offer fast and reliable delivery, even for large product catalogs, which greatly enhanced the customer experience and cemented the company's dominance in online retail. Furthermore, Amazon's introduction of Amazon Prime showcased its commitment to customer-centric services. By offering unlimited fast shipping, exclusive deals, and access to a vast library of digital content, Amazon Prime has created a loyal customer base and contributed to substantial revenue growth. The success of Amazon Prime demonstrates the company's ability to identify customer needs and develop innovative solutions that provide value and convenience.

Apple Inc. is known for its innovation and exceptional performance. One example is the launch of the iPhone. When the first iPhone was introduced in 2007, it revolutionized the smartphone industry. Apple's careful integration of hardware, software, and design resulted in a groundbreaking product that quickly gained widespread popularity. The iPhone's success propelled Apple to new heights, establishing the company as a leader in the mobile market and significantly increasing its revenue and market value. Another example of Apple's superior performance is its retail strategy. Apple Stores are known for their sleek design, exceptional customer service, and seamless integration of products and services. By creating a unique and immersive retail experience, Apple has consistently achieved success. This success can be attributed to Apple's focus on providing a premium customer experience and showcasing its products in a way that highlights their value and functionality.

Tesla, the electric vehicle and clean energy company, has achieved consistent performance by disrupting the automotive industry and pioneering sustainable transportation. One notable example is the launch of the Model S. With its long range, high performance, and cutting-edge design, the Model S showcased the viability of electric vehicles as a practical and desirable alternative to traditional gasoline-powered cars. The Model S received critical acclaim, won numerous awards, and significantly contributed to Tesla's brand recognition and market value. Additionally, Tesla's focus on building a comprehensive charging infrastructure played a crucial role in the company's success. Tesla Supercharger stations provide fast and convenient charging for Tesla owners, reducing range anxiety and addressing one of the major barriers to electric vehicle adoption. By investing in charging infrastructure development, Tesla has demonstrated its commitment to supporting the entire electric vehicle ecosystem, further bolstering its position as a leader in the industry.

These three business examples illustrate how Amazon, Apple, and Tesla focused on their performance goals, which directly led to them achieving these monumental results. Moreover, it's the consistency with their performance in executing various strategies of supply chain optimization, product innovation, and infrastructure development that raises the performance bar of their competitors as well as our expectations.

Dick Gould

Competing at a championship level in any activity sports or otherwise requires a leader who can consistently get the best out of each and every member of the team, as well as out of the team as a whole, but particularly at the right times. There are many elements involved in a team's success, such as preparation, setting expectations, managing egos, and creating a culture of winning, but whether in sport or business, eventually, it all comes down to performance at crunch time on the court, on the field, or during a sales call. To perform well, one must be able to produce at a very high level *at a specific time*, and often in collaboration with the coach.

As a leader, it is imperative to constantly encourage people to try their best to get better and improve. This often means helping them prove to themselves that their best is usually far greater than they thought it could be. But there are far more moving parts to this process of competing at the highest level than just expending great effort. For example, relishing a challenge often means overcoming our fear of failure. Finding a way means not knuckling under what seems to be overwhelming circumstances. When it all comes together, win or lose, it's satisfying to know that one has put forth one's absolute best effort and has gotten better in the process.

"The Stanford Way" of first-strike tennis means being aggressive, even when being tentative feels safer. Accepting coaching is being open to input when your impulse is to do it by yourself. Being a competitor means overcoming the habit of resting on your laurels or wallowing in defeat and instead looking ahead to the next challenge. Various elements of competing have one thing in common: not only are they difficult, but they are very often counterintuitive because they involve some degree of discomfort.

My job is not to make it easy, but to push players into these areas. Only by being in a challenging situation with some regularity do we begin to feel more comfortable with it. Consistently forcing yourself, your players, and your team out of everyone's comfort zone is not just important for playing tennis, or any sport, or any endeavor; it's also critical for both the coach and the players if they are to win championships, and for anyone who wants to reach their potential and succeed beyond what they thought possible.

Dick Gould
Head Coach, Stanford University Men's Tennis Team
(1967-2004)
17 NCAA National Team Championships

ELIMINATE UNFORCED ERRORS

Most games are lost rather than won. Before you can win a game, you have to not lose it. So, how can you put your team in the best possible position to win? A big part of it is eliminating unforced errors. Let's take a look at football. When I'm watching football, it's not just about making spectacular plays, but it's about avoiding mistakes that can be prevented. Unforced errors can be defined as *mistakes or penalties committed by a team that are not a direct result of the opponent's actions. It is the result of one's own mistakes made by an individual or organization without external pressure or influence.* Minimizing or ultimately eliminating unforced errors is crucial because they can have a significant impact on the outcome of a game. These errors can include penalties, turnovers, missed assignments, dropped passes, fumbles, missed tackles, mental lapses, or poor coaching decisions. Every play matters because sometimes it comes down to a matter of inches. I've watched teams setting up for the game-winning field goal, and a careless penalty is called on the offense, which pushes them back five yards. The kicker kicks the ball and watches in heartbreak as the ball hits the goalpost and bounces off, causing that team to lose the game. Had there been no penalty and had the kick been attempted five yards closer, they would have won.

By eliminating unforced errors, a team can maintain control, sustain drives, and prevent the opposing team from capitalizing on their mistakes. Team members should strive for perfection in their performance. While they might not achieve perfection, they will definitely be playing at an extremely high level, and through their disciplined preparation and execution, teams can maximize their chances of victory.

Jimmy Johnson is the first head football coach to win both a college football national championship and a Super Bowl. In 1987, he led the Miami Hurricanes to a national championship victory and won back-to-back Super Bowls with the Dallas Cowboys in 1992 and 1993. Johnson has emphasized the significance of eliminating unforced errors in football games and has often stressed that minimizing mistakes is crucial for achieving success on the field. Johnson strongly believes that avoiding unforced errors leads to consistent performance. By minimizing mistakes such as dropped passes, missed assignments, or unnecessary penalties, a team can execute its plays more effectively, increasing the likelihood of success. Unforced errors can have a direct impact on field position. Turnovers, fumbles, or interceptions can give the opposing team a significant advantage by granting them a better field position. Johnson stresses the need to protect the football and make smart decisions to maintain field position. Unforced errors can also disrupt the momentum of a team. A dropped pass or a missed opportunity can deflate morale and give the opposing team an emotional boost. Johnson emphasizes the importance of maintaining positive momentum by eliminating self-inflicted mistakes. According to Johnson, avoiding unforced errors requires mental discipline and focus. Players must maintain concentration throughout the game and execute their assignments with precision because one mental lapse can cost you the game. Johnson also believes that coaches play a significant role in reducing unforced errors. Proper preparation and effective coaching can help players minimize mistakes. Coaches must instill a culture of discipline and accountability, strongly emphasizing the importance of error-free football, which will enhance their chances of winning games.

In the business world, unforced errors can occur in various aspects of a company's operations, strategy, or decision-making. Let me share some examples of unforced errors that companies may make. Companies can make unforced errors in their marketing and branding efforts, such as poorly executed advertising campaigns, offensive or insensitive messaging, or inconsistent branding across different platforms. These errors can lead to reputational damage and loss of customer trust. Another example is introducing a product without conducting thorough market research or failing to address customer needs. Companies may invest significant resources in developing a product that ultimately fails to resonate with the target market, which will lead to financial losses. Companies can also make unforced errors in customer service by providing inconsistent or poor support, mishandling customer complaints, or ignoring feedback. These errors can lead to customer dissatisfaction, negative reviews, and a decline in customer loyalty. Another example is in operations and the supply chain. Errors can occur when companies experience inventory shortages, logistical inefficiencies, or quality control issues. These errors can disrupt production, delay deliveries, and impact customer satisfaction. Companies can also make unforced errors in strategic decision-making by failing to adapt to changing market conditions, overlooking competitive threats, or making poor investment choices. These errors often result in missed opportunities, loss of market share, and decreased profitability. Another example is when unforced errors occur in internal communication and processes, such as inadequate employee training, ineffective collaboration, or lack of clear communication channels. These errors can lead to misunderstandings, delays, and reduced productivity.

Successful businesses focus on minimizing these unforced errors by fostering a culture of continuous improvement, conducting thorough research and analysis, seeking customer feedback, and prioritizing effective communication and collaboration.

At its peak in 2004, Blockbuster Video consisted of 9,094 stores and employed approximately 84,300 people. Let's take a look at the reasons why Blockbuster Video failed and filed for bankruptcy. Blockbuster failed to adapt to the changing market conditions in the video rental industry, particularly the shift to digital streaming services. The company was slow to embrace online video rental and streaming, which allowed competitors like Netflix to gain a significant advantage. Netflix has had a market cap in the hundreds of billions of dollars.

Another reason was Blockbuster's large physical footprint with thousands of stores, which required significant operating costs, including rent, utilities, and staffing. This obviously made it difficult to compete with online rental services that had lower overhead costs. Blockbuster also did not innovate enough to keep up with changing consumer preferences and market trends. It relied too heavily on its traditional business model of renting physical videos and did not invest enough in developing new technologies or services. The rise of Netflix and Hulu provided customers with more convenient and affordable options for watching movies and TV shows and surpassed Blockbuster in popularity and market share. Although Blockbuster experienced incredible growth during the 1990s and early 2000s, there were numerous unforced errors in leadership that contributed to its downfall.

MY 1% PRINCIPLE

How do good teams become great? How does someone who is great become extraordinary? It happens when you push beyond your limits. You are capable of doing more and achieving more than you think. My 1% Principle is simple to understand and leads to extraordinary results. All you need to do is start by being 1% better at something today than you were yesterday. Then tomorrow, you're up to 2%. The next day, you're up to 3% better. It's having trust in the process of improvement, which compounds into something quite substantial over time. It's focusing on one tiny action today to get you one step closer to where you want to be tomorrow. Self-improvement isn't a destination. It's a process that never ends, which becomes part of your superior culture of excellence.

Here are more ideas: Can you give 1% more effort today than you did yesterday? Can you accomplish 1% more than last week? Can you improve by 1% on a current weakness? Can you add 1% more knowledge by learning something new today? It's as simple as running one lap on the track. The next time you're on the track, run one lap plus a quarter lap. The next time, run one lap and a half. Next time, run one lap plus three-quarters. Soon, you'll be running one mile. Before you know it, running five miles will be routine, and perhaps even running a marathon might become a possibility. But how did it all start? It started with the 1% Principle.

What if you're in the gym lifting weights? You might begin by doing two sets of ten repetitions of bicep curls at a comfortable weight. One week later, you might increase the weight or keep the same weight and add more repetitions. A week after that, you keep pushing your limits smartly, and you are well on your way to improving your strength.

Bruce Lee and one of his students would run three miles every day. One day, they were close to hitting their usual three-mile mark when Bruce said, "Let's do two more." Extremely fatigued, his student responded, "I'll die if I run two more." Bruce's response to his student was, "Then do it." After running the two extra miles, his student was completely exhausted and a bit angry because of Bruce's comment. "Quit, and you might as well be dead," Bruce explained. "If you always put limits on what you can do, physical or anything else, it'll spread over into the rest of your life. It'll spread into your work, into your morality, into your entire being. There are no limits. There are plateaus, but you must not stay there; you must go beyond them. If it kills you, it kills you. A man must constantly exceed his level."

The point is this: Whatever you do, you can always do more. But do it in a smart way. If you haven't run for two years, don't do a ten-mile run. If you haven't been in the gym for a while, don't overdo it. That's how careless injuries happen. You might have the right intent for improvement, but it's not about doing big things immediately. It's doing the little things that lead you toward achieving the big things. Here's an example of a little thing. At sea level, water is extremely hot at 211 degrees, but at 212 degrees, it boils. When it boils, you also have steam. When you have steam, you can power a locomotive. That's the big difference that one extra degree makes.

When I became head coach, I would consistently focus on using my 1% Principle to improve my team and myself. I always keep in mind the quote, "Do not follow where the path may lead. Go instead where there is no path and leave a trail." We can learn from other successful people and championship teams, but making yourself and your team unique to outdo what others have done puts you in a position to accomplish extraordinary things. The big positive effect for everyone is that it causes a higher tide where all boats rise. Successful people and teams will learn and examine possibilities they never thought could be accomplished. This is critically important because there are still many things in life that haven't been discovered, invented, or achieved. To push your limits in everything you do and imagine the possibilities of what could be, you must erase the lines of what has already been proven and accomplished.

I strongly believe that sometimes the smallest step in the right direction becomes the biggest step of your life. I have seen this with many people as well as in my own life—a 1% step in the right direction can set us on a trajectory for unprecedented achievement and success. By committing yourself (daily, weekly, monthly) to the 1% Principle, you become more open and exposed to different and new possibilities, and therefore, you'll have better outcomes in your life.

Section 3: The 4 P's for Achieving Success

Now that you've completed the 4 P's for Achieving Success, please take ten minutes to honestly rank yourself and answer the questions. The purpose of the assessment is to help you identify action items that will enable you to move forward with your leadership journey to becoming a superior leader. Below, you will find questions with corresponding gray boxes. Please use these boxes to rate yourself on a scale of 1-10 (1 being "needs improvement" and 10 being "superior") on your ability to do the specified task. Then, answer the corresponding free-response question.

How would you rate your ability to have empathy for your team members?

What are ways you can enhance your team member's well-being by viewing them as people first versus employees?

_____

_____

_____

How would you rate the quality and effectiveness of the Professional Development Coaches provided for your organization?

What is one thing you can do in the next quarter to provide superior coaching for your team?

_____

_____

_____

How would you rate your ability to maintain poise under pressure?

What can you do to maintain your composure during a crisis situation?

_____

_____

_____

How do you rate your ability to use the 3 Cons (Contribute, Consistency, and Confidence) to enhance your team members' commitment?

What are some ways you can improve the 3 Cons with your team members?

_____

_____

_____

How would you rate your ability to build meaningful relationships with others?

Who are three people with whom you can enhance the quality of your relationship, and what specifically can you do to improve your relationship with each person?

_____

_____

_____

How would you rate yourself in being open to hearing creative ideas and different solutions?

What can you do to encourage your team members to contribute their ideas and solutions when exploring new possibilities?

_____

_____

_____

How would you rate your current level of self-fulfillment in life?

What are some examples of ways you can enhance your fulfillment in life?

_____

_____

_____

How do you rate your ability to create the ideal plan to achieve superior goals?

What is the single biggest process improvement you can implement to achieve superior results?

_____
_____
_____

Rate your skill level at driving incremental performance for yourself and your team.

If you could pick two areas to drive a 1% improvement today, what would those be?

_____
_____
_____

Performance goals influence results. How would you rate your ability to focus on performance goals?

What are two specific things you can do to optimize the consistency of your team's performance?

_____
_____
_____

Add up your total score for this assessment and enter your score here.

THE 6 KEYS FOR PEAK PERFORMANCE

section 4

Chapter 12

KEY NO. 1
PHYSICAL

"You can practice shooting eight hours a day,
but if your technique is wrong, then all you become
is very good at shooting the wrong way.
Get the fundamentals down and the level
of everything you do will rise."

—Michael Jordan

THE PHYSICAL KEY DEALS with how good you are at physically doing your job in two situations: you as an individual and you with your team. You are a reflection of your team, and your team is a reflection of you. If you're leading a business team, how good are you physically at doing your job? If you're coaching a sports team, how good are you as a coach? How would you rate yourself on a scale of one to ten? Now, how would you rate your team on a scale of one to ten? These are two different yet important situations for you to reflect on. The point is this: You are responsible for yourself, and you are responsible for your team.

There's a gigantic difference between being a great person and a great leader. As I mentioned earlier, there are many head coaches and CEOs who have the right principles, values, and disciplines for themselves, and they might even be extraordinary as individuals, but they struggle with transferring those same principles, values, and disciplines to their team. I've seen this happen a ton with people in leadership positions who deeply care about their team and just need help coaching them in a better, more effective way.

HIT IT IN

In soccer, you need to score goals. In basketball, you need to shoot baskets. In tennis, you need to hit it in! It's all about fundamentals. The physical fundamentals you and your team have are the necessary foundations to give your team a chance to succeed. In business, how good are your frontline team members in dealing with current and potential clients? Are they speaking with them in a professional and caring way? Do they have great communication skills? Are they offering different options and solutions to solve problems? These are some examples of basic fundamentals for any successful business. Or are they making careless mistakes? And do these mistakes happen often? Are there complaints from clients because of how your frontline team members spoke to them? Are you losing clients? Is there dysfunction among team members? It's your responsibility as the leader to coach your team members properly. They're a reflection of you!

Focusing on the basics and keeping things simple is paramount. My players would frequently hear me say the words "hit it in" before stepping on the tennis court for a big match. Let's think about it. In tennis, you have to hit it *in* to win. You cannot hit it out and win. Hitting the ball in one more time than your opponent gives you that chance to win. You might hit it high or low, or hard or soft. Whatever you do, if you want to win, hit it in. There are only two ways to win a point in tennis: you hit a winner, or your opponent makes an error. It's as simple as that. So, I posed this question to my players: "Is it easier to hit winners on every point or for our opponent to make errors?" They all agreed that we might hit some winners, but the majority of points we win will be because our opponent makes errors because of our solid performance. And it's true that most teams achieve victory not because of the big plays they make but because of the errors they don't make.

Now, think about your own team in business or sports. What are the most basic fundamentals you need to give your team a chance to succeed? Sometimes, things become complicated and seem to evolve into unnecessarily complex situations. Your job as the leader is to make certain that everything is kept simple and clear. If you don't, it often leads your team members to feel overwhelmed, assuring that they will definitely not perform anywhere close to their potential.

Let me explain this concept even further. How do we hit it in? Where do we aim our shots? There are two things that make tennis challenging: the net and the lines. It's unbelievable to me when I see players aiming one inch over the net or trying to hit it two inches from the lines and then getting upset when they miss. I'll ask them, "Can you hit that shot in ten times out of ten? Of course not! If you're that risky, you're probably going to miss more shots than you make. You might make three out of ten but, is that a good percentage to help you win?"

Another thing that I would often say is "big shot, big target," meaning I want my players to be aggressive and confident when going for our big shots, but I want them to aim those shots at a big area on the court. I would often say, "Aim for a big target area instead of a small target area, and we will hit it in a lot." The tennis professionals on TV do this same thing all the time. It's relevant no matter what level of player you are. This is a very basic yet valuable concept and completely relates to anything you are striving to achieve. This is an example of how I kept things simple with advanced players, and you can do the same with your team. Strip it down to the basics and always remember the most important fundamentals that your team needs to do that will lead to success.

CLIMB THE MOUNTAIN

We had great structure in our tennis practices, and I had my team doing many things that our competitors were not doing. Before every practice, we would do various stretches together. We would then go over to the school track for a variety of running exercises to help improve the aerobic part of tennis, then to the steep hill near our tennis courts to sprint up the incline and jog down (eight to twelve times at varying distances).

These things were done before my players even picked up their tennis rackets to begin hitting balls on the court.

In order to enhance what we did on the court, I needed my players to get tougher and stronger physically off the court. When some players start a tennis match, they often play very strong through the first set and usually midway through the second before fatigue sets in and they begin to run out of gas. This obviously affects their performance, focus, and consistency. I wanted my players to finish the match as strong as they started it.

When I required my players to get in the gym, lifting weights two times a week, it helped them not only physically but also mentally. They knew they were doing more than their competitors and felt like they deserved to win. That feeling of "deserving to win" is a powerful one. I was also mindful that their first priority as students was school, and I helped them learn time management. They had a demanding school schedule, but everyone can make time to exercise for fifteen or twenty minutes on a given day by planning ahead. Depending on their schedule, our players would get in the gym for fifteen minutes to an hour to do their workouts. Now, even if they had time constraints and could only do the minimum time commitment, a lot of these fifteen-minute workouts led to many extra hours of preparation. Physically improving our conditioning, footwork, strength, flexibility, and balance greatly enhanced how we performed on the tennis court, giving my players opportunities for peak performance.

Think about what you are currently doing physically to help the people on your team. Now, think about ways to enhance this physical part. How can you make them stronger and better so that they can attain peak performance throughout the entire day? What can you do to ensure they can go from one task to the next without getting fatigued? It's important in everything you do to start strong and finish strong. You should be able to complete your last task of the day as well as you did the first one. The following are some examples to help your team members maintain productivity and focus in the workplace:

- Stay hydrated: Dehydration leads to decreased focus and energy levels. Team members should be drinking enough water before coming to work and throughout the day.
- Healthy snacks: Encourage your team members to eat healthy snacks like fruits, nuts, or yogurt to help sustain energy levels and avoid sugar crashes.
- Manage emails: Team members should set specific times to check and respond to emails rather than constantly interrupting work to read every new message.
- Avoid Multitasking: Multitasking can often reduce productivity and increase errors. Team members should focus on one task at a time.
- Stretch and breathe: Encourage your team members to do deep breathing techniques and stretching exercises in between tasks to reduce stress and enhance mental clarity.

If you work hard and smart, you will consistently put yourself and your team in favorable situations for peak performance. Being prepared and physically ready for what you will encounter today is completely under your control.

For example, have you ever been on a challenging hike? Your chances of completing a successful hike up to the top of the mountain depend on how prepared you are for it. You'll start strong but might become physically fatigued along the way. Drinking water, eating snacks, and having lunch will keep your energy levels high throughout the hike. And how amazing and gratifying is the feeling you get when you reach the top of the mountain? Well, when you start the hike, the goal is to make it to the top. Not just halfway or a hundred yards away. Get there. Go all the way! Everyone feels challenged physically. It often takes proper preparation and relentless perseverance to achieve your goal and make it to the top of the mountain. And once you're there, how beautiful is the view and feeling of accomplishment? So climb that mountain and do what many others don't.

TAKE THE PUNCHES

How much can you physically endure? How many punches can you take? Anyone can throw them, but not everyone can handle being punched. In boxing or mixed martial arts, you never know when you're one punch away from winning or getting knocked out. The only way to get tougher and better is to put yourself through adversity and uncomfortable situations. Think about it. It might not be easy at first, but if you're prepared and ready to rise to the challenge, you can handle the punches. By dealing with it, you actually become stronger, tougher, and better from that experience.

When you set a goal and want to achieve something of significance, it rarely comes easy. I used to share a story about traveling with my players. If I'm taking a trip from Honolulu to New York (with a connecting flight in Dallas), there are certain challenges that might arise. After arriving at the airport, there might be a long line at check-in and another long line going through security. Once on the plane, there might be an unexpected delay even before takeoff. Once we're in the air, there could be an unreasonable, disruptive passenger giving headaches to the flight attendants, as well as the rest of us. We also might experience turbulence and strong headwinds. Once we arrive in Dallas, we might have only ten minutes to make our connecting flight, only to find that the gate is in the next terminal. After barely making it on the connecting flight, there might be another delay because the pilots need the mechanics to check something in the plane. Once we're in the air, it's a smooth flight until we experience turbulence again and, with some severe crosswinds upon landing, finally arrive in New York.

How much adversity can you really handle in reaching your destination? How much can you tolerate in striving to accomplish your goal? How many unfortunate situations can you deal with and still stay positive? How many roadblocks can you overcome? The most successful leaders and teams stay fixated on their destination and are determined to succeed no matter how tough the challenges might be to get there. They can take multiple punches because they are resilient and have relentless perseverance in achieving their goal. I have found that if you want something badly enough, you will adjust, redirect, and find a way.

THE MIKEY LIM AND SKYLER TATEISHI STORY

I had a player named Mikey Lim, Robbie's younger brother by two years, who won the state singles championship in his junior year. Now, he was a senior, team captain, and the number one player on our team, and I wanted him to help me build the confidence of junior Skyler Tateishi. Skyler was number two on our team, and I knew the following year, he would most likely be number one after Mikey graduated. Mikey and Skyler were the top two players on the team by far. I talked with Mikey and asked him to take Skyler under his wing and help him develop as much as possible through the season. Being the great team player he is, Mikey agreed without hesitation. Skyler looked up to Mikey, and I knew they would push one another, ultimately helping the other player improve.

Throughout the season, it was amazing to see how much Mikey was helping Skyler. It inspired the other junior and senior players on our team to help mentor the freshmen and sophomores. As a coach, I loved seeing this. The younger players were getting more confident in themselves, and the upperclassmen felt great, knowing that these younger teammates were the ones who'd be filling their shoes next year or the year after. It was like I had multiple assistants all working toward the same goal.

Once the regular season finished, we were ready for our league championship tournament. Mikey was the number one seed, and Skyler was number two. Yes, you can already guess what happened. They both got through their draws, made it to the singles championship, and ended up playing against each other. Throughout the season, Mikey had always beaten Skyler in practice matches. But, on this occasion, anything could happen.

I sat in the front row on the bleachers next to the 'Iolani School athletic director, who observed that this should really be the state championship final. I agreed with him. They were battling, and the level of play was incredibly high. They were hitting powerful groundstrokes with very few unforced errors. Toward the end of the third set, the match was nearing the three-hour mark. It was so close and exciting, and I still had no idea who would win. They both gave it their all, and it literally came down to one or two points, which really came down to one or two shots. Skyler seized the opportunity, took a chance, executed, and won. As he walked to the net to shake hands with Mikey, Skyler looked like he was half excited and half sad. He respected Mikey greatly, and it was the first time he had beaten him. For his part, Mikey looked like he was genuinely happy for Skyler and extremely sad and disappointed at the same time.

On the ride home, I asked Mikey what his thoughts were, and the first thing he said was, "Wow! Skyler played awesome. He was tough!"

"Yep! You helped make him tough."

Mikey went on to say how happy he was for Skyler to break through and win the league championship. He also said that he was disappointed in himself for not being able to find a way to win and missing some key shots on big points. I told Mikey how proud I was of both of them and that it was sad that somebody had to lose. As happy as he was for his teammate, I could sense that he was beginning to feel really bummed.

Mikey had been last year's state singles champion, seeded number one in the league championship, and lost to the teammate that I'd asked him to take under his wing. "If you could choose between winning the league championship or the state championship in two weeks," I asked him, "which would you choose?"

"The state championship, of course."

"There you go!" I said. "This is a good wake-up call for you. Sometimes, a tough loss like this is a blessing in disguise. If you won today, you might assume that everything is OK with your game. But after this loss, you'll focus on those details that you need to polish up. What's done is done. That loss is in the past. Focus on improving every part of your game in the next two weeks and continue to help Skyler, and he'll be helping you as well."

Mikey agreed, and when he left, he said simply, "Thanks, Coach!"

I could see that he had the right mindset and was fully committed to improving himself, Skyler, and the rest of our team. Our team practices resumed a few days later in preparation for the state championship on Oahu, and it was intense and a whole lot of fun. When the tournament began, Mikey was there watching and cheering on Skyler in all of his matches, and Skyler did the same for Mikey. The support they showed to each other and their teammates was wonderful to see. That's what a real team is all about. As it turned out, Skyler lost in the semifinals, and Mikey went on to win his semifinal match on the other side of the draw. And yes, Mikey dominated the final, winning his second state singles championship. The following year, a confident Skyler was extremely dominant, winning the state singles championship, and I clearly remember Mikey calling him on the phone from college to congratulate him. They were both outstanding champions and very selfless, which became contagious among their teammates for years to come.

♦ **MIKEY LIM AND**
SKYLER TATEISHI

Chapter 13

KEY NO. 2
MENTAL

"Focus on the possibilities for success,
not on the potential for failure."

—Napoleon Hill

THE MENTAL KEY DEALS with how good you are at focusing and concentrating on your job and completing your tasks. Noise and distractions are things that people with average mental focus experience. Great leaders with exceptional mental focus can block out any noise and distractions to complete the task at hand. Think about when you're at a restaurant in a conversation with someone and the waiter drops a stack of plates and glasses across the way—do you look? Or do you continue on with your conversation as if nothing happened?

The common response is to look and see what happened. But, if you're extremely focused, nothing will disrupt or deter you from the task at hand.

The great Dallas Cowboys football coach Tom Landry said, "There is only a half-step difference between the champions and those who finish on the bottom. And much of that half step is mental." I completely agree. Time and time again, I've seen how little the differences are between being a champion and being a finalist. It's consistently having the right mental frame of mind and the ability to focus on the here and now. Philadelphia Eagles quarterback Marcus Mariota said, "It's crazy how close the margins are in the NFL. Especially at the quarterback position, a decision that you make in a matter of seconds can ultimately determine the outcome of not only the game, but maybe the season."

MENTAL TOUGHNESS

In my youth, I would often hear people say that sports are ninety percent mental and ten percent physical. I think that's probably true in most of the things we do in life. Having the right mindset and perspective makes all the difference. All successful leaders and teams have mental toughness. You've heard those two words before, but what exactly is it? Mental toughness is *the ability to create and maintain the right kind of internal feeling, regardless of the circumstances.* The brain controls the body, so controlling your thoughts and having the right internal climate gives you the opportunity for consistent peak performance.

It doesn't matter if a bad call is made against you and you feel cheated. It doesn't matter if you receive bad news and feel disappointed. It doesn't matter if you get injured and feel frustrated. We've all experienced these situations in life. What matters is how you respond. Are you resilient? Can you focus on the present instead of worrying about the past or the future? Do you have mental toughness? In life, it's inevitable that we will face various adversities.

Let's take a look at some specific examples. You might have experienced going for a job interview and then receiving the news a few days later that you didn't get the job. You might feel like you deserve a promotion in your company, and then a co-worker gets awarded the promotion instead of you. You might be in a romantic relationship and deeply in love with your partner, and then your significant other wants to break up with you. Sometimes, things aren't meant to be, and you need to find the internal mental strength to move forward.

Mental toughness is also definitely necessary in sports. In tennis, I would share with my players that we need our physical toughness to weaken our opponent in a match, and our mental toughness will make them crack, causing us to win. Our opponent might be able to match us physically, but we will have the clear advantage mentally. We might also have to overcome challenging situations such as being benched, coping with a sickness, or dealing with spectators who are cheering against us. Average athletes will let these and other situations affect them in a negative way. Great athletes will always find a way to be motivated and consistently perform at high levels regardless of the challenge they're facing.

Owning mental toughness builds the foundations for long-term success, and it's a choice you can make for yourself. Former Navy SEAL commander Jocko Willink said, "If you want to be tougher mentally, it is simple: Be tougher. Don't meditate on it." I completely agree with him. If you want to be tougher, then be tougher. It's really a simple decision. It's very recognizable and obvious to identify teams that are mentally tough. These teams made the conscious decision to be mentally tough, which became a habit and part of their identity.

Stephen Hill

When I was a young boy, I discovered one of my favorite singing groups, New Edition. I was a bit younger than them, but they were in their early teens when they treated their fans to their first single, "Candy Girl." Being that they got their start at such a young age, New Edition was pretty much my generation's version of the Jackson 5. Over the years, their "Popcorn Love" songs matured into soulful R&B hits that were the soundtrack to my first loves/crushes and heartbreaks. Early on, their lyrics and videos helped me navigate what would become a lifelong journey of love followed by heartache and vice versa.

Anyone with a mother can tell you that love is a beautiful thing. Whether it be love for a person, a beloved pet, a favorite destination, or a prized possession, love is perhaps the greatest form of expression we have in this world. After the first love we experience with our parents and family, we get old enough to experience romantic love, and if we allow ourselves to remember that feeling, we know it's one of the most innocent, pure, and powerful forms of love we have and will ever experience. What I didn't know as a teen was that losing a love like that is what would prepare me to be the man I am today.

Love makes us pay attention. It makes us experience with every fiber of our being. In my opinion, experiencing love is perhaps what sits at the very foundation of our existence. It feels incredible, and when something we attach that feeling to is no longer accessible, we feel empty, lost, and forlorn. If you allow yourself to sit with those feelings for an extended period of time, you can become depressed. On the same token, if you allow yourself time to heal and remain open to it, you will afford yourself the opportunity to experience love again.

As an actor, I have found a form of expression that I love that isn't romantic, but it is something I love just as dearly. I have now been an actor for over twenty years, and it is the longest relationship I have had with anything. What this love has taught me is that love in its purest form is a spiritual energy one can find anywhere, anytime. But for some reason, we attach it to specific things that are tied to the identities we create for ourselves. This is where our passions are born. I have been acting for over twenty years now, and many times over, my love and passion for acting have been the only fuel I had to keep me going. Whenever the disappointments and the rejections start to take a toll on me, that's when I have to focus even harder on my love for my craft. I've allowed myself to quit twice in my career for about a week or two each time, and my love for it made me re-engage. In my darkest hours, I had to trust. I had to have faith that the best is yet to come. Thoughts of despair will undoubtedly come up, but you have to train yourself to see beyond and light a torch of mental fortitude to guide you through the darkness.

I remember a time when New Edition was going through some growing pains. In the midst of it all, they released a new song accompanied by a new video. In the video, the group members passed around a newspaper with the headline reading, "New Edition. Have They Lost It?" The name of the song: "Can You Stand The Rain?" As I write this passage you are reading now, the show I've worked on for five seasons, Magnum P.I., was just canceled a few weeks ago. The writers of my industry are on strike, and I just got word this morning that we actors are now officially on strike, too. To say the least, my industry is in shambles. There are many broken hearts dealing with the uncertainty of work in their respective fields of creativity. Passions are being tested in ways many have never had them tested before. As New Edition sings, "Sunny days . . . everybody loves them . . . but tell me baby . . . can you stand the rain?" These are the moments to strengthen the mind and hunker down and weather the storm. Rain will inevitably always come, but beyond the clouds, beyond the storm, like love, the sun is always there waiting to connect with you again. I was in the fifth grade when "Can You Stand The Rain?" was first released, and New Edition never lost it, and neither have I. Love is never truly lost; only new expressions of it are consistently found. Allow faith to be your guide.

Stephen Hill
Actor, Magnum P.I.

PRIORITIZE YOUR PRIORITIES

When you wake up in the morning, the first thing you should think about is asking yourself three important questions: Who do I love? What do I love? What do I love about myself? The reason is it immediately puts you in the right mindset by being thankful and grateful for everyone and everything you have in your life, and you begin your day with a positive attitude. Because we lead busy lives, if we don't reflect on these important questions, we can be easily sidetracked into feeling stressed and negative about the things that lie ahead. This is a very critical habit because it keeps you focused on the big picture of life instead of getting irritated and frustrated about petty things that occur throughout the day. This mindset and routine will keep you centered in striving to take care of the people and achieve the tasks that are most important to you.

When you're able to prioritize your priorities, it keeps you on track to achieve your goals. Some people have so many things on their to-do list that they rarely make a dent in it. Investor and philanthropist Warren Buffet has a simple three-step process for this. First, he'll write down a list of his top twenty-five goals. Second, he'll circle the five most important goals. Third, he'll cross off and completely eliminate the other twenty goals, even if they're somewhat important to him. Buffett's reasoning is that those twenty goals are lower in priority and actually take away his energy and focus in achieving the top five priorities. The only way to accomplish your top five goals is to put all your effort, energy, and focus into them. The other goals are actually distractions that inhibit you from accomplishing your most important goals.

Urgency is also a determining factor in your priorities. A friend of mine is an emergency room doctor who shared with me his system regarding which patients he takes care of first. He uses the example of a stoplight with the colors red, yellow, and green.

- Red signifies immediately life-threatening.
- Yellow is serious but not immediately life-threatening.
- Green is minor.

His system is simple and clear because he prioritizes the degree of urgency. He says that he needs to differentiate threats from non-threats by focusing his efforts on the reds. I often see people who react to everything as if it is red. They seem to feel constantly busy and overwhelmed because they can't recognize which situations require their immediate attention. The lesson here is to *know your reds!*

MISTAKES VS. FAILURES

Mistakes will actually make you a stronger, better person. Everyone makes mistakes. It's part of living and learning. You learn what not to do next time to avoid making the same mistake twice. There are causes and effects for every action. A leader may make a mistake that results in bad or unfortunate experiences for the team. And oftentimes, these effects might cause team members to feel turned off. Too often, employees or athletes find themselves trapped in an unfortunate situation for too long, which may even lead them to look for a different profession or sport, all because of one person who negatively affected them. It would be sad if you were the person that caused others to feel this way. But what if you're a leader who just needs help and wants to improve—to become a stronger, more positive figure, rather than unintentionally or unknowingly leading in a counterproductive way?

There's a big difference between mistakes and failures, but having the right perspective and mindset in dealing with either one is what really matters. A good leader knows that when they make a mistake, it's actually a learning experience. When they fail at something, it's an opportunity for improvement and future success. Henry Ford said, "Failure is an opportunity to more intelligently begin again." Failing at something and having it become a regret actually causes you to retreat and prevents you from moving forward. A leader will train his or her team members to view mistakes as learning experiences to improve themselves instead of failing and feeling regret. Failure needs to be viewed as feedback. It tells you what's not working so that you can figure out what does. If you don't try anything, you're absolutely guaranteed not to fail. You're also guaranteed not to grow. *Rich Dad, Poor Dad* author Robert Kiyosaki said, "Winners are not afraid of losing. But losers are. Failure is part of the process. People who avoid failure also avoid success."

It's imperative to learn from the experiences of others. In the long process of inventing the light bulb, Thomas Edison famously said, "I have not failed. I've just found ten thousand ways that won't work." Can you imagine if he didn't have the proper perspective? We might all be living in darkness when the sun goes down. Michael Jordan, one of the greatest basketball players ever, said, "I've missed more than nine thousand shots in my career. I've lost almost three hundred games. Twenty-six times, I was trusted to take the game-winning shot and missed. I've failed over and over and over again in my life. And that's why I succeed." Hockey's great Wayne Gretzky said, "You'll always miss one hundred percent of the shots you don't take."

It's important to try things to help yourself grow and not have any regrets about trying them. Amazon founder and chairman Jeff Bezos said, "I wanted to project myself forward to age eighty and say, 'OK, I'm looking back on my life. I want to minimize the number of regrets I have.' And I knew that when I was eighty, I was not going to regret having tried this. I was not going to regret trying to participate in this thing called the internet that I thought was going to be a really big deal. I knew that if I failed, I wouldn't regret that. But I knew the one thing I might regret is not ever having tried. I know that would haunt me every day."

In business, everything starts with the owner or CEO of a company. In sports, everything starts with the head coach. In both cases, this leader will be in a position to affect others on their team either in a positive or negative way, which directly affects the morale of the team and the performance of every team member. There are so many diverse situations in which people lead other people. In education, for example, the president of a high school is the overall leader of that institution. The principals are in charge of the school supervisors. The supervisors are in charge of the school's teachers. The school's teachers are in charge of their students. For students to have the best possible experience and to develop their full potential depends heavily on the leadership of the president and everyone in between. Think about your own experiences and how you would describe leaders that you've worked for in business or played for in sports. As a leader, you always have a choice in how you lead and instill the right mental focus in your team members.

THE ROSS INOUYE STORY

During my first season as head coach in 1994, I had a senior on my team named Ross Inouye, who was ranked number one in the boys' 18 division in the state of Hawaii. He had great character, was highly respected, and was liked by everyone. Once our season finished, Ross asked me if I could train him in private tennis lessons to prepare him for tryouts at Stanford University in the fall. We set up a schedule where I could train him three times a week during the summer—twice in private lessons and once in an advanced group training session.

Ross's goal was to make the Stanford tennis team, which was the top college team in the United States. Ross had won hundreds of matches because he was a very consistent player, but we needed him to be more aggressive and add more power to have a chance to compete at that level in college. As an incoming freshman, he could be playing against men three or four years older than he was, and therefore, we needed to raise his level of play quickly. The transition from high school to college is challenging in academics, but even more so in athletics. Ross trusted me and was fully committed to working on improving these parts of his game for the next three months.

Once the Stanford tennis tryouts concluded, Ross called me on the phone and said that he had good news and bad news. I didn't know what to think, but I asked him to give me the good news first.

"Coach, I beat a couple of nationally ranked players in tryouts, and the good news is I finished at number twelve."

"That's great news, Ross! Stanford has so much team depth and outstanding players from top to bottom. Finishing at number twelve is a fantastic accomplishment. What's the bad news?"

"The bad news is the coach said they're keeping only ten players on the team this year."

I couldn't believe it. I felt devastated, as though I was the one who didn't make the team. I could only imagine what Ross was thinking and feeling.

I said, "Ross, I'm so sorry. We had prepared you, and you worked so hard these past few months, sacrificing other things in order to get your tennis game to that next level. How are you, and what are you thinking?"

"Coach, I'm OK. When I come home during Christmas break, can you train me in privates and group again? I want to keep working on my game through this year, train with you all summer, and try out for the team again next year."

⟡ ROSS INOUYE

"Yes, you know I'll help you any way I can. But what if the same result happens?"

"It very well could, but if there's a chance I can make the team, I want to take that chance. I'm so close, and I know I can do it."

When Ross was a sophomore, he called me again on the last day of tryouts. "Coach," he said, "I have good news and bad news."

I said, "Not again! You're killing me, Ross! Tell me the good news."

"Well, I played awesome in the challenge matches, beating a bunch of nationally ranked players, and the good news is I finished tryouts at number nine."

"Don't tell me the coach is only keeping eight players!" I said. "What's the bad news?"

"Coach, there is no bad news. They're keeping ten players. I'm on the team!"

I said, "Ross, I am so happy and very proud of you. I feel like I made the team, too! Your mindset and commitment through this year, having a goal and going after it no matter the odds, is truly admirable and extremely inspirational."

"Thanks, Coach," he replied. "Thanks for helping me and believing in me. I couldn't have done it without you."

Ross was on the Stanford tennis team for three years and has two national championship rings. By the way, while he was there, a guy by the name of Tiger Woods was on the Stanford golf team, and many of the golf and tennis players were good friends with each other.

Ross's accomplishment is tremendously inspiring because of his mental focus on going after something that was important to him. I am so grateful that I was a part of this priceless experience for him, and I've shared this story with countless players over the years to inspire them and give them hope to go after anything they want in life.

Chapter 14

KEY NO. 3
EMOTIONAL

"Emotions can get in the way or get you on the way."

—Mavis Mazhura

THE EMOTIONAL KEY DEALS with how good you are at controlling your emotions and being aware of the emotions of others. Some people make irrational decisions because of how they feel at that moment. It's definitely good to show your passion if you're able to control your emotions. The greatest leaders always make decisions based on reason, not emotion. Coaching your team to be aware when people become emotional and to take some time afterward to recover from that experience allows them to control themselves and the situation in a positive way. Remember, you always need to control the situation instead of the situation controlling you. Having emotional awareness is necessary for you and your team to have peak performance.

ATTITUDE VS. MOOD

Don't be confused between attitude and mood. A mood is a reflection of your attitude. If you change your attitude, you can change your mood. People with poor attitudes often end up in a bad mood. Others with a positive attitude often experience good moods. That's the power of your attitude and keeping a positive perspective and outlook in life. Anger, frustration, and depression are mindsets that are often temporary, but they can evolve into bad habits and affect your lifestyle. A positive attitude allows a chain of events to happen. It leads to having happy thoughts, favorable experiences, good feelings, better results, and winning. Now, think about what would happen if you had a bad attitude right now. How would that negativity affect your mood, feelings, thoughts, experiences, results, and your life?

In order to have emotional toughness, you need to control your attitude and keep it positive all the time. It needs to become a habit. When it becomes a habit, you will have control over your thoughts and control over your life. You will then be able to control your destiny and accomplish extraordinary results. Plus, nobody wants to hang around with negative, hopeless people. So listen to me right now, and don't be one of those people.

The legendary actor Morgan Freeman said, "Self-control is strength. Calmness is mastery. You have to get to a point where your mood doesn't shift based on the insignificant actions of someone else. Don't allow others to control the direction of your life. Don't allow your emotions to overpower your intelligence."

Being aware and sensing when others around you are having negative emotions allows you the opportunity to help them. You can be the sunshine on their cloudy day. In order to achieve goals or anything significant in life depends on your perspective toward it. Keeping a positive outlook keeps you on the right track. No one has ever won a championship by being grumpy, depressed, and negative. If you like losing and failure, choose a bad attitude. If you want to win and achieve greatness, choose a positive one.

NEW EXPERIENCES, NEW FEELINGS

If you don't try anything new, everything in your life will stay the same. A parent who exposes their son or daughter to a variety of sports and activities allows their child the opportunity to try new things to see what they like and don't like. It gives them the chance to have new experiences in the hope that they will find something they are passionate about and truly love. The same is true about relationships. A man or woman looking for a soul mate will not find one by staying at home. They need to go out to different places and meet new people. If you haven't found love with a partner, you definitely won't find them by staying at home and being isolated. Opening yourself to new experiences gives you opportunities to meet different people, experience new feelings, and live a better, more fulfilled life.

When you have these new experiences, it leads to an entire spectrum of new feelings. The more experiences you have, the better. Feeling the width and depth of various emotions will ultimately help you in your life, and you will be able to help many others. Many of us have experienced the thrill of victory as well as the agony of defeat. Experiencing the agony makes us appreciate the victories even more. It's about the highs and the lows. You appreciate winning even more after some tough emotional defeats. These experiences ultimately make you a better, tougher, and stronger person for going through difficult adversities in life.

Some years ago, my friend Reynold and his wife, Allison, wanted a Maltese puppy and found a breeder who had a litter of three male pups. After selecting one and calling me on the phone with excitement, they suggested that I go look at the puppies as well. I went the next day, and one of the two puppies was extra happy to see me, kissing me and showing me lots of attention. He basically chose me, and there's no way I could have said no—they were so adorable!

When I was able to bring him home a week later, I named him Ace (yes, an obvious tennis connection), and I had watched all of Cesar Millan's videos the week prior to prepare me for this big commitment as it wasn't just about me anymore. I wanted to care for Ace in the best possible way and give him a happy, healthy life. Ace went everywhere with me, and because of his lovable personality, he made lots of friends—both dogs and humans.

Three years later, during a regular doggie checkup, the vet told me that Ace had a heart murmur that we needed to keep an eye on. I was definitely concerned upon hearing the news, but Ace seemed as happy as ever, looking forward to our daily adventures. He loved hiking, taking car rides, going to the beach, and, of course, playing with his doggie friends. One day, after I'd finished private tennis lessons with my students, I noticed that Ace's breathing seemed a little different. He usually ran up the stairs, but this time, he waited at the bottom for me to carry him up. This was very odd, and later that night, his breathing seemed more exaggerated. In the morning, I took him to the vet, who told me to give Ace medicine only after eating. Well, this was the first time that Ace hadn't had an appetite and had eaten nothing, which meant that I couldn't give him the medicine. That night, his breathing worsened, and, extremely worried, I took him to the emergency pet hospital. The doctor immediately put Ace in an oxygen chamber, with a diagnosis of possible pneumonia. I was told they'd keep Ace with them that day and overnight to monitor his breathing. I was to go home and remember that no news from them would be good news for me.

At my condo, hoping and praying for the best, I watched as time passed from 8 p.m. to 9 p.m. and then to 10 p.m. I'd received no call from the doctor and began to feel a bit relieved and hopeful that Ace was experiencing a relatively normal sickness and was on his way to a full recovery. I dozed off, and my phone rang at 1 a.m.

"Rusty!" the doctor said. "We need you to come to the hospital right away! Ace took a turn for the worse and died, but we performed CPR, and now he's come back."

When I arrived at the hospital, the doctor took me to the back to see Ace. He was lying on his side, unconscious, with a tube in his mouth, and was breathing extremely heavily. His eyes were open, and I knew he knew I was there with him. I was crying and kissing his face, hoping that this was just a bad dream. The doctor consoled me, saying how rare it was for a dog to come back after CPR. I was so happy and grateful that he had! And then the doctor said, "Ace came back to say goodbye to you." Soon after, the beeps on the machine began to slow, Ace's eyes began to close, and he passed away.

It was the absolute worst feeling I've ever had in my life. I felt like I lost a part of my heart that day, and that missing part will never be replaced. I miss Ace tremendously and think about him every day. My years with him were the happiest years of my life. It's incredible how a dog can mean so much. Bringing him home that first time was the best decision I've ever made. He taught me deeper meanings about enthusiasm (because he was always so happy to see me), loyalty, caring, and love. Even though losing him was the worst feeling I've ever experienced, the joy and happiness I had with Ace were truly priceless. So, believe me when I encourage you to experience new things because they can give you the chance to grow and discover powerful new emotions that will stimulate your life in unimaginable ways.

◊ ACE

THE KEVIN CAULFIELD STORY

A player who has passion, listens well, and works hard is someone any coach would love to have. In addition, a player with amazing quickness and footwork, great shot consistency, and high intelligence makes that player even more valuable to a team. That's the kind of player Kevin Caulfield was to our team. By his senior year, he had been voted captain and was our number-one player. He was well-respected by his teammates and competitors because of his strong mind and great physical toughness on the tennis court. If I'm being really picky and critical, Kevin had only one weakness—his emotional responses to certain players.

Now, let me convey this clearly so that you completely understand. Kevin had emotional toughness most of the time, but one particular competitor from Maryknoll School, who was a year older than Kevin, could really rattle his emotions. He seemed like a nice boy off the tennis court, but on the court, he behaved differently and would get under Kevin's skin. I mean, his behavior was really bad. He would cheat on purpose by making bad line calls. He would question every line call Kevin made. He would ask what the score was after Kevin called the score aloud. He wouldn't give the balls nicely to Kevin in between points. And he would call Kevin names that weren't nice. I believe he did all of these unsportsmanlike things because he wanted to win at all costs. Now, put yourself in Kevin's shoes. Who wouldn't get irritated and frustrated with an opponent like this?

During Kevin's junior year, he played this boy twice in the regular season, winning one and losing one. This boy was a really good player who didn't have to resort to this type of behavior to win matches. In fact, I believe he could have been an even greater player and competed at a much higher level had he behaved properly and respected the etiquette of tennis. But his unacceptable behavior greatly affected Kevin and how he competed against him. Kevin was well aware that the Maryknoll player pulled these antics just to irritate him, and everyone watching could clearly see the effects they had on him. This kept Kevin from playing up to his full potential and made him more vulnerable to defeat.

At the state championship in Wailea, Maui, Kevin and this boy won their early-round matches and would compete against each other in the quarterfinals. I knew Kevin felt uneasy going into this match because he already knew he was about to be treated badly yet again. So the key was to get Kevin in the right mindset to totally control his emotions from the first point until match point, something that he hadn't been able to do in previous matches. We already knew all of his opponent's tricks, so we knew what to expect. My challenge was finding the most effective way to help Kevin deal with it.

"This boy has tried every trick in the book against you," I told Kevin. "So, the good news is we know what to expect. The bad news is I don't know how you'll respond. You know he does those things because he knows he can't beat you without them. People like that want to get a reaction from you. They see how their actions affect you in a negative way. That's why they do it. My challenge to you in this match is to be 'cool as ice.' Show no emotion. Let him do what he'll do and show him that nothing affects you. If you can do this, it will drive him nuts. The spectators will see how bad his attitude and behavior really is, and I have no doubt that you will win."

"Coach, that makes complete sense. And you're right. I haven't been able to control my emotions against him for an entire match."

"Kevin, I know you can do it, and I know you love a challenge. And think about this. This is the last time you'll ever play against him because he's a senior. And if you beat him, his high school tennis career is over. Wouldn't that feel sweet and amazing?" I looked into Kevin's eyes, and I could see an aura of calm intensity within—he would rise to this challenge.

"Coach," he said, "I'm ready."

I felt proud watching Kevin walk onto the court and even prouder watching him compete. Sure enough, his opponent cheated Kevin by making obvious bad line calls, but Kevin still showed no emotion. His opponent unnecessarily questioned every line call Kevin made, and Kevin made it clear he was unaffected by this. His opponent tried to irritate him by asking him what the score was after every point, when Kevin had clearly verbalized the score. Still, Kevin maintained his poise and focus. In between points, his opponent tried to disrupt Kevin's rhythm by hitting or tossing balls to the far area of the court instead of giving them to him nicely, forcing him to walk further to retrieve them. He also called Kevin names on the changeovers, and yet Kevin was impressively cool as ice. But after all of this expected adversity, his opponent was out of tricks and out of time, and Kevin totally dominated, winning 6–3, 6–2.

It was an extraordinary performance of emotional toughness, which showcased his character and focus. It was inspiring for his teammates and the spectators to see Kevin's superior culture of excellence and his superior disciplined details come together to achieve this incredible display of peak performance. I was proud to see Kevin transform himself in this match into a leader who became a strong team captain for us in his senior year, following in the footsteps of former captains Skyler Tateishi and Mikey Lim, both of whom Kevin greatly respected.

KEVIN CAULFIELD (RIGHT) WITH SKYLER TATEISHI

Chapter 15

KEY NO. 4
STRATEGICAL

"Always start at the end before you begin."

—Robert Kiyosaki

THE STRATEGICAL KEY DEALS with how good you are at figuring out the most effective strategies to use that will help you achieve your goals. I have seen many teams work extremely hard but still adopt the wrong plan and fail. Every successful person works hard because hard work works. Working hard is a prerequisite for success. What's more, leaders and teams who work smart set the foundations for peak performance. But in order to work smart, you consistently need to have the right strategies to achieve your goals. And remember, direction is more important than speed. If you're headed in the right direction and can figure out the correct strategies to get where you want to go, you'll achieve your goal eventually.

WORK BACKWARD

One of the big reasons for our twenty-two consecutive state championship victories was that we had a goal, and I had to work backward to figure out how to achieve it. Obviously, winning the state championship was our team's overall goal, and I would examine all the details that we could control ourselves. For example, there were three distinct parts of our season: the regular season, the league championship, and the state championship. To have the best chance to win the state championship, our players had to have the best possible seedings. The order in which they were seeded in the state championship depended on how we finished in our league championship. Getting the best possible results in our league championship depended on our players' seeding in that championship. And those seedings depended on the results we had during the regular season.

Getting the desired results during our regular season depended on our lineup against other schools in order to get head-to-head victories, which directly affected seeding. It wasn't just about randomly writing names on paper and exchanging the lineup with the coach of the opposing team. I would examine all the possibilities of various lineups and the possible effects and outcomes. Everything had to be deliberate and completely calculated.

It's important to break things down in detail and clearly explain it to your team. For example, in order for my team to win the state championship, we need to win a lot of tennis matches. Before we can do that, we need to win *one match*. In order for us to win that one match, a player needs to win two sets. Before he can win two sets, he needs to win *one set*. In order to win that set, he needs to win six games. Before he wins six games, he needs to win *one game*. To win that game, he needs to win four points. Before winning those four points, he needs to win *one point*. And the only way you have a chance of winning that first point is in practice, right here, right now.

That's how important practices really are. Your team members need to understand this, and it's easier for them to see when you break it down, starting with the goal and then working backward. During a match, it's also important for your coaching staff and players to understand that whether you won or lost the last point, the most important thing now is the next one. Understanding this is crucial so that the athlete can maintain his present focus and be at his best for the next point. After all, that's the one thing he can control that will affect whether he wins or loses. And being at his best for the next point depends on what he does in practice, right here, right now. Making a shot in basketball can earn you two points, or three if you're behind the arc. But in tennis, as in baseball, volleyball, and soccer, it's one point, one run, one goal at a time; there are no three-pointers.

Everything should focus on that next point. Training your athletes to give their best physically, mentally, and emotionally for each and every point or play makes all the difference. This is the mentality that must be instilled in practice so that your athletes can perform when it really counts in competition. It all depends on disciplined practice and proper training. The athlete needs to understand that they must practice the same way they play. Practice does not make perfect. What if you're practicing the wrong things? Perfect practices give them the chance to achieve peak performance.

Having fun and enjoying helping each other in practice is necessary for building your team for competition. My own practices are also designed to be tough so that playing matches feels much easier. And another thing: If players are getting too fatigued in matches, then they probably aren't preparing correctly in practice. My team knew how important every single minute of every day in practice was for us to achieve our goal. They understood that it was about these superior disciplined details and that every quality practice we did got us one step closer to winning that state championship.

STAY COMMITTED

Sometimes, you might have a winning strategy even if you start off losing. If you're running a marathon, the goal is to win the marathon, not the sprint. Some people often win the sprint but lose the marathon. If you're running an actual marathon, depending on your strategy, you may be content in fifth place for most of the contest until the final two miles, when you turn up the speed and pass the four frontrunners to win the race. We've all heard the saying, "It's not how you start, but how you finish." (But don't get me wrong—I always prefer a good start *and* a strong finish.)

The point is this: In a football game, your team might have the lead at halftime. You are winning, but you haven't won yet. On the flip side, the other team is losing but hasn't lost yet. You need to play the entire game. Staying committed to the strategy you believe in for the entire game—if you feel it's working—could very well earn you the victory.

People often say, "If it ain't broke, don't fix it." I've seen a number of businesses and sports teams change a winning strategy unnecessarily, which results in losing or giving up much-needed momentum. It's important to understand and be aware of why you are winning or why you are losing. Oftentimes, a player of mine might be losing 3–4 in the first set of a singles match. Well, changing our strategy at that moment might not be the smart thing to do. He's losing the sprint, but everything might be going according to our master plan to win the marathon. Even if he loses the first set, he can still win the next two sets to win the match. It's crucial to stay committed to your strategy if you feel it's the right one, regardless of the score.

ADJUST THE SAILS

If something is clearly not working, it's time to adjust the sails and make a change. If my player loses the first set 1–6, changing our strategy might give us hope in turning things around for the better. Time is also of the essence. During the two-minute coaching break after the first set, I would make a change in our strategy to put my player in a better position to win. In terms of different strategies, we always have a Plan A, B, and C. This is part of being prepared and coaching my players to coach themselves. If they can recognize when a strategy change is necessary, maybe they can do so even before talking with me during the coaching breaks. Then, we won't waste time using an ineffective strategy, and we will be able to compete better, increasing our chances of winning.

Speaking of time, sports such as football, basketball, and soccer have time clocks, while sports like volleyball, golf, and tennis don't use them. Because time is an issue in basketball, for example, it definitely affects your strategy depending on who's winning or losing and how much time there is left in the game. A team with a ten-point lead and one minute left in the game might execute a more reliable, less risky strategy to use the clock to their advantage. The losing team might have to be extra aggressive and foul more because the score and time dictate their strategy to keep that last bit of hope alive.

Volleyball, on the other hand, is different because time is not a factor. To come out on top, you need to win a certain number of points, which wins a set, and winning sets wins the match. You can be down on match point and still come back and win the match. There's no stalling and running out the clock. You need to win the last point to win the match. Therefore, the element of time is often a factor in determining the most effective strategies for you to achieve success. The most successful businesses are thinking long-term. They want to win the marathon. They want to be in business forever, which should be the goal of any company. Just look at how many businesses have closed and gone bankrupt. Remember RadioShack and Tower Records? And my earlier example about BlockBuster? What's a big reason for their failure? It's often not recognizing when to adjust the sails and use a different strategy. Having awareness and being able to adapt to different styles and trends in the marketplace allows the best companies to stay on track for long-term success.

ONE THING BETTER

During my junior year at Creighton, we went on a road trip to play against Drake University on their campus in Iowa.

Coach Ed put me at number one singles, and my opponent was an outstanding player—he was so good that he was also on Canada's Davis Cup team. When I looked across the net, it was obvious to me that he was a much more accomplished player than I was. He had better groundstrokes, volleys, serves, and returns in addition to being taller and faster.

I thought to myself, *Do I have a chance? How can I win?* On paper, he's definitely going to beat me. Luckily, we don't play a tennis match on paper. We play it in person, face-to-face. So, what do I do against him? What kind of strategy can I do to put myself in a position to win? Through the years, I learned that I don't have to be better than my opponent at everything. I just have to be better at one thing and keep doing that one thing over and over again. Coach Ed was a master of preparing us for matches, and I knew that I was very fit thanks to our many extra hours of conditioning and lifting weights.

So, I came up with a strategy to give me hope—to give me that chance to win. I decided that my strategy would be to play a very long match. I wanted to keep him on the court for four hours if I could. You never know what could happen. He could get injured or experience cramping. He could get frustrated and upset with himself. He could get tired and impatient. These were definite possibilities in a long match, but if I lost quickly in a one-hour match, I wouldn't even give these scenarios a chance to materialize. I thought about four-point situations—three that would favor me and one that wouldn't. The three that would be good for me were winning a short point, winning a long point, and losing a long point the reasoning being that I could play a long point and, if I lost it, still affect his conditioning. The one situation that wouldn't favor me was playing a quick short point that I lost (because I'd lose the point and not affect his conditioning). Executing this strategy would involve a bit of mathematics. If I directed all of my groundstrokes toward the middle of the court, hitting heavy topspin shots and penetrating slices, I could bisect the angle of his shots so that I could at least touch the ball. Conversely, if I hit a shot to the corner and I didn't hurt him with it, he would have a greater angle to hit a winner against me, and I probably wouldn't even touch the ball. With this strategy, I could play long points (maybe twenty to thirty shots per point), which would lead to playing longer games and a longer match.

On the first point of the match, I executed the strategy perfectly, playing a very long point that involved more than twenty shots. I was committed and continued doing this every single point. I wanted conditioning to become an issue. I was hopeful that my physical toughness would start to affect his mind. We were both playing brilliant tennis in front of a massive crowd of people who were all cheering for my opponent, by the way. The downside for me was that he won the first set 7–5. The upside was it lasted over an hour, and things were going according to plan.

I felt encouraged and was convinced that I knew I had the right strategy to give me a chance to win, even after losing the first set. In the second set, I began to execute my shots even more precisely with more pace and depth down the middle of the court. My goal was to hit shots higher and lower to him, to keep his contact with the ball out of his preferred power zone, just above waist level. Our rallies were grueling, and we were both getting winded. I knew that he wanted to beat me badly, especially playing on his home court in front of his fans. But what he didn't know was that I wanted to beat him even more. The match was now at the two-and-a-half-hour mark, and I had set point to even the battle. After another long, tough point, he missed his forehand long, and he threw his racket toward the net. I won the second set 7–5, but, more importantly, I witnessed a crack in his armor.

In the third set, I stayed committed to my strategy and was extremely focused mentally during and in between points. He, on the other hand, continued throwing his racket out of frustration and started yelling at himself, saying, "This match should have been done two hours ago!" I thought to myself, *Yeah, I got him.* He couldn't take it anymore. He was upset and mad at himself that I was in a position to win. He knew that he was a better athlete and player than me, and it was eating him alive. The battle was just beyond the three-and-a-half-hour mark when I found myself with a match point. Needless to say, it was another long, tough point, and he finally hit his backhand into the net. I won the third set 7–5, walked up to the net to shake hands, and headed quickly for the exit. Looking back, I saw him grab all five rackets out of his bag and slam them into the concrete, cracking every racket. I had a big smile on my face and a satisfying feeling of accomplishment inside.

This is a story that I've shared with countless players over the years to inspire and help them find a way to win. Think about how this applies to business. You don't have to be better than your competitor at everything. You just have to be better at one thing and do that one thing extremely well. The most successful leaders and teams find a way to win even if the odds are against them. So, remember, always bet on yourself!

Chapter 16

KEY NO. 5
TACTICAL

"Good tactics can save even the worst strategy.
Bad tactics will destroy even the best strategy."

—George S. Patton

ONCE YOU HAVE THE RIGHT STRATEGY, you need to use the correct tactics to execute that strategy. Think of strategy as the general framework needed to accomplish your goal and tactics as the little details to help you get there. Some leaders are good at figuring out the right strategy for their team but still might suffer a defeat because the right tactics weren't used. The greatest leaders and teams have disciplined details and connect the dots completely when determining their strategy and tactics to achieve victory.

STRENGTHS VS. WEAKNESSES

In competition, any time you can use your strengths against your opponent's weaknesses will greatly favor you. In tennis, for example, if your opponent's forehand is stronger than their backhand, a typical strategy might be to play as many shots to the opponent's backhand as possible. But how do you do it? Which tactics do you use to allow that scenario to happen as often as possible? If you just direct every shot toward the backhand corner, a smart opponent will adjust and ultimately run around the backhand to play more forehand shots from the backhand corner.

So, here's the answer. If you're competing against someone equal in ability to you or even better than you, smart shot selections are critical. For example, one tactic might be to play a shot to your opponent's forehand corner. Yes, I know that's their strength. But, once they are in the forehand corner, it completely opens up the backhand corner for your next shot, which will favor you. You might even be able to hit two or more consecutive shots to their backhand before having to go to their forehand again, opening up the backhand side again. Another tactic might be shot variety—hitting with different spins, depths, heights, and speeds. If your opponent likes playing tennis with a certain rhythm and pace, using shot variety will drive them nuts. Your opponent might like it when you hit the ball really hard over and over again. Their shots might come back to you even harder and faster. Changing your tactic by using shot variety might greatly favor you against an opponent like this.

People exude more confidence in themselves when they know they're good at something. Everyone has certain strengths, whether they know it or not. We also have certain weaknesses, which provide an opportunity for improvement. But let's focus on strengths. The advantage for most successful teams is they're able to use the strengths of their individual team members to collectively help their organization. Always remember that *individual strength adds to team strength.*

For example, if a company's executive team is comprised of ten people, each with one unique strength of expertise, the tactics their CEO employs with them can be vital to the company's success. In order to get peak performance from each team member, the CEO must have a culture where everyone truly enjoys working together, respecting and cherishing each other's strengths. When the executives deeply appreciate each other, it sets up tremendous opportunities to encourage a growth mindset, using various tactics to be more effective and efficient, which leads to peak performance. Looking at things from a different perspective is a good thing. The greatest leaders are always open to different solutions and new possibilities. As the leader, the CEO can facilitate open and constructive discussions to leverage the strengths of individuals to help the team excel. Helping and supporting each other while empowering the leaders to drive a deeper purpose and meaning in their work creates an array of tactical options to complement the overall strategy for the team's success.

ADAPT TO YOUR TEAM

Why do some teams with incredibly talented team members lose? And why is it that some teams with only average team talent win? When you have amazing talent on your team and you lose, it's usually because the leader isn't adapting his or her plan to maximize that talent in the best possible way. I've seen many athletic coaches and business leaders fail because they want to stick with their own plans and have their team members adjust instead. However, the best coaches will adapt their plan to consistently highlight the talent of the individual players to put the team in the best position for success. Knowing the strengths of the people you have and using the best strategic and tactical options to complement your team's talent will always put you in a position to win.

In football, for example, a lower-ranked team might defeat a highly-rated team, and it's viewed as a major upset. What is considered an upset? It's when a team with less talent beats a team with more. That's why sports competitions are held on a field or court instead of played on paper looking at each team's individual talent and assuming who should win. I've had many occasions when I looked across the net and recognized that my opponent had more talent than me, yet I was able to win with smart play, using effective strategy and tactics.

When I was a kid playing Little League baseball, I noticed how good coaches would put players in the right positions, and other coaches would mistakenly put their players in the wrong ones. It doesn't make sense to put an exceptional catcher in right field or a superstar pitcher at second base. Same thing in business. A team member who is an outstanding salesperson should be in a sales position, potentially training and developing other team members to improve their sales techniques. Being able to adapt and use the strengths of your team will consistently put you in favorable positions to achieve success.

SETBACKS ARE OPPORTUNITIES FOR COMEBACKS

We've all experienced setbacks at some point in our lives. Whether you've had an injury, a heartbreaking defeat, or an occupational change, it's your mindset that first determines in which direction you're headed. If you have the right mindset and are determined to rise up and recover from the setback, tactics are the little things to keep you moving forward in the right direction. It will help you connect the dots and keep you focused on becoming even stronger than you previously were. Remember, little things make big differences, and big things are often accomplished when you take care of the little things first.

Let me share with you a few setbacks encountered by some notable people. Oprah Winfrey was demoted from her job as a news anchor because the executives said she "wasn't fit for television." Walt Disney was fired from a newspaper for "lacking imagination and having no original ideas." The Beatles were rejected by Decca Recording Studios, who said, "We don't like their sound. They have no future in show business." Michael Jordan, after being cut from his high school basketball team, went home, locked himself in his room, and cried. Henry Ford had two failed car companies prior to succeeding with Ford Motor Company. Albert Einstein wasn't able to speak until he was almost four years old, and his teachers said he would "never amount to much."

During my junior year in college, I tripped over my feet in tennis practice, and as I was falling to the ground, I braced my fall with my right hand. It was an instinctual reaction, and I knew it was a serious wrist injury (and yes, I am right-handed). After visiting the hospital, the doctor informed me that I had a chipped bone and a torn ligament in my wrist. He put a cast on me that came nearly up to my right shoulder to let the ligament heal. It was a major setback for me. I felt extremely disappointed, as I'd been playing amazing tennis and was enjoying great momentum with my game.

The doctor said I'd be in a cast for two months. (After the first month, I was re-casted with one that came up just below my right elbow.) This was truly depressing for me and affected more than just my tennis game. Writing was a huge challenge, as well as taking a shower and having to wrap my right arm in a plastic bag taped near my shoulder so the cast wouldn't get wet. Sleeping was also an issue, but the worst part was watching my teammates compete and not being able to practice and play with them. Fortunately, I quickly adopted the right mindset to focus on everything else I could do to stay in good physical shape. During tennis practice, I would run, use the stationary bike, and do lots of sit-ups and leg raises to keep my abdominals strong, as well as a ton of plyometric and flexibility exercises.

After two long months, the cast was removed, and I immediately began rehab. I was determined to come back stronger than ever and wanted to make sure that the bone chip and ligament had healed properly. I would see the trainers five days a week for my rehab, and I was disciplined to do their suggested additional exercises on my own. After two months and three weeks of no tennis, I was finally able to start hitting tennis balls again, and I felt a new appreciation for the game and being healthy. That was the first time I had a major injury that kept me from playing tennis, and I didn't take anything for granted after that. I learned an important lesson—setbacks are opportunities for comebacks.

Kobe Bryant is one of the greatest basketball players of all time, and he suffered a major setback when he tore his Achilles during a game late in his career. It's one of the worst injuries that can happen to an athlete because of the long rehabilitation process. Let me share with you the mindset of a *superior achiever* dealing with this major setback. Shortly after the injury, Kobe posted on Facebook, saying, "All the training and sacrifice just flew out the window with one step that I've done millions of times. The frustration is unbearable. The anger is rage. Now I'm supposed to come back from this and be the same player or better at thirty-five? How in the world am I supposed to do that? Do I have the consistent will to overcome this thing? Maybe I should break out the rocking chair and reminisce on the career that was. Maybe this is how my book ends. Maybe Father Time has defeated me—then again, maybe not! Feels good to vent— let it out—to feel as if this is the worst thing ever. Because after all the venting, a real perspective sets in. There are far greater issues and challenges in the world than a torn Achilles. Stop feeling sorry for yourself, find the silver lining, and get to work with the same belief, same drive, and same conviction as ever. One day, the beginning of a new career journey will commence. Today is NOT that day! 'If you see me in a fight with a bear, pray for the bear.' That's 'mamba mentality'—we don't quit, we don't cower, we don't run. We endure and conquer!"

THE CHRIS MA STORY

In 1995, a year after partnering with senior Taylor Tom and winning the state doubles championship as a freshman, my sophomore singles player Chris Ma went undefeated during the regular season. At the state championship on the Big Island, he continued his streak by winning match after match. After a convincing victory in the semifinals, Chris was ready to face the number one ranked player in the state of Hawaii in the boys' 18 division, a player who was also the defending state singles champion and the tournament's number-one seed from the Big Island.

Chris was ranked number one in the boys' 16 division, and both players were used to winning. His opponent had a multitude of weapons in his tennis game. Among his many strengths, he was extremely athletic with a powerful forehand and serve and played exceptional, aggressive tennis. He really had no weakness. So, what would our strategy be? How could I put Chris in a position to win? I told him that this would obviously be a tough challenge, but I knew we could find a way to win. Luckily, Chris looked forward to challenges. He loved it when an opponent played his best tennis, challenging Chris to do the same.

So, I shared with him that we needed to do two things as often as possible. First, to direct more shots to his opponent's backhand because his forehand was very lethal. Second, to be patient in the point by varying the heights of our shots—hitting higher and lower shots with the goal of keeping it out of his power zone, which was a little bit above his waist level. I believed that these two situations would favor Chris in a way where we would win the majority of the points. And, of course, if we won the majority of the points, we would win the match. Chris agreed and walked confidently onto the court.

There was a tremendous, lively crowd around the court, eagerly awaiting an intense battle between these two champions. In the first twenty minutes, his opponent destroyed Chris, 6–0. The spectators were shocked at how lopsided this match was. Chris could not even get into a position to have a chance to execute our strategy. He couldn't even get into a rally. He'd return his opponent's serve, and the shot after that was either a winner or a forced error. When Chris served, his opponent would either hit a return winner or force an error from Chris on that shot or the next. It wasn't pretty. It was painful to watch. Almost every point finished with a maximum of three or maybe four shots at the most.

After every point Chris lost, I could feel hundreds of eyes watching me to see my reaction. So, I stood there cheering him on with a positive expression, though my insides were churning as I imagined what Chris must have felt. I was convinced that we had the right strategy, but we needed to have the right tactics to let him get to the point to execute that strategy.

Immediately after losing the set point, I walked quickly onto the court for the two-minute coaching break. I said, "Chris, I know we have the right strategy, but he's just not letting you play. It's all about math and our first two-shot selections. We need to bisect the angles of the court and be precise tactically with our first two shots. When you're serving, hit every serve down the middle. Whether he hits his huge forehand or backhand, he's making contact from the middle of the court, which means you'll touch the ball. And if you can touch the ball, you can get to the point to execute our strategy. Also, when you're returning serve, hit every return to the middle of the court for the same reason in bisecting the angles of the court.

"In the first set, you would hit a neutral ball to a corner, and he would either hit a powerful forehand from his forehand corner, or he'd run around his backhand and hit his favorite inside-out forehand."

I could see that this made perfect sense to Chris, and I walked off the court, ready to watch these tactical adjustments in action.

The second set was a completely different story. Chris was executing his shots exactly as we'd discussed. It was amazing to see. Every point became a display of what looked like hard, heavy-hitting shots to the average tennis fan, but it really was all about tactics and execution. The spectators could not believe their eyes, as it seemed to be a completely different match than what they'd witnessed in the first set.

"What did you tell Chris?" one of them asked.

Not wanting to share any of our secret details, I simply said, "I told him how to win."

Chris won the second set, 6–3, and I again walked onto the court for the split-set coaching break. I said, "Chris, you're tough, and I'm proud of you. Keep doing everything you're doing with your first two shots, but let's add one more thing. I noticed that when your opponent is going to hit a running backhand, his shot is neutral, which doesn't hurt you and gives us an opportunity to be aggressive. When you see that situation, move forward quickly to play a volley from on or inside the service line. You'll be on offense, and you'll definitely win the majority of those points." He agreed, and then it was time to start the third and deciding set.

I overheard some of the spectators saying they couldn't believe how Chris had turned things around. The third set began the way the second one had ended. Chris showed great determination and was executing our tactics and strategy perfectly. Finally, he was up 4–3 with a breakpoint opportunity. Everyone could see that Chris was wearing his opponent down physically, which was leading to mental cracks. I was feeling great watching all of this, but the next thing I saw was Chris lying down on the tennis court. He was in pain with severe leg cramps. I couldn't believe it.

The umpire called an injury time-out and allowed me back onto the court with the trainer. We immediately began massaging Chris's legs to alleviate the pain. Chris needed just five more points to win the match. He only needed to play five more minutes of tennis to win the state singles championship. Once the umpire called time, the trainer and I walked off the court, and the boys were ready to continue this epic match.

But the cramps continued, and Chris was having great difficulty moving—yet he didn't want to retire from the match. He lost the next three games and the third set, 6–4, then hobbled toward the net to congratulate his opponent. Needless to say, it was sad to see such a fantastic match end this way. As I sat down next to Chris, we talked about what had just happened. "Coach, you were right about the strategy, and the tactical adjustments worked great. I had it. I just needed five more points."

"I know!" I said, knowing we'd been completely prepared for this match. "I don't understand why you cramped. We hydrated properly for a week, and it baffles me that you had cramps. Why do you think it happened?"

"Maybe it's because I didn't eat breakfast."

I almost fell out of my chair. "What? Why didn't you eat breakfast?"

"I was feeling kind of nervous and didn't really have an appetite."

"Oh my gosh, Chris! You need to eat to have energy, whether you feel like it or not."

"Well, Coach, at least we clinched the state team championship yesterday." This kind of selfless thinking typified why Chris was such an amazing team player for our team. He went on to win the state singles championship the following year as a junior, and as a senior, he won the state doubles championship. In fact, that state singles championship match that he cramped up in as a sophomore was his only loss during his entire varsity tennis career.

CHRIS MA

Chapter 17

KEY NO. 6
ENVIRONMENTAL

"When a flower doesn't bloom, you fix the environment
in which it grows, not the flower."

—Alexander Den Heijer

THE ENVIRONMENTAL KEY means creating the right
atmosphere for your team, even as you deal with outside forces
beyond your control. As head coach, I wanted to create a safe and
friendly environment for my players and their families, as well
as the other students and their families, so they always looked
forward to coming to our tennis facility. It was so gratifying to
consistently see so many students and parents socializing with
one another in such a positive, welcoming environment. This is
such an important part of peak performance. Even if you have

the other five keys, if your team doesn't feel right about their environment, and if they can't properly deal with forces beyond their control, they won't perform up to their full potential.

IT'S YOUR PEOPLE

In order to have the right team environment, everyone needs to play a role. To help the team achieve its goals, every individual needs to contribute to making an impact. Everyone wants to be a part of something special and significant. That's why people love participating on a team. But that's only if the team leader is fair and truly cares about the well-being of each individual. As the leader, it's your responsibility to create a healthy, safe, and positive atmosphere because they're *your* people. It's just as you'd do with your family at home—your team is your second family away from home.

Creating an environment that fosters collaboration and cohesion allows your team the opportunity to accomplish anything they set their minds to. Moreover, encouraging them to contribute innovative, creative ideas—thereby helping the team find different and better ways to achieve goals—deepens the commitment of each team member. My twelve players, the assistant coach, and every player's parents had roles on our team, which built strong team support for everyone involved. In creating your environment, it's extremely vital to acknowledge the behaviors you value. At Punahou School's annual athletic awards assembly, each coach would present one team member with the Most Inspirational Player award, as voted upon by his or her teammates. And local businesses might have their own annual or semiannual awards, acknowledging team members who demonstrated special resiliency, teamwork, creativity, perseverance, integrity, compassion, humility, and courage. At Punahou's tennis complex, the sportsmanship trophies on display were significantly bigger in size than the championship trophies. In these and other ways, leaders can create a positive environment and highlight the accomplishments of their team members, fostering the atmosphere that they want to create and, more importantly, sustain.

In the University of Oregon's sports complex, Hawaii football star Marcus Mariota's Heisman Trophy is on display. What's fascinating is the inverted pyramid at the base of the trophy. At the bottom of this pyramid, near the point, is the name Mariota. Stacked above that are various layers of recognition: names of Little League baseball teams Mariota played with, names of numerous coaches who helped him, and names of teachers and other mentors who believed in him. At the very top level are the names of every teammate from the 2014 Oregon Ducks football team. Every player on offense, defense, and special teams is listed on the base of Mariota's Heisman Trophy.

If you view this incredible display from above, you'll also see a rendering of his home state. Mariota has noted that all of Hawaii's people played a key role in his success in winning the prestigious Heisman. Those people helped and encouraged him to believe in himself, which made him the person he is today. This amazing display showcases how important coaches and a positive team environment can be in helping someone excel to reach his or her full potential. Best of all, it can be contagious, sending the right message to others who want to strive for the same superior excellence.

THE BUCKY JENCKS STORY

Having a team-first mentality is absolutely necessary. Because tennis is an individual sport like golf, swimming, and track, I wanted everyone on my team to be part of something greater than one person. I wanted the team to be bigger and more important than any one individual, including myself. The only way to put the team first is to make sure that all members feel they're contributing to making the team better and holding each other accountable for every action—or nonaction.

Let me share a story with you. In 2003, a few weeks before leaving for the state championship on the Big Island of Hawaii, the top two players on my team were suspended from Punahou School. The school administration informed me that these two were no longer on my team and might be expelled. I had no idea what had happened, but I soon learned that athletes from another school had vandalized the cars of some of our own top athletes. In response, some of the players on our soccer and track teams—as well as my top two players—decided to retaliate. They vandalized the other school by spray-painting graffiti around its campus. Understandably, Punahou School has a zero-tolerance policy for situations like these.

So now my team had gone from twelve players to ten, and we were on our way to the Big Island. While at the state championship, other teams and coaches were asking my players and me about what had happened. They'd been hearing all kinds of false rumors, and the story was evolving into something far different than what had actually happened. Bucky Jencks, who was number three on my team, instantly stepped up and became a leader. Bucky was a super-talented athlete in soccer, track, and tennis. Everyone on our team respected Bucky, an ultimate team player who always put the team first. As a freshman, he won the state doubles championship with his partner, senior Mike Bruggemann. Now, as a junior, Bucky found himself on stadium court playing for the state singles championship.

Bucky is a person with extraordinary character and is liked by everyone. His opponent from the island of Kauai liked and respected him too, but he also defeated Bucky in that championship final. In defeat, Bucky represented our school and team with ultimate class. During the trophy presentation on stadium court, Bucky asked the tournament director if he could use the microphone to address the crowd. First, he congratulated his opponent for winning and playing incredible tennis. Second, he thanked the tournament director, umpires, volunteers, fans, and all the families in attendance supporting their sons and daughters. Third, Bucky said, "I want to address the unfortunate incidents you're probably aware of between a few athletes from Punahou and another school. Their actions are unacceptable. It's a reflection of a few students who made a poor choice. It's not a reflection of the entire school. As I hope you saw in this tournament, my teammates and I represented our school and families to the best of our abilities. This is who Punahou School is, and this is who we are as Punahou students. Please don't let the unfortunate actions of a handful of students taint your view of us or our school."

Upon handing the microphone back to the tournament director, Bucky received major applause and a standing ovation from everyone there. His meaningful words provided much-needed clarity. Players from the other school involved in the incident approached our boys' and girls' varsity players to shake hands and hug. It was such a beautiful thing to see. Out of a thoughtless, stupid choice of a few came a closer bond of respect and appreciation between players representing both schools. Needless to say, I was so proud of Bucky for being proactive and doing what he did. By putting his team first, he not only united every school and athlete, but he consequently held himself, our team, and everyone there to an even higher standard of excellence.

BUCKY JENCKS

EXPECT THE UNEXPECTED

I liked seeing my players practice in the toughest conditions. Practicing on an extra hot day with high humidity or in very windy conditions made my players tougher and better in dealing with such challenging situations, should they be a factor on match day. On a very windy day, for example, I'd often tell my team, "We might not be able to play our best tennis on a day like this, but neither will our opponents. To gain the advantage, we just need to deal with the wind a little bit better than they do to get the upper hand. Even though we might not feel or play at our peak, we can always give it our best." Heat, cold, wind, humidity, light drizzle, and snow flurries are environmental conditions that many athletes experience during competition, and I would frequently remind my team that the best excuse is the one you never make.

But what about in the business world? Can you deal with the pressure of deadlines, shifting market conditions, and other unforeseen circumstances that can and will arise when you least expect it? If you always expect things to go smoothly and according to plan, you will consistently be disappointed. The key is to expect the unexpected. If you have the mindset that you expect adversity and challenges on a daily basis, you'll be able to deal with them in a much more favorable way. Problems are inevitable. You must condition yourself and your team to be problem solvers.

Think about the environment you're in right now. Is it very hectic and chaotic? Do you constantly feel stress and pressure? Do you get sidetracked because things arise that need your attention, which causes you to alter your plan for the day? If your response to these questions is yes, then you were probably expecting your day to go according to plan. But whether you're in sports or business, things rarely do. You must be able to adapt and adjust if you want to be productive and succeed. The best leaders and teams are prepared for everything and anything that could happen and know how they will respond. They're expecting it. They understand their internal and external environments and can properly deal with the unexpected. They become comfortable in what others perceive as uncomfortable situations.

LOOK WITHIN YOURSELF

During my senior year at Creighton, we traveled to Lake of the Ozarks to play the University of Missouri. It was a gorgeous sunny spring day at a beautiful country club. We usually played six singles matches first, followed by three doubles matches next, with the best of nine winning the day. However, another dual match before ours was running overtime, and because there were three courts available right then, the coaches decided to play the three doubles matches first.

My partner, Rick Faust, and I played great together and won in straight sets. Our team had a 2–1 lead after the doubles matches, and we were feeling hopeful going into singles. Coach Ed had me at number one singles against Missouri's number one, who boasted a high national college ranking. Time was ticking away in my college tennis career, and I had only a few more months before I graduated, so I wanted to savor each and every match I played. Playing college tennis while traveling to different parts of the country was one of the best experiences of my life. Needless to say, I was fired up and ready to give it my best against Missouri's best.

My opponent was a super strong, talented player who appeared to have no weaknesses. In fact, he and I had the same style of play, and winning would depend on who executed better. I honestly felt that he was a notch better than me, although I was playing the best tennis of my entire college career. I had poise and confidence in myself, and as the match began, I rose to the occasion. I was matching him shot for shot, and if I could sustain that, I believed I had a chance to win. In all honesty, if we played each other ten times, I felt that he'd probably beat me nine times out of ten. But I didn't have to play him ten times. I didn't need to beat him ten times. I just needed to beat him one time—today!

The first set was an incredible display of power, control, finesse, and fight. We both were executing heavy, aggressive groundstrokes and taking advantage of shorter balls and putting those shots away with piercing volleys and punishing overheads at the net. After an hour and fifteen minutes, he used one of those volleys to close out the first set 7–5. The first set was so close I felt it could easily have gone my way had I executed two or three shots better.

The second set was much like the first. In fact, we were both exhibiting the first five keys of peak performance brilliantly. Physically, he and I were showcasing our entire arsenal of shots, grinding out every single point and using good footwork to continue hitting these precise shots with power and finesse. Mentally, we seemed about equal—our concentration and focus on the task at hand were like a mirror image. Emotionally, we were both controlling our internal climate and getting pumped up, using it to fuel us at the right moments. Strategically, we both seemed to have an identical plan. It would just come down to which of us would carry it out better. Obviously, he felt that he could play his game to beat me, and I felt I could play mine to beat him. Tactically, we were trying to do the same things to each other; it would all depend on the execution. And on that score, I connected on some important points and won the second set 7–5.

Just before the third set, I looked over to the side of the court and saw my entire team sitting there next to the Missouri team. It dawned on me that the rest of my teammates had completed their matches and that mine was the last one to finish. We had already passed the two-and-a-half-hour mark, and the crowd was getting loud and rowdy. My teammates were looking at me, yelling, "Let's go, O Captain! My Captain!" (That was an Ethan Hawke line from the *Dead Poets Society,* and that's what the other players called me as team captain.) The Missouri team was yelling encouragement to my opponent, as were most of the other spectators. That was the moment my opponent and I realized the team match score was tied 4-4, and we were the deciding match.

This was when the sixth key about the environment became very evident. The only spectators cheering for me were my coaches and teammates, a total of nine people. The other two hundred-plus onlookers were cheering for my opponent. In fact, it no longer felt like a tennis match, with the usual etiquette. It felt more like a football game, with some extremely vocal fans. That's just how it was, and I had to deal with it.

In the first game of the third set, I ran wide to hit a backhand, rolled my left ankle, and fell to the ground. I tried to walk it off, but I immediately knew that this was a bad injury. I mean, it was really bad! I could barely put any weight on my left foot. Looking over at my teammates, I could see their faces in shock, and their hopes of a huge team victory evaporated. I felt completely deflated and majorly disappointed, but I wasn't about to retire from the match. It didn't even cross my mind, even though I couldn't step into my forehands, push off my back foot to hit backhands, or spring up on my serve. Dejected, I began to think, *I can't, I can't, I can't!* and I quickly fell behind, 0–4.

Then, as I was preparing for the next game, I looked over and saw how defeated my teammates looked. I felt helpless and defeated as well, like I was letting them down as their captain and teammate. I was two games away from losing the match, but more painfully, our team match. A victory would have been the biggest win in our team's history, for sure.

As I was toweling off by the back fence, Coach Ed walked over and said, "Instead of worrying about the things you can't do, focus on what you still *can* do!" Then he walked away. He said this in a very powerful and forceful voice, the only words he spoke to me during the entire match. I digested what he'd said and thought, *That's brilliant! If I can't step in on my forehands, I can put all of my weight on my right foot and hit open stance forehands. If I can't push off my back foot on my backhands, I can put all the weight on my right foot and hit open stance backhands. If I can't spring up on my serve, I can put all the weight on my right foot and make a lower contact to serve.*

I figured out these adjustments, and they all made perfect sense. But was it too late? Up to this point in the third set, my opponent had made me run extra because of my injury and limited court coverage. It actually took him out of his game plan because he figured the injury meant he was on his way to victory. But after Coach Ed's words of wisdom, I won the next game. After winning that one, I thought, *At least I won't lose this set 6–0.* Then I won another game and was down 2–4, and on the next changeover, I was only down 3–4. Now, the environment was getting really crazy. Everyone in the crowd was screaming, banging seats, just making noise. It was intense, and even though I'd won those three games, I was still two games away from losing.

Maybe it was the adrenaline, but now I was also executing my shots better after making those adjustments. My opponent was definitely feeling the pressure because I was coming back! With all the drama, this match was going to be epic, even if I ended up losing. It was at this moment I realized I wanted to beat not just my opponent but all of the two hundred-plus people cheering against me. And the only way to do it was to continue to fight for every single shot in every single point. I wanted to win this match for Coach Ed and my teammates and make it the most monumental college match that these spectators had ever seen.

After winning the next two games, I was ahead 5–4. As I sat on the bench drinking water on the changeover, I looked across the court at my teammates. I was using them as inspiration, reflecting back on all the hard work, sweat, and pain we'd experienced together to get to this moment. From that point on, there was no denying me. After winning match point, I felt overwhelmed as I shook hands and hugged my opponent at the net. I had earned his respect, along with that of all his supporters, and they congratulated me as I left the court. They told me that I'd shown heart, determination, resiliency, and toughness. They told me they were inspired by my comeback, especially in that boisterous pro-Missouri environment.

The next day, I was on the front page of the sports section of the *Omaha World-Herald*. Coach Ed had a quote in there: "It was a good learning experience for our younger players. They were all there sitting and watching the whole thing. He was beaten. It was a really good comeback." Coach Ed's advice to me that day is something that I'll never forget. I've used it countless times with my players to inspire them to always focus on what they can do, not what they can't.

Section 4: The 6 Keys for Peak Performance

Now that you've completed the 6 Keys for Peak Performance, please take ten minutes to honestly rank yourself and answer these important questions. The purpose of the assessment is to help you identify action items that will enable you to continue with your leadership journey toward becoming a superior leader. Below, you will find questions with corresponding gray boxes. Please use these boxes to rate yourself on a scale of 1-10 (1 being "needs improvement" and 10 being "superior") on your ability to do the specified task. Then, answer the corresponding free-response question.

How would you rate your physical ability to do your job?

What can you do to improve your physical performance of your job by five percent next quarter?

_____

_____

_____

How would you rate your mental ability to do your job?

How can you improve your mental toughness when facing adversity?

_____

_____

_____

Rate how aware you are of the three most important questions you should ask yourself each morning to put you in a superior mindset.

Answer these important questions: Who do I love? What do I love? What do I love about myself?

_____

_____

_____

How would you rate your ability to identify the "red light" priorities in your day (or situations that require urgent attention)?

What are the top three urgent priorities that demand your attention today?

_____

_____

_____

How would you rate your ability to control your negative emotions?

What is one example of a time when you expressed a negative emotion to a team (or team member), and how would you do this differently today?

_____

_____

_____

Rate how good you are at figuring out the best strategies to accomplish your goals.

What is one strategy you can add to accomplish your next round of goals this quarter?

_____

_____

_____

How would you rate your ability to consistently find ways to win?

What's the one thing that you can focus on that you can do better than your competition?

_____

_____

_____

Rate how good you are at figuring out the correct tactics to complement your strategy.

What are your personal strengths that will give you opportunities for success?

_____

_____

_____

How would you rate your ability to deal with setbacks?

In the past, what was a setback you experienced, and what did you do to emerge stronger?

_____

_____

_____

Rate your skill level at creating an environment that shows people that they matter (acknowledging people)?

What are three areas where you can create or enhance a positive working environment for your team?

_____

_____

_____

How would you rate your ability to be prepared for unforeseen circumstances?

In the past, what was a major unexpected event you experienced, and what can you do to prepare for something similar next quarter?

_____

_____

_____

Add up your total score for this assessment and enter your score here.

THE 8 KEYS FOR SUSTAINING SUCCESS

section 5

Chapter 18

KEY NO. 1
THE CHARACTER
OF A CHAMPION

"Character is the foundation stone upon
which one must build to win respect. Just as no worthy
building can be erected on a weak foundation,
so no lasting reputation worthy of respect
can be built on a weak character."

—R.C. Samsel

IN SPORTS, EVERY COACH can help build and improve
the character of their athletes, which can help them achieve
success in both their sport and in life. In business, every leader
can help build and improve the character of team members,

which will help them in the workplace and in their lives. The coaching philosophy for all coaches should be to strive to develop champion athletes of good character. The same leadership philosophy can be applied in the workplace to help employees be the best people they can be and represent the organization in the best possible way. Focusing on building character gives everyone the chance to perform to their maximum ability and potential. They will be thinking and acting in ways that put themselves and the team in the best possible position for success. This needs to be done as early and consistently as possible.

In soccer, you often see a team of five- and six-year-olds being coached by a parent with limited knowledge of the sport. This parent coach has a critically important role in instilling certain things in these young players. The players need to have fun, and they need to learn the basic fundamentals of soccer and the importance of teamwork. Most importantly, they need to start building the kind of character that will help them in athletics and in life. But much too often, the parent coach is focusing on winning and only on winning. This can have adverse effects as these young boys and girls begin to think that only winning is important. This might lead them to have a mindset to win at all costs. This might cause them to cheat to win. It might cause them to be mean to their opponents in order to win. It can even cause them to be mean to their own teammates if they see that only the stronger players are consistently in the starting line-up. It might cause an unhealthy climate among teammates instead of creating a healthy climate where individuals are working together and helping each other improve.

We sometimes wonder whether professional athletes are indeed good role models. We see some of these professionals reach the pinnacle of achievement and success in their sport and then see them fall from grace, the direct result of flawed character. It's obvious that these professionals are exceptional athletes, yet individuals of questionable character. This might even keep them from playing or competing at an even higher level and achieving even greater success. Can you imagine these athletes going back in time to when they were five years old, playing their sport for the first time, and having a coach instill in them that character should be their number one focus, that they are to win with humility and lose with grace? How much different would each of their lives be today?

DEVELOP YOUR PHILOSOPHY

All coaches or leaders should have a philosophy that they instill in their teams. But is their coaching philosophy effective in achieving the goals and results they want for their team? Or are they going about it the wrong way? Are they focused too much on winning, which might be hindering their team from achieving its maximum potential? Is their philosophy helping or hurting the development of the members and the team as a whole? A leader must first identify what is really important for his or her team. What can you do to put your team in the best position to succeed? What degree of excellence do you want for your team? And how do you then introduce the correct process for coaching and leading your team? What legacy do you want to leave to your team members?

When I became head coach of the Punahou School boys' varsity tennis program back in 1994, my team philosophy was to develop champion athletes of great character first and great tennis players second. I shared with my team that it is most important for us to exhibit character, respect for others and ourselves, unimpeachable ethics and integrity, and constantly strive for superior excellence. I already had some good athletes, but what's a good athlete with poor discipline or bad character? Definitely not one that I'd be proud of. I wanted to set a high standard for that 1994 team, to serve as a model for teams to follow for years to come.

I don't agree when people say it doesn't matter if you win or lose—"just have fun and enjoy the experience." It does matter if you win or lose. Winning is important. If it weren't, we wouldn't keep score. But you need to do it correctly. In my youth, I remember having a Snoopy tennis poster in my room with the message, "It doesn't matter if you win or lose, until you lose." I learned something very important about myself by competing in baseball, soccer, and tennis. I learned that winning was fine with me, but I absolutely hated to lose. It's something that I still feel to this day. Trying your very best to win is a good thing because it requires you to formulate a plan, execute a strategy, deal with stress and adversity, solve problems, and put yourself and your team in the best position to be successful.

I also don't agree with giving trophies to everyone who participates in a tournament. It devalues the meaning of a trophy for those who work hard to earn one. What's more, those who don't win—especially those who finish last—are embarrassed because they know they really don't deserve a trophy. At our annual Punahou School Junior Novice Tennis Tournament, we displayed the trophies on the first day of the tournament so the players and their parents could see them when they checked in. They noticed that there were some big, tall trophies and others that were much smaller. Upon closer inspection, they also noticed that the big, tall ones were the sportsmanship trophies, and the smaller ones were for the champions and finalists. Our top priority was to show how important sportsmanship and good character are. Our participants began to understand this too—they all wanted to be chosen as the sportsmanship winner and take that big, beautiful trophy home. The effect was significant. Our top priority became their top priority because they knew the tournament committee valued sportsmanship more than winning. Consequently, their good attitudes, behavior, and respect for opponents helped all of them perform at a much higher level—which then put them in more favorable positions to win.

CONSTANT THIRST FOR GROWTH

Many people have asked me about the sports I've played and how I developed my own character and leadership traits. In my youth, I first played baseball. I liked the sport because many of my school friends played, and it was fun learning skills such as throwing, pitching, catching, and batting. Thanks to baseball, my hand-eye coordination improved a great deal, and I especially liked pitching and playing second base. After a few years of baseball, soccer became an interest of mine because, again, many of my friends played that sport. I liked the movement and fast action, although I didn't care too much for all the running involved. Yes, I know—if you play soccer, you run all the time. My footwork, movement, and conditioning were greatly improved from playing soccer, as they should have with all that running in practice and in games. After a few years of soccer, I began to take an interest in tennis. My mom started playing, and I would go to the tennis courts with her to try it myself. It looks easy enough on television, so I thought it would be no problem for me. I quickly realized how difficult and challenging tennis is. I began to visualize how much fun it is to hit home runs in baseball and started trying to do the same thing on the tennis court. Mom immediately put a stop to that and said that if I wanted to play tennis, I would have to learn the sport correctly by taking tennis lessons. So, I did and quickly realized that the skills I'd learned in baseball and soccer greatly complemented what I was learning in tennis. I began to improve tremendously in the sport when I realized that all I had to do to win was hit the ball in one more time than my opponent. I thought to myself, *I can do that!* So, the hand-eye skills that I practiced in baseball and the footwork skills I learned in soccer helped me in tennis.

In baseball and soccer, I'd observed that you could have one or two great players on your team and still lose a lot of games. But in tennis, it all depended on me—I couldn't blame anyone else if I lost. I earned all the glory when I won, and I accepted all the blame when I lost. It was also clear that if I wanted to be great at tennis, I could be. No one else could tell me that I couldn't be great because it all depended on me. I liked having this control over my own destiny even though I started playing tennis relatively late, in the ninth grade. In high school, varsity soccer and varsity tennis had overlapping seasons, which forced me to choose one sport over the other. I chose to play varsity soccer for Damien Memorial High School in the ninth grade while I continued to practice tennis as much as I could. I began to enter tennis competitions and won my first two novice tournaments in the same week. Because I won at the novice level, I soon had to move up into open tournaments and compete against the top-ranked players in the state of Hawaii, many of whom had been playing tennis since the age of five or six.

Obviously, I had a lot of catching up to do, but I really enjoyed the challenge of competing one-on-one in singles. I then began to play varsity tennis for my high school, from tenth grade all the way until I graduated. My goal during my first year of competitive play in tournaments was to be one of the top twenty in Hawaii. At the end of the year, I was ranked number eighteen. My goal during my junior year was to make the top ten. I was ranked number eight. My goal during my senior year was to make the top five. I achieved a number four state ranking and earned a partial tennis scholarship to attend Creighton University in Omaha, Nebraska. That was the first year that the Creighton coach, Ed Hubbs, could offer partial tennis scholarships. So, I chose Creighton for its good academic reputation and the opportunity to compete in Division I college tennis. As an entering freshman, I flew by myself to Omaha, where—not having visited beforehand—I expected to find red barns and farmers wearing overalls. But as the plane came in for a landing, I looked out the window and saw a big, attractive city down below, and I just knew that my college experience was going to be a good one.

My personal character development began with strict discipline from my parents, mainly my mom, and was also influenced by Hanalani School, which I attended from preschool until eighth grade. After that came Damien High, which was considered the strictest Catholic school in the state. Needless to say, a sense of discipline and respect for others was instilled in me from the start. Through those elementary, intermediate, and high school years, I observed my baseball, soccer, and tennis coaches closely. I learned many positives and negatives about what *to* do and what *not* to do as a coach. I learned about the variety of ways they made sports fun—including hard work. I learned how important communication is between the coach and players and how to bring out the best in team members. I learned that not everyone can be coached the same way because players have different personalities, and different triggers must be used to get players to respond optimally and to the best of their ability. Of all the coaches I had during this time, I felt the biggest impact and learned the most from Coach Ed at Creighton. Coming from Hawaii and going to Nebraska was a big change for me, but also an exciting one. I was independent and had to learn to do things, including my own laundry, for the first time.

When I first started with Creighton's tennis program, Coach Ed had entered our team in the Nebraska Open tournament in Omaha, where many other college teams would compete. This was Coach Ed's first real look at his new players, other than seeing them on a Betamax recruiting tape. Yes, Betamax—the technology before the VHS tape. (And yes, VHS was the technology before DVDs, which came before Blu-ray.) Because of the many freshman orientation events I had to attend, I didn't have much time to practice tennis before the tournament. After winning my first two rounds, I developed a big blister on my right hand during my third-round match. I'm right-handed and had played with blisters before, as many other players have, but this one was really bad. The blister was in the middle of my hand, and it was ripping and bleeding along the crease of my palm with every shot I made. Needless to say, it was very painful. But even more painful was the fact that I was losing to an extremely tough opponent, and the blister was my excuse. I retired from the match in the second set and went back to my Swanson Hall dorm room. At 5:30 the next morning, my phone rang. It was Coach Ed telling me to get my butt into his office in ten minutes. I brushed my teeth and ran fearfully over to his office, suspecting that my retiring from a third-round match because of a blister might be unacceptable in college.

"Did you retire from a match because of a blister?" Coach Ed demanded as soon as I walked in. "Where is this blister?"

I held out my hand, and he pulled it toward him, tapping his index finger on the blister. "Does this hurt?" he asked.

I didn't want to admit it at first, but then I nodded. He simply said, "Never, ever retire from a match because of a blister." I assured him that it would never happen again and left his office to head to the tennis courts for our early morning practice. I taped up my hand and prepared myself for a tough session.

The following year, we played a match outdoors in Missouri after spring break, and the temperature dropped twenty-five degrees in two hours. Snow flurries started, and it was freezing. It was easily the coldest match I have ever played. I wore two T-shirts, a long-sleeved shirt, a reverse weave sweatshirt, and my team jacket over all of that. I also wore double socks, my shorts, cotton sweatpants, and my team sweatpants over it all, and it was still freezing cold. My ears were numb, and I was feeling miserable. I definitely didn't want to be out there playing tennis. My opponent beat me 6–2, 6–2, because I put up no fight against someone I should have beaten by that score.

Five minutes or so after every match I played, Coach Ed would usually stop to talk with me. This time, as I sat outside the court, watching my teammates play, trying to get warm, he walked by without saying a word. I immediately knew I had done something unacceptable again, and I feared what he might do this time. He walked by again without saying a word, but then he doubled back and began yelling at me in front of everyone. He said I was weak and gutless and some other words I'm sure he invented—a tirade that seemed to last nearly five minutes. Then he walked away without me getting in a single word. As I sat there digesting what had just happened, I realized everything he'd said was true. I *was* weak and gutless and all the other words he'd invented. It was an extremely important turning point for me, and I began to understand Coach Ed. He was trying to make me tougher and stronger, a player who could be the leader of our team. I subsequently became team captain for the next two years. I figured out that Coach Ed was really helping mold my character. He didn't want me making excuses because of a blister or cold weather. He wanted me to give it my best no matter how tough, distressing, or uncomfortable the situation might be. He knew that my teammates would emulate me and begin to have that same fight.

CHARACTER IS CONTAGIOUS

Great leaders are not born. They are made. They are made through the influence of others. Let's take a look at three-time Super Bowl Champion head coach Andy Reid of the Kansas City Chiefs since 2013, who was previously the head coach of the Philadelphia Eagles from 1999-2012. Coach Reid is widely regarded as one of the greatest coaches in the history of the National Football League. He is the only NFL coach to win over one hundred games with two different teams, appear in four consecutive conference championships with two different franchises, and have the most wins for those same teams. During his time as head coach, eleven of his assistants became head coaches in the NFL—two of them also went on to win Super Bowls.

For all these people, the experiences they encountered on their own journeys through life, including their time with Coach Reid, shaped them into who they are today. They learned what works and what doesn't. They learned what is effective and what is ineffective. This is how great leaders are made.

Obviously, good parenting is very important in establishing a strong foundation for building character in a child. It doesn't matter if a coach begins his coaching relationship with a kid at age five, ten, or fifteen; parents definitely play a key role from the beginning. And they continue to play that role in helping reinforce the right character traits the child learns through sports. A good coach with the right values can greatly enhance and build on that early foundation. As I mentioned earlier, a child playing sports spends more time with the coach and team than he or she spends in school with a math, science, or English teacher. This means that the coach has a major impact on the child. It is both a huge responsibility and a great opportunity to help instill the correct discipline, values, and morals that shape the players' character. Likewise, the general manager of a business also needs to instill the correct discipline, values, and morals in the staff, which will strengthen the team bond and help the team accomplish its goals. Putting your team members in the best position to be successful and doing it the right way with great character becomes contagious and fosters a positive, safe, and fun environment.

CHAMPIONS ARE DEFINED BY OTHERS

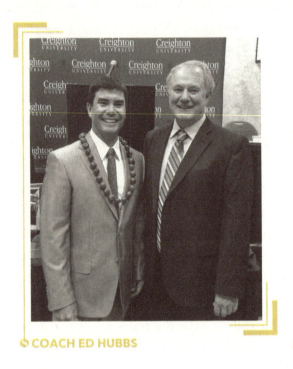

♢ COACH ED HUBBS

Great leaders breed more leaders. That's what Coach Ed did for me at Creighton. On April 9, 2014, I flew back to Omaha from Hawaii as the very first tennis player inducted into Creighton University's Hall of Fame. During my Hall of Fame speech in front of nearly one thousand people, I was so very proud to highlight Coach Ed (I had him stand to be recognized by everyone there) as the main reason for my winning one hundred thirty matches in the number one and number two positions in my college career. Everything I learned from him was priceless, and I used his lessons as guidelines for coaching my own teams. Respecting others, having integrity, and being courageous, ethical, resilient, determined, inspirational, honest, and positive were a few of the many character traits that Coach Ed instilled in me. His focus and dedication in helping me compete, act, think, and behave properly unlocked my potential in tennis and shaped my leadership qualities.

After graduating from Creighton with a communications degree in 1991, I came back to Hawaii, became certified with the United States Professional Tennis Association, and began teaching tennis. My intent was to pursue law and become an attorney, but the lawyers who took lessons from me wore glasses that appeared three inches thick. I asked them what their typical day was like, and they all said that they read all day in the office. But I didn't want to read things I had to read; I wanted to read things I liked to read. So, that was the end of my pursuit of law, and I continued teaching tennis instead. I quickly began to develop many of our state's top-ranked junior players. Plus, I got to wear shorts and be outdoors in Hawaii every day.

In 1994, I was offered the head coaching position for the Punahou Boys' Varsity Tennis Team. I was twenty-four years old. The most important thing I wanted to do was instill the importance of character in my team. I told them we would constantly strive for excellence by having integrity, ethics, honor, humility, positivity, respect for others, courage, inspiration, and the determination to compete with every ounce of our being. I told the boys I only had two team rules—Lateness and Listening. And while they were all listening, I quickly added that we would have no verbal, ball, or racket abuse. In order to play our best tennis, we needed to control our thoughts, mouths, and hands at all times. If we can do this, we have a great chance of controlling the tennis ball. Any violation of the Listening rule would result in one hundred push-ups. Any violation of the Lateness rule would result in running "snakes" on the bleachers. It's simply amazing how quickly doing one hundred push-ups or running snakes cures the listening and lateness problems.

Self-discipline and team discipline became important goals for me to constantly instill and enhance in my players. Do the right thing—whether or not someone is watching should make no difference. I gave my team an example by telling them if they walked by a piece of trash without picking it up, someone would see that and assume that our entire team did it. Instead, it's very easy to pick up that piece of trash, drop it in a garbage can, and continue on your way. Another example happens when it rains and we need to dry the tennis court. I told my players that we should be proactive by grabbing a squeegee and being the first ones on the court to help dry it off rather than waiting for our opponents or someone else to do it. It's the simple, little things that make big differences. It's a discipline that must be carried out on and off the tennis court.

Two weeks into our season, we were up against a much weaker school, and I kept my top four players out of the line-up. As I watched one of my senior singles players competing in a match on center court, I noticed he was badly disrespecting his opponent. I closely observed his behavior during the match, in which he acted as if his opponent was absolutely wasting his time. My player served, and his opponent missed the return. The opponent served, and my player made the return. His opponent hit the next shot out. This was a pattern that happened over and over again throughout the match. After finishing the match in a very brief twenty-five minutes, my player walked up to me, saying, "Coach, I won, 6–0, 6–0!"

My response was, "All right, you're off the team." When he asked why, with a shocked and confused look on his face, I said I didn't want any of my players behaving and acting that way—that his actions were shameful and disrespectful and would poison our team. I sent him home, and he telephoned me later that night to apologize and ask if he could rejoin the team. I told him I'd talk with the team in practice and that *they* would decide whether to give him a second chance. The next day, I shared our conversation with the team and let them talk among themselves for five minutes. I asked the boys what they'd decided, and they said they wanted to give him a second chance. I said I'd call him that evening with the news, and he could rejoin the team the next day. When he came back—wow, what a turnaround in attitude! He apologized to the entire team for his actions during his match, and after that, the difference was like night and day. He got it and understood clearly what Punahou boys' varsity tennis was all about.

This incident unsettled some of the younger players on the team, who looked up to this senior player and figured if it could happen to him, it could happen to anyone. So, it was a valuable learning experience for both the individual and the team. They began to learn that our team was not so much about our victories as it was about our character. Of course, we're going to strive to win, but by doing it the right way. Most athletes want to be good at their sport, and some athletes want to achieve mastery. But it isn't done with an attitude that focuses on winning at all costs. It's done with an attitude that focuses on simply being a good person and striving for superior excellence with character—which incidentally unlocks their true potential as athletes.

THE CHRIS MA STORY (CONTINUED)

Earlier, I talked about Chris Ma, but let me share more about him. In 1994, my first year as Punahou's head tennis coach, he was a freshman who beat all of our top senior players in tryouts to earn the number one spot on our team. Chris had been ranked number one in the state of Hawaii ever since he began competing in the ten and under division. He already had many good character traits instilled in him by his parents and previous coach and was well-liked by everyone. I felt it was my responsibility to continue to enhance and reinforce the discipline and character traits that were important to me in building the identity of our team. This philosophy would help not only Chris but also every member of our team.

Once our tryouts were completed, I needed to submit a team roster at our coach's meeting, deciding which players would represent our team in singles and doubles. From twelve players, I needed to select four singles players and four doubles teams. I had five players picked for singles but still needed to decide who would play doubles. As I sat on the bleachers mulling it over, Chris walked by and asked me what I was thinking about. I shared the dilemma I faced in deciding who played singles and doubles. I was trying to put myself in their shoes and make certain that everything was done fairly to give both the players and the team the best possible experience. I explained to Chris that we had two seniors who had won the state doubles championship the previous year, and I imagined they now wanted a chance to win a singles championship. We had another senior who was ranked number one in the state in the boys' 18s division; if I were him, I would also want the opportunity to play for a singles championship. And we had another senior who was really exceptional at singles but often struggled in doubles.

And then there was Chris, who had beaten all four seniors to earn the number-one spot on our team. In effect, this gave me five players whom I really wanted to play singles, but one of whom would need to play doubles. Chris completely understood my dilemma and, without hesitation, said, "Coach, I'll play doubles!" I reminded him he had earned the right to be our number one singles player, and I assumed he would want to—in fact, would expect to—play singles.

"If I can help the team in doubles," he replied, "then I'll play doubles, and the four seniors can have their chance in singles." I was caught completely off guard as this would solve my dilemma and let me submit our team lineup for the season. Chris's offer showed me how much of a team player he was. At our team meeting the next day, I shared the dilemma I faced and gave high praise to Chris in front of everyone. It was the perfect opportunity to demonstrate that we should always do what was best for the team rather than for ourselves. As great as Chris was in tennis, he showed he was even better as a person. Due to his character, he quickly earned respect from me and everyone else he came into contact with. He went on to become the model player for our tennis program, and I would share the Chris Ma story with every team that followed.

And by the way, Chris partnered with senior Taylor Tom that year—a player who had lost to his teammates in the previous state doubles championship—and went undefeated the entire season, winning the state doubles championship final, 6–0, 6–1.

Chapter 19

KEY NO. 2
DISCIPLINE DRIVES PERFORMANCE

"When you want something you've never had,
you have to do something you've never done."

—Thomas Jefferson

DISCIPLINE CAN BE DEFINED as *the practice of training people to obey rules or a code of behavior.* Let me be clear—discipline is training others to act, think, and behave correctly. It is not punishment. Goals cannot be achieved without discipline. We all feel differently every day. You can't allow yourself to only do certain things when you feel good. You need to have the discipline to do things when you don't feel like it. In other words, having discipline means forcing yourself to behave differently than you feel. If you only did things when you felt good, you wouldn't get much done. I believe that ninety percent of discipline is just showing up. Disciplined people keep their promises and commitments. They do not procrastinate. They know that discipline means *doing* things. It's getting things done. It must become a habit, one that is done consistently to achieve one's goals.

SIMPLE RULES, CLEAR CONSEQUENCES

A great leader establishes simple rules with clear consequences. As I stated earlier, my two rules are Listening and Lateness. These are two very simple rules but extremely meaningful in sports, business, and life. It is critically important to explain the consequences clearly to your team so there's no confusion if any violations of team rules occur. If a player is caught not listening, the first offense earns fifty push-ups. If it happens a second time or any time thereafter, it's one hundred push-ups. One minute late is late. For our team, the consequence of being late was five snake runs on the stadium bleachers. Snakes is a conditioning exercise in which you run up the stairs, across the bleachers, down the next set of stairs, across the next section of bleachers, up the next set of stairs, and so on. It's amazing how quickly one hundred push-ups solve a listening problem or how five snake runs on the bleachers cures the lateness problem. I chose these consequences to help build both their strength and conditioning, which the players need to be doing anyway. The method of discipline needs to be a positive one that will help them improve rather than a consequence that is only viewed negatively.

During our practices, we often played various tennis games for conditioning and also employed a variety of footwork exercises. Communication is critical so that conditioning is not mistaken as punishment. For example, I would say, "When we finish this next game, *everyone* does ten sprints, but the winning team can choose to do only half that number." When explained correctly in this way, winning the game and doing half the conditioning is viewed as a reward. Compare that with saying, "The winners of this next game can do five sprints, while the losers will do ten." In this sense, losing and conditioning are paired negatively and seen as punishment. I don't even use the term "losers." Rather, I use the word "unfortunates." As mentioned earlier, some of our disciplines involve no racket, ball, or verbal abuse. I would always say, "We can do ninety-nine things right, but if we do one thing wrong, then everyone will only remember that one thing." This is important because this philosophy holds the entire team accountable. If there's a lapse in judgment by a player who swears out loud and commits verbal abuse that others can hear, it appears to outsiders that all of our players swear like that. This discipline is important because it doesn't matter if it's my number one player or my number twelve player committing the verbal abuse. Everyone lives by the same standard.

ACCOUNTABILITY IS EVERYTHING

The rules are for everyone on your team, and everyone must hold each other accountable. Discipline must be enforced consistently. Otherwise, your rules become meaningless, and your respect will begin to deteriorate. Everyone is treated the same, and you, as the leader, must not play favorites. This allows the whole team to have the best possible experience, and not just the top athletes, while the rest of the team experiences an erosion in morale—one in which the team starts feeling like less of a team. Rules and discipline are imperative in building the framework for character traits you want to instill and enhance in your team. You can't afford to send mixed messages by enforcing the rules only part of the time. But everything you do must still be reasonable and fair. Put yourself in their shoes so that you can never be accused of being otherwise.

For example, practice for our tennis team started at 3:45 p.m. Remember, one minute late is late. At 3:44, all of my present players were aware of the time and calculating who wasn't there and how many snakes that individual would be doing on the bleachers. Oftentimes, we'd see players cutting it close, sprinting to be with the team before the clock struck 3:46, thereby sparing themselves the additional exercise. The point, of course, is punctuality. They were learning that it's important to be punctual. Punctuality is necessary and something that would definitely help them in life beyond tennis.

How many times do you see a coach explaining a drill to the team while some of the players continue to talk with each other and not pay attention to what the coach is saying? This is when the listening rule comes in handy. If I'm explaining the next exercise, and I say, "Austin and Jake will be playing the crosscourt forehand game on court four," and Austin says, "Which court?" Then my response is: "You weren't listening. That's a violation of our listening rule. That's one hundred push-ups." This is what I mean when I say that one hundred push-ups cure the listening problem. Just think how much better your team will be at focusing and listening to what you say the next time you explain a drill or game. This is a discipline and standard that must be consistently enforced by the leader.

LEAD WITH POSITIVITY

I'm a big believer in catching a team member doing something good and highlighting that action or behavior to every other member of the team. People do good deeds all the time. Compliment them. Acknowledge them. This becomes contagious because it reinforces to others what you are striving for. Other team members will have a greater tendency to want to do good deeds as well. As you know by now, I'm all about superior disciplined details. So, when it's time to collect all the tennis balls after practice, and I see Matt going out of his way to run two courts over to get one lonely ball, I make it known to everyone that this kind of detail is what I appreciate. It is a part of our superior standard of excellence. When it's ball collection time at the next practice, more players will have a tendency to follow Matt's lead.

I also love highlighting a player who encourages a teammate who might be struggling mentally or emotionally that day. It's all about helping and supporting each other by doing things that you would want others to do for you. Many leaders catch a team member doing something wrong and then embarrass that person by admonishing him or her loudly and generally making a scene. This isn't good. I do the opposite. When I catch a team member doing something wrong, I talk with him discreetly at a low volume. But when I see a team member emulating something we're striving for, I make certain that everybody hears me. This is healthy for everyone and helps the team focus on what *to do* as opposed to what *not to do*.

THE JASON CHANG STORY

Here's an exception in talking discreetly to a player at a low volume. During my first year as head coach of Punahou's boys' varsity team, I received a phone call a week after the state championships.

"Hi, Coach Rusty! It's Jason Chang. I was wondering if you had any time in your schedule to work me in for private lessons?"

"Jason," I replied, "I'm sure you know about my standards and expectations for behavior from students. I've watched you compete in the tournaments, and I know you're a good player, but I'm not sure it would work out. To be honest, your behavior and attitude are the opposite of what I try to teach."

"I'm really willing to try," he answered. When I heard that, I decided to give him a chance and worked him into my schedule for lessons. I knew it was going to be a big challenge to help him make the kind of turnaround that would help his tennis and ultimately impact his life. I also knew it would be a process that would take some time.

Jason was just finishing tenth grade when I started teaching him privately. He was already a good player, ranked number eight in Hawaii in the boys' 16s division and number one on Iolani School's boys' varsity tennis team. Prior to that phone call, what I'd observed from Jason in tournaments was extremely poor behavior and bad discipline. He frequently committed all three abuses—verbal, racket, and ball—and often yelled and caused a scene on the tennis court during competition. It was bad. And this is why I responded the way I did when he called. He was definitely on the wrong end of the spectrum and needed major help and guidance. Jason played with a lot of passion and fire because he loved tennis. But nobody had taught him discipline—how to control himself mentally and emotionally. During our first lesson, I remember clearly explaining to him the Listening and Lateness rules, that there would be no verbal, ball, or racket abuse, and what the consequences would be if there ever were. Jason was willing to make a change, and I told him that it would take some time for him to completely control his behavior.

So, the process began. There were definitely some flare-ups along the way and phone calls to his parents, especially after I added Jason to my advanced group training lesson with his peers. They were all extremely competitive with each other because they all hated to lose, even in our group tennis lessons. They all played against each other in tournaments and were all highly ranked in Hawaii. I knew this was exactly what Jason needed every single week, and he consistently showed up for his weekly private lessons and weekly group lessons.

Having a high standard for Jason to strive for, plus the opportunity to interact with peers who were all striving for our superior standard of excellence, really helped reshape his focus and priorities. I told him he was nowhere near reaching his potential in tennis because he held himself back by letting unnecessary situations affect his performance. When he would fall behind in a match, for instance, he played differently than he did when he was winning. My challenge to him was to compete the same way whether he was losing, winning, or tied, and to keep a good attitude and control his behavior at all times. Hearing these things over and over again every week had a huge positive effect on Jason. I told him he needed to adjust his focus from competing against opponents to bettering himself. He needed to realize that he was not going to win every single point and every match for the rest of his life. But he could give it his best by trying to put himself in a position to win. That, after all, is what makes sports exciting—being in a position to win. Sometimes we win, and sometimes we don't, and that's okay.

His senior year, Jason competed in singles at the state championship tournament in Wailea, Maui. In the semifinals, he played another one of my players, Chris Ma, who was then in his junior year. The match lasted just under three hours. It was an incredible display of groundstrokes, movement, and heart. Chris defeated Jason, 7–5, 7–5. They both showed great respect for one another, and it was a fantastic test to see how far Jason had come and for him to see what the bright end of the spectrum looks like. Needless to say, I was extremely proud of him and his display of character in the face of such stress and adversity. Jason's transformation was validated when he earned the number one ranking in the statewide boys 18s division after he graduated from Iolani.

My training and guidance for him didn't end there; we now started to prepare him for college tennis at the University of California at Irvine. That summer, during a group training lesson, Jason was having a bad day, had a major flare-up, and threw his racket against the fence on the far side of the tennis court.

"Jason, get out of here!" I yelled across the court. "You're number one, but you still can't control yourself after all this time and effort. Get out! In fact, leave your rackets here and just start running around the block!"

Now, the street where our tennis courts are located was circular, and running one time around the circle covered 1.1 miles. I continued the group training, and all the other players were working extra hard, probably because they'd never heard me yell like that before. But they all knew why I did it and how Jason had been before I started his lessons. And they knew that if a rule was violated, it didn't matter if you were ranked number one or number thirty. It was a great reminder for all of them of the high standards we set for ourselves. The younger players were also reminded of the consequences when rules were violated. As I continued the lesson, I saw Jason running by, trying to make sure that I saw him. I did but looked away, and he continued running—a second time, then a third time around. After he'd covered 3.3 miles, I told Jason to get back on the court to resume training. He was back on track, probably frightened that I yelled at him in front of everyone, and he never had a flare-up after that. Today, Jason is a doctor in Honolulu and married with three children. I'm so very proud of the person he became, and he has shared with me that he leads his medical staff with many of the same principles, rules, disciplines, and standards that he learned in tennis.

Chapter 20

KEY NO. 3
ALWAYS IN CONTROL

"People who say it cannot be done should not
interrupt those who are doing it."

—George Bernard Shaw

IT'S INEVITABLE—there are some things over which you
have no control. You're in a traffic accident because the guy
behind you is careless and runs into you. You're stuck in bumper-
to-bumper traffic because someone else had an accident. Your
flight is delayed or even canceled because of bad weather. But
while situations like these are completely out of your control,
what you can control is your own reaction. You can choose
to react rationally or irrationally. You can choose to react by

stressing about the situation or by staying calm and letting go of stress.

So, how does an effective leader respond at such times? She controls the situation rather than letting the situation control her. One of the best ways to do this is to expect the unexpected. It's imperative to envision the different turns that a certain situation can take and to plan for how you will deal with them. Unforeseen circumstances can and will happen, and you need to be prepared for all scenarios.

What if a team member gets injured? Or if someone gets sick? What if you fall behind early in a game? What if you establish a big lead? What if the officials make bad calls against your team? What if the entire crowd is against you? What about competing in challenging weather conditions? You need to accept it and deal with it rather than complain and make excuses. Both teams must deal with challenging weather conditions; the key is to have your team deal with it better than your opponent. The point is great leaders are well-prepared for all scenarios that can and will happen. They already have a plan B and plan C and have trained their team members to prepare and respond in the same way.

LEARN TO DIFFERENTIATE

Let's consider our choices in various situations. We can plan ahead, or we can choose to be unprepared. We can accept a bad attitude or choose to assume a good one. We can choose to behave appropriately or choose to behave badly. We can choose to be lazy, or we can choose to give one hundred percent of our effort. We can choose to give up, or we can choose to bounce back. We can choose to respect others, or we can choose to disrespect them. We can choose to be weak, or we can choose to be strong and tough. We can make do with low standards or choose a high standard of excellence for ourselves. We can choose to be distracted, or we can choose to focus on what we want to accomplish. We can choose to rush things, or we can choose to be patient. We can choose to cheat, or we can choose to have integrity. We can choose to lie, or we can choose to be honest. We can choose to be mean to others, or we can choose to be kind. We can choose to be selfish, or we can choose to be humble. We can choose to be a bad sport or choose to exhibit sportsmanship.

In other words, there are many things that team members can control and must be able to differentiate for themselves. And as their leader, you need to identify and explain that they do have choices—and consequences for their choices. Leaders need to be role models and make the proper choices themselves by walking the walk to talk the talk. It determines the identity you want for your team and the legacy you want to leave them with.

READ EMOTIONS

Emotional awareness means *being aware of other people's emotions as well as your own.* A strong leader must always remember to base decisions on reason, not emotion. Having emotional awareness is always better than reacting quickly and regretting it later. Never do something permanently foolish just because you're temporarily upset. This starts with the leader and trickles down to every member of the team. I have watched countless sports competitions where one team is losing—not because the other team is doing things to win, but because the losing team is defeating themselves with their negative attitude. So, when you find yourself in a hole, stop digging. And if your team is on the winning end of this scenario, don't get in the way of your opponent when they're shooting themselves in the foot!

Having emotional awareness requires having control of your thoughts. When you have control over your own thinking, you can have control over your life. Leaders with emotional awareness are conscious of their own emotions and able to manage their feelings properly. Maintaining poise, no matter what the situation may be, is paramount. Leaders also need to be aware of the emotional state of other people. Understanding why a person is behaving or feeling a certain way is important in being able to help them. Having empathy for that person will create a connection with them because they'll realize that you understand why they're feeling the way they are.

IGNORE THE NOISE

Let's face it: Apart from the winning team and its supporters, many people enjoy seeing a victorious streak come to an end. They want to see a champion defeated by an underdog. They want to see a number one team lose. They're jealous of your success—and when your team is in the public eye, the sports media can add pressure by highlighting your accomplishments and *their* expectations. All of this might add unnecessary stress to your team. It's up to you to keep the focus on what's important to the team's success. When adverse situations appear, team members need to focus on tightening their bond with each other in order to overcome that challenge together. Here are some examples of noise and distractions.

- Media Attention and Public Pressure: High-profile championship teams are often under intense media scrutiny, with journalists dissecting their every move. Interviews, analysis, and media speculation can be distracting and create added pressure.
- Fans and Social Media: The passionate support of fans is a double-edged sword. While it can provide energy, motivation, and support, it can also lead to the team feeling the weight of heightened expectations.
- Injury Concerns: Injuries can disrupt a team's rhythm and cause anxiety among team members. Championship teams often face the challenge of coping with the injuries of key members while maintaining their performance standards.
- Personal Issues: Team members have personal lives beyond the team, and can sometimes lead to publicized personal problems or controversies. These behavioral issues need to be handled properly in balancing personal matters with professional responsibilities.

There will always be distractions and noise, both externally and internally, but you need to be proactive in preparing for these and other issues. Championship teams maintain their focus on what they can control and always keep their eyes on the prize. These teams understand that the real measure of their success lies in their internal standards, not in the noise or opinions that may arise externally. While external recognition and validation are nice, true champions are driven by their intrinsic desire to be the best they can be.

I always had twelve boys on my varsity team, but I never had the same twelve boys the following year because the seniors graduated. So, winning the state championship and then having some of those players return while adding new players who make the team creates a whole new team of twelve. The fact is, not all twelve of them won that state championship. I explain to them that this is why we're not really defending a championship— we're trying to win a championship with a new team of players. This becomes their focus because they understand that they want to *earn* a championship together as a new team. This minimizes the pressure of defending a championship and keeps a proper perspective on what they want to achieve together as a team goal.

YOU OWN YOUR THOUGHTS

Control your thoughts, and they become words. Control your words, and they become actions. Control your actions, and they become habits. Control your habits, and they become character. Control your character, and it becomes your destiny. And all of this evolves because of a single thought. Your thought. Control it and own it.

When you can perform a skill in your sport but have trouble executing it in competition, it's not a physical thing. It's a mental thing. Physically, the athlete can do it. He has done it thousands of times. But mentally, he's doubting himself or experiencing fear, which inhibits him from performing that skill during competition. Coaches must have pressure simulations in their practices to help their athletes. Players need to practice the same way they will play in competition. They need to maintain the right internal climate, no matter what the situation. For example, I'd tell my players that the ideal internal temperature is between eighty-six and eighty-eight degrees. Any less than eighty-six or any more than eighty-eight is not good. They need to identify their ideal internal intensity level and must be able to summon that at any time.

Earlier, I talked about Bucky Jencks, but let me share more about him. As I previously shared, Bucky was super talented in tennis, soccer, and track. He was someone everyone liked and who always brought a healthy level of excitement with him. He had good character traits, but I felt I needed to help him contain his high energy level and channel it properly. In 2000, during a regular season match at Iolani School, I had Bucky playing in the first doubles position. Before the match started, he and his partner were feeling extremely confident that they would win, and win easily. He was overly excited and wanted badly to win the match without losing a single game.

Well, Bucky and his partner won the first set, 6–0, but the second set was a much different story. They lost a game, and Bucky began playing badly—I mean really badly. His internal temperature was well above the 88-degree mark, probably near the boiling point, and I would guess he hit triple digits in the second set. Bucky and his partner lost that set, and they came off the court for the ten-minute coaching break before the third set. Bucky's face was bright red, and he went on and on about how "lucky" his opponents had been to win the set. He kept this up until I said, "Bucky, quiet! I need you to stop talking and lie down on this bench!" He complied, and I made sure everyone left him alone. I needed him to stay there, to breathe and relax for five minutes. I needed him to calm down and get his internal climate under control.

After five minutes, I gave him two strategic points to focus on. As he started to walk back onto the court, he paused by the gate and said, "Coach, that was brilliant coaching." I smiled, shaking my head, and he and his partner won the third set, 6–1.

BE READY

An effective leader has total control over how his or her team is prepared. It's always better to be over-prepared rather than under-prepared. Great leaders have a habit of preparing so well that they know there's nothing more they can do. Vince Lombardi, the legendary head coach of the 1960s Green Bay Packers, was extremely detailed and meticulous in his preparation during football practices. He often told his team to "run it again," as he was convinced they would have an advantage over other teams if they were doing more than their competitors and if they worked harder and smarter. Coach Lombardi put his team through tough practices with great discipline because he believed that ninety-nine percent of the work and training that goes into winning a Super Bowl happens during practices.

I believed the same thing. I would plan every tennis practice the night before in order to be prepared and maximize our practice time. There were times when I told my team that we'd already won the championship, even before the state tournament began, because our preparation was so good. I wanted to give them confidence and belief in themselves. I knew we were doing things that no other team was doing, and I wanted them to feel like they deserved to win. We were ready and just needed to go out there and execute on the court, trusting in ourselves and in our preparation.

Legendary Boxer Muhammad Ali believed that a fight was won not in the ring but in the time spent preparing for the boxing match. He said, "The fight is won or lost far away from witnesses—behind the lines, in the gym, and out there on the road, long before I dance under those lights." The Chinese general and philosopher Sun Tzu said, "Every battle is won before it is fought."

It's always better to be prepared and not have an opportunity than to have an opportunity and not be prepared. The more prepared someone is, the luckier they tend to be.

It is true that *luck is what happens when preparation meets opportunity.* Many people perceive successful teams as being lucky sometimes. If and when luck does happen, it's because the leader takes a proactive approach to preparing the team for any possible opportunities. A great leader makes things look easy. But while he or she makes leading look easy, nothing of significance that you want to achieve ever comes easy. Great leaders spend countless hours preparing behind the scenes to make their teams look refined and polished. Great leaders are consistent in making sure the team is well-prepared for anything and everything.

Chapter 21

KEY NO. 4
COURAGE AND CONVICTION

"Courage doesn't mean you don't get afraid.
Courage means you don't let fear stop you."

—Bethany Hamilton

YOU WILL NEVER CROSS THE OCEAN unless you have the courage to lose sight of the shore. Great leaders have the courage to make tough, difficult decisions and will stand up and do the right thing at all times. They make these courageous decisions based on their values and principles, and they never compromise their belief in what they know is right. This is what great leaders do.

Whether the situation appears simple or complex, great leaders always have the courage to make the best decisions based on integrity and ethics. This is often a test of the leader's character, which can either deepen the bond with the team or cause that bond to erode. Having the courage to do the right thing might not make everyone happy, but they will all respect you. They'll know where you stand, what kind of person you are, and what kind of team you want. Here's a quote I like to remember: "Standing alone doesn't mean I'm alone. It means I'm strong enough to handle things all by myself."

OWN YOUR DECISIONS

It's very important to firmly establish your role as the leader. When Vince Lombardi first became head coach of the Green Bay Packers, he immediately went to work defining the role of his players and his own role as head coach. Instead of putting the responsibility of winning on the players, he assumed that duty himself. He communicated to his team his expectations for their commitment and hard work during training, but he also outlined his own responsibilities in teaching and pushing them to maximize their potential. By taking on the burden of winning himself, Lombardi removed pressure from the players and allowed them to focus on being their best on the field. This also built trust between him and his team—that if both sides focused on their roles, they would be in the best possible position for success.

I made it a point to do something similar with my teams. I told them that I would take all the blame if we didn't win the state championship. My players knew I was the leader, responsible for preparing and guiding them for our matches through our season. I wanted to reduce the team's stress level and pressure to win. When we did win, I gave the credit to the players for their on-court performance, as well as to the other players who were watching, supporting, and cheering their teammates on from the sidelines. I held myself accountable when we lost matches because, as the leader, it was my job to prepare the team to be successful. I didn't want my players to have to shoulder the blame for a loss. Instead, I would assume there was something more I could have done or said to them before or during the match. Whatever the case, the leader takes full ownership of how the team performs.

In business or in sports, when there are problems and deficiencies with your team members, the problem is usually not them. It's usually you. Remember—everything starts with the leader. If there's dysfunction and low morale on your team, it's a reflection of you. Ineffective leaders will blame the team members. Great leaders will blame themselves, take responsibility, and find ways to solve the problem.

BE HONEST

It takes courage to have open and honest communication with your team members. Honest feedback is extremely important. I always say that I don't give good feedback or bad feedback. I give honest feedback. This has helped me tremendously because during competition, when the pressure is on and my players look to me for coaching and guidance, my advice is very meaningful to them because they know I'll be honest with them. "I know how you can win this match," I tell them. "If you do this and this, you will win." They believe me and trust me and will try their best to execute that strategy.

In order to give honest feedback effectively, you need to understand your team members' personalities. There are so many different personality types. Not everyone can be coached in the same way. Not everyone can be communicated with in the same way. You need to know what triggers certain individuals and how to communicate with them effectively. I've had players who are extroverted and always very pumped up. Sometimes, they're *too* pumped up, and I need to calm them down so they can perform at their best. Other players who are introverted and mellow need to be pumped up for the opposite reason.

Having honest communication with your team members is important because if you do it tactfully and make them realize you're trying to genuinely help them, they'll know that you care about them. *It's best to give at least two compliments before offering constructive criticism.* Not everyone enjoys receiving constructive criticism, but if communicated properly, it will be taken more as helpful feedback rather than criticism. Such feedback is viewed by team members in the context that you are helping them improve rather than cutting them down. Following up with them is critical; it reinforces the importance of improvement in a particular area of concern. If your team member knows that it's important to you as the leader, then it becomes even more important to them.

Great leaders also provide an avenue for team members to have open and honest communication with them. Communication works both ways, and great leaders take advantage of the fact that it's not a one-way street. It's good for team members to give the leader feedback. It helps give the leader insight into what team members are feeling and thinking. It helps the leader understand the pulse of the team. And it helps the team know that their opinions and feelings matter. This truly takes courage on the leader's part. Just as you might have constructive criticism for your team members, they will have constructive criticism for you. This open communication keeps you constantly in touch with the team's vibe. It also puts you on track toward building a "real" team in which each member feels special because everyone is contributing and improving for the good of the team—including the leader. Just remember, a smart person knows what to say. A wise person knows whether or not to say it.

MAKE EVERYONE MATTER

When I was in high school, I often practiced with some good friends on the Punahou School tennis team. When I met with them at Punahou's tennis complex, I was able to observe many of their varsity practices. I noticed that their team wasn't really a team. It was more like a group of individuals who were *sort of* on a team. They didn't seem to want to practice together because they all appeared to have rivalries with one another. And when they did practice, they wouldn't give each other their best. And yet, they definitely would when they practiced with me. I also noticed that the team members were extremely divided and that the "team" was severely fractured. Communication between team members was minimal; they just didn't look happy to be together.

When I became head coach, I wanted to make certain that we would have a "real" team on which everyone mattered and everyone was important. We would have open and honest communication in which team members could share their feelings with each other, and everyone realized that the team collectively was bigger than any of them individually.

So, during my first week of practice, I talked to the players about my observations of—and concerns about— past teams. I noted that in the past, a player wouldn't want to practice or give his best with another player because they had a rivalry and often played each other in tournaments for ranking. The effect of this situation is counterproductive in a team environment because it erodes the togetherness of the team and certainly doesn't help an individual develop his potential. I needed them to understand that the better one player gets, the better the other player gets, and vice versa. Helping each other be better individually helps the team collectively. It would take courage on their part to do this. Our focus would be the team and how everyone could contribute to the team every single day by trusting and helping each other.

And when, not if, an issue of concern arose, we would talk openly to resolve it. As I said in Chapter 6, most problems occur because of misperceptions, miscommunication, misunderstandings, and misinformation. I told the boys that open and honest communication with each other is necessary for helping dispel negative feelings toward one another and helping the togetherness of our team. It's inevitable that we're going to play one another at times in tournaments. When we do, we go out there and respect each other, give our best effort, and are still friends again once the match is over, regardless of who wins or loses. And in terms of coaching, when we do play each other in singles or doubles, I will watch the match but not coach during the match. It's the fairest, cleanest way. They know each other very well, and it avoids any possible coaching controversy, favoritism, or misperceptions.

As a player, I saw early on how important a coach can be to a team. In my youth, I played on a Hawaii Youth Soccer Association team in the central Oahu community of Mililani. Our team was comprised of all the top players from the American Youth Soccer Association teams in town. Our coach, Coach L, had great soccer knowledge and good experience as a coach and former player. Our practices were tough, and we practiced specific skills and plays every day. Coach L knew all our strengths and weaknesses and which positions we should play to give our team the best chance of winning. And win we did!

We won a lot during two seasons with Coach L. However, two months before the start of our third season, Coach L's work schedule changed, and he could no longer coach our team. Mr. A filled in, and we lost every game we played. We had the same players on the team, the only difference being that the new coach and his son were added to the roster. Mr. A didn't know how to practice us, which positions to play us in games, nor when to use substitutions. Moreover, although his son was the weakest player on our team, Mr. A showed blatant favoritism by moving him into the starting lineup. Needless to say, we weren't having fun anymore and no longer looked forward to practices and games as we used to.

The following season, Coach L returned, and we were winning again, having fun, and looking forward to every practice and game. We appreciated and respected Coach L even more after our experience with Mr. A.

Please note that even though Mr. A coached our third season, we called him Mr. A instead of Coach A. He had authority over us but lost our respect from our very first practice. After seeing how impactful the coach really is to the team, I vowed to myself that if I ever became a coach, I would have the awareness, compassion, professionalism, and empathy to help lead my team the right way, to the best of my ability.

EMBRACE THE ENVY

When someone throws a brick at you, don't throw it back. Use it to build a house. I have witnessed many jealous people doing things that good people just don't do. Again, you have a choice in how you respond to such situations. It's a test of your character. A fool takes a knife and stabs people in the back. A wise man takes a knife, cuts the cord, and frees himself from the fools. I share this with you to urge you to have class and *always* take the high road. Fools want to drag you down the dirt path and get you all muddy. Don't give them that satisfaction. Here's another bit of advice: Weak people seek revenge. Strong people forgive. Intelligent people ignore.

I have had countless students and players who achieved the number one state ranking, a state singles championship, a state doubles championship, and national rankings. But I am most proud of my impact in helping them become great people in society. Through the years, many of these players told me about other players or other parents disrespecting them or saying mean things about them behind their backs. They couldn't understand why. I explained to them that others were envious of them because they were winning, accomplishing great things, and showing great character. People have been envious of me too. But that's just how some people are. If we weren't winning, if we weren't doing anything of significance, why would anyone else care? They wouldn't. Envy happens when you're in the spotlight and achieving what others perceive as success.

Knowing this, you have a choice to let them affect you or not. You can control how you respond. Embrace the envy. I would tell my players that I couldn't care less about what jealous people thought of me because I didn't waste time thinking about them for even two seconds. Don't let such people rent space on your internal hard drive. The next time someone talks behind your back or says something mean about you, take it as confirmation that you are doing something significant and are someone that they probably admire. If not, why would they spend time talking about you in the first place?

Because of my honest communication with my team, they know that I'm there to help them in any way possible. In a way, it makes them feel secure. Many players have told me that I'm more than a coach to them—I'm almost like a second father. What a compliment!

THE CHRIS IWAMURA STORY

I began teaching private and group tennis lessons to Chris Iwamura when he was in the seventh grade at Punahou School. He already had great character traits and some good tennis ingredients in him. What I found even more impressive was that he was extremely coachable, super fun to work with, and constantly strove for excellence. He wanted to be great. He was willing to take risks and try anything and everything to make his tennis game better. If there was a more effective way of doing things, he wanted to do it. I showed him more advanced stroke and footwork techniques, and he did them. I showed him different strategies and various tactics, and he did them. He was the opposite of complacent and an absolute joy to coach.

Chris was a strong singles player, but he had a big passion for doubles. He became one of the greatest doubles players I've ever coached. While on my boys' varsity team, Chris made it into the state doubles championship finals all four years. As a freshman, he won with Bucky Jencks. Over the next two years, he won with another fine player, Nick Leong. And through these years, he continued getting stronger and stronger because he had the courage to take risks to improve his tennis game. As a senior, he partnered with a player named Matt Nakagawa. Both Matt and Chris were a little too risky with their serves, causing some unfortunate double faults on key points in the state doubles championship. That's the only match Chris suffered a defeat. But I always admired Chris because he played to win rather than playing not to lose, and one of the main reasons for his success was his courage to take calculated risks.

Fast-forward to today: Chris's parents, Harvey and Betsy, were the former owners of Honolulu's iconic Rainbow Drive-In. Remember, I mentioned that Chris already possessed great character traits before I started training him in tennis? Well, that's because of his parents. While he was being groomed to take over ownership and management of Rainbow Drive-In, his parents had him learn every single facet of the business first. I've seen him working at every position in the restaurant, including cashier, cook, manager—even taking out the garbage. By learning every job, he earned the respect of the other employees. Because of his hands-on experience, they know Chris understands what they're thinking and feeling.

◊ CHRIS IWAMURA

I'm so proud to have coached Chris and to have helped him learn life lessons on the tennis court. Having the courage to take calculated risks made Chris the person he is today. I visit Rainbow Drive-In on a weekly basis to satisfy my plate lunch craving and consistently interact with his employees. All of them say he's a great owner and leader who cares about his people, and they are grateful to have him at the helm.

Chapter 22

KEY NO. 5
YOU CREATE
THE ENVIRONMENT

"Helping one person might not change the world,
but it could change the world for one person."

—Anonymous

LEADERS ARE RESPONSIBLE for creating a team's "environment." But is that environment positive or negative? Is it good or bad? It's the leader who sets the tone for creating an atmosphere in which team members feel cared for, safe, excited, passionate, and productive and are able to flourish and accomplish the team's goals. You want your team members to feel like they belong. You want your team members to really love what they're doing and the people they're doing it with. You want them to feel there's nowhere else they'd rather be at the moment. You want them to feel a deep connection to the mission and the purpose of the team's goals and to believe that everyone plays an important role in accomplishing these goals together.

The environment you create for your team directly helps the growth and success of each team member. For example, if you associate with people who get straight A's in school, work hard, have high standards, and expect to accomplish great things, you'll likely start to have the same expectations for yourself. But what if you're hanging around people who are lazy, have no goals in life, or use drugs? Chances are you'll begin to go down that same road sooner or later. You're the same person, but now you're in a different environment with different influences.

In business, it is said that you need to take care of the people who take care of the customers. This is true. And often, if your business is quite large, you also need to take care of the people who take care of their people who take care of the customer. The head coach of a basketball team will want to take care of his assistant coaches, players, nutritionists, strength and conditioning coaches, and administrative staff in order to have a more favorable chance of winning. Everyone working together in a good, positive environment increases the probability of success in achieving the team's goals.

LISTEN FIRST, SPEAK LAST

One of the biggest communication problems is that we don't listen to understand. We listen to respond. Great leaders will listen carefully to what their team members are saying. By listening, you allow your team members to voice their opinions and share their concerns (whether privately or as a group), which helps their connection and deepens their commitment to the team. This is critical. What you don't want is a team member who's unable to share his or her concerns. This can cause them to drift away until, sooner or later, their commitment to the team no longer exists.

Listening takes time, but it allows you to read the pulse of your team. You get an immediate vibe on how they are feeling, and they get a vibe on you as well. Listening is a skill. Most people in leadership positions have no problem talking, but many of them forget to listen. Let's take a look at the reasons why this is important.

When you *listen first*, you have the opportunity to gather information and gain a better understanding of the situation. This will allow you to absorb the ideas, perspectives, and concerns of others. Listening first also demonstrates respect for others and shows that you value their input and are willing to hear them out. This empathetic approach fosters better relationships, collaboration, and trust, and people are more likely to engage with you when they feel heard and understood.

More importantly, great leaders often *speak last*. They listen to the opinions of others first before they give their own. Rushing to speak without fully understanding the context or the other person's viewpoint can lead to misunderstanding and miscommunication (remember these are two of the 4 Misses we need to avoid!). By listening first, you greatly reduce the chances of misinterpreting information or jumping to conclusions, and you're able to clarify any uncertainties and respond more effectively.

When you listen to others' perspectives, it enables you to identify common ground, bridge gaps, and find areas of agreement. By considering different viewpoints and incorporating them into the conversation, you can work toward building consensus and finding mutually beneficial solutions. Plus, people have different experiences, insights, and knowledge that you might not possess, which can expand your own understanding.

I remember something very interesting that the Dalai Lama said about listening: "When you talk, you are only repeating what you already know. But if you listen, you may learn something new." Speaking last ultimately helps you as the leader because you get to hear the opinions and views of others first. It helps others feel that they are being heard, and it helps you understand what they're thinking and feeling before you give your own feedback. And most importantly, it promotes meaningful, healthy, and productive interactions.

Just remember—you don't have to be right for someone else to be wrong. Another person might have a different point of view. For example, if we are standing facing each other and we look down at writing on the ground, I'll see the number "6," and you'll see the number "9." In another situation, I'll see the letter "M," and you'll see the letter "W." And still in another situation, I'll see the number "7," and you'll see that it's not a number, but the letter "L." If someone has a different point of view that differs from you, try to understand *their* perspective. Try to see what they see—and why they see it. Both of us could be right.

PROTECT YOUR PEOPLE

Great leaders are genuinely interested in their team members. They want to help them in every possible way. They care deeply about *their* priorities and goals. When you're talking with someone in person, they can feel whether or not you really care about them. Let me make you aware of something: All of us have cell phones—but, if you're checking your cell phone while you're talking to someone, that person in front of you knows that your priority is your phone first and him second. If you truly care about him, you'll set the phone on silent (even keep it out of sight) and really focus on and commit to the conversation at hand. This is hugely important because it makes it clear that he is your number one priority. The greatest gift you can give someone is your time. When you give someone your time, you're giving them a portion of your life that you'll never get back.

Great leaders will always support their people. They will constantly ask their team members if they need anything. Team members will understand that what they're doing is important enough for you to be following up with them. This doesn't take much time to do, but the impact is huge because you're showing that you care about them and what they're doing. When you focus on the well-being of your people, you're demonstrating that you value them as individuals, not just as workers. This fosters a sense of loyalty and commitment to your organization and directly enhances employee satisfaction, engagement, and retention. You definitely won't get the desired results or even come close to accomplishing your team's goals without focusing on your people. Pay attention to the well-being of your team members, and you'll give yourself a chance to reach the goals you're striving for together.

Great leaders make their team members feel safe. Great leaders take care to protect their team members. The environment you create fosters this feeling of safety and care. There have been countless times when I've walked out to the parking lot after a practice or game to find a player waiting to be picked up by a parent who is obviously late. When that happens, I always wait with him, even if it puts me behind schedule. It's the right thing to do. It's what I would want if I were in that player's tennis shoes, waiting under a dim light under the cover of darkness with no one else around.

When your team members feel safe, they will communicate their concerns and vulnerabilities more freely. The bonds and relationships between the leader and team members become greater and deeper. They will trust you and be loyal to you. (In business, developing such a trusting environment also encourages employees to want to get to work and do their jobs because they look forward to being there.) This kind of atmosphere prompts an athlete to get to practice and work hard because she looks forward to being there. She knows that you listen and that you care, and she feels safe because of the environment you've created. She feels that she's truly a part of a team and plays a key role in accomplishing the team's goals. This environment will eventually allow your team to accomplish extraordinary goals both individually and collectively.

Most of us have heard the analogy about the importance of getting the right people on the bus. I like to use an airplane analogy. You need to get everyone on the plane in the right seats in order to soar high above the clouds and reach your destination. The captain of an airliner has a co-pilot, a flight crew, and passengers. The leader needs to put everyone in the right role and in the right seat. By doing so, everyone on the plane knows that the leader cares about them because they're all in it together. Everyone's on the same plane, headed for the same destination, in a healthy environment, and every person is a reflection of the same superior standard of excellence.

Sylvia Luke

As Lieutenant Governor for the state of Hawai'i, I get invited to many events. I always enjoy meeting members of the community, whether to celebrate, commemorate, engage, or learn. One event I attended had a fantastic emcee. He was personable and charismatic and could connect with the audience in such an intimate way. He commented that someday, he'll be replaced by artificial intelligence, or what we commonly refer to as "AI." The AI revolution is just beginning, and while there are many pros, I started to think about the nuances we'll miss when AI becomes the norm . . . possibly even for leaders.

No matter how advanced artificial intelligence becomes, AI will never be able to capture the one-of-a-kind mixture of emotions, past experiences, level of reflection, and lessons learned that make us who we are. AI couldn't capture the emcee's uniqueness or adapt to the audience the way he could. So, when I think about building the right environment for my team to thrive and succeed, it really boils down to creating a space that fosters individuality.

When I was elected Lieutenant Governor, I knew I wanted to tackle key policy areas to create great change for the state of

Hawai'i. Each person on my team brings their backgrounds, experiences, and strengths to work together toward a common goal. But this is only possible by creating a safe space for each person to be themselves, share their ideas, make mistakes, and grow. Someone who worked closely with me once said, "You're kind of like an individual magnifier. You find a way to bring out the best in others." The comment made me think of a quote by Helen Keller, "Alone we can do so little; together we can do so much."

In a safe space that embraces individuality, it's so much easier to encourage collaboration, break down silos, and achieve goals together. As a leader striving for excellence, I'm committed to building trust with my team and creating an environment that believes who you are is important to the work we do together. By embracing our differences and individuality with appreciation and humility, we become more empathetic team members making the way we approach our work extremely personal and meaningful, which leads to incredible results. In our case, we make a tremendous impact on the communities we serve. That's something AI cannot easily replicate as we strive to become superior leaders.

Sylvia Luke
Lieutenant Governor, State of Hawaii

GIVE EVERYONE A ROLE

Personal growth leads to team growth. Do your job and accomplish the things you're responsible for doing. Everyone plays a crucial role in achieving the team's success. Every person wants and needs to feel valued and appreciated. It's the leader's responsibility to make everyone on the team feel important. In order for team members to feel important and part of the team, the leader must clearly identify each person's role and how he or she can contribute toward making the team better. We have twelve players on the boys' varsity tennis team, and I want the twelfth player to feel just as important to the team as my number one player. For example, I tell the team that when we compete in the state championship, every match we win counts as one point toward the team championship point total. That's regardless of whether you're playing singles or doubles and regardless of whether you're our number one singles player or part of our number four doubles team.

At the beginning of the season, I speak individually with each player. I ask them to tell me what they think their strengths and weaknesses are. Their responses often surprise me, and they give me good insights into what they think of themselves. After listening to each player's self-assessment, I then share my view of what he's good at and what needs improvement. I identify and focus on his strengths and explain that we need to keep practicing and building upon them—as well as working on some weaknesses. The players who made the team most likely did so because of their strengths.

One might have a strong forehand and serve. Another might have a good, solid all-court game. Yet another might have exceptional shot consistency and conditioning. Whatever the case, we need to identify it so the player knows what he's good at. This makes him feel good about himself, it creates a good learning environment for him, and he knows exactly how he can contribute to the team.

As head coach, I also have clearly defined roles for assistant coaches. The assistant coaches must share the same values and discipline as the head coach, which helps the cohesiveness of the team. The head coach might often exchange ideas with the assistant coaches, but the final decision always lies with the head coach. There will be difficult and challenging decisions to be made, but they must be made fairly and with integrity.

Tryouts, for example, must be handled fairly. Who will make the team? It's often easier in tennis because we have two players in a singles match—one who wins and one who loses. In golf, two players can play a round, and the one with the lower score wins. In swimming and track, the athletes race with a clear winner in each event. It can be more subjective in some sports like baseball, football, basketball, and volleyball, which makes it more challenging. Every year in our tennis team tryouts, it seems to come down to thirteen players competing to be on a twelve-man team. I put myself in their shoes. Rather than the coach deciding which player he likes better, I feel the fairest way is to play a sudden-death match. I know it's brutal, but it's fair. I know that if I were them, I wouldn't want the coach to make a judgment call on who makes the team. I would want to control my destiny and settle it on the tennis court.

The sudden death match has several benefits. First of all, the winner makes the team and earns instant respect from his teammates since none of them would want to be in that pressure situation. Second, the winner instantly gets tougher and enjoys a big boost of confidence, knowing that he rose to the occasion and earned his spot on the team. Third, everyone feels bad for the player who lost because anyone who plays sports knows how it feels to lose—especially when everyone is watching and keenly aware of the stakes. I always suggest that our team members go out of their way to give encouragement to the player who lost when they see him the next day on campus. Fourth, players who lose the sudden death match often use the experience as motivation to be better. They bounce back by working harder and smarter so they can make the team the following year and avoid the sudden death match again.

As head coach, I also have clearly defined roles for parents. Many parents want to help but need to be educated along the way because the experience is new for them and their son or daughter. The head coach needs to give them do's and don'ts. Once tryouts are completed, we have a meeting with all players and parents. We require at least one parent of every player to be present at this meeting, in which we go over the schedule and the upcoming season in general. This is when we define the parents' roles. Of course, we strongly encourage them to come and support the team at matches. Parents can also help provide food and drinks for the players after matches and can select a team parent to coordinate this. Parents are not coaches. Parents should not talk with coaches regarding lineups or playing times because they need to understand there's a good reason for everything we do. Parents should schedule medical or dental appointments around the practice and match schedule. Parents should give the head coach advance notice of any trips or conflicts that may affect practices or matches. If there are other concerns, parents should feel free to contact the head coach directly. By clearly defining their role, the coach is able to better concentrate on guiding the team.

THE BERNARD GUSMAN STORY

I first met Bernard Gusman the summer after I graduated from high school when I was asked to join the Junior Davis Cup training clinic at the Turtle Bay Resort on the North Shore of Oahu. The top five players in the state in the boys' and girls' 18s and 16s divisions had been invited to this weekend event, and they all showed up. It was the best tennis clinic I've ever attended. Bernard had us doing drills and games that were very challenging but also super fun. We were working together, pushing each other hard, and helping one another. It was very competitive and cooperative. Bernard created a great, comfortable environment for us. The tennis training was so good that we were all quite sad when the weekend came to an end.

In 1992, four months after I joined Punahou as a tennis pro, Bernard was appointed the school's Director of Tennis. I was super excited that he would be the program's new leader as he possessed so much knowledge of the sport. I couldn't help but reflect back on that memorable tennis clinic he had conducted more than four years earlier. Much of the current staff was nervous about the personnel changes; nobody knew who would be kept on or let go. I quickly saw that Bernard had a high standard of excellence and a great vision for developing the full potential of Punahou tennis. The school had eight courts, and we developed programs for players of every age and ability level, in addition to our intermediate, junior varsity, and varsity tennis teams for boys and girls. It was absolutely impressive. There were a lot of moving pieces, but Bernard found a way to make everything work perfectly. He even started a kindergarten tennis program where all one hundred fifty kindergarteners were introduced to tennis. Little did we know at that time how important this program would be. We developed many players who started taking tennis in kindergarten and went on to be state singles and doubles champions and achieve number one state rankings.

Consequently, Punahou School tennis became one of the best, most respected programs in the United States. Many coaches and leaders from the mainland and other countries would come to Punahou to talk with Bernard and observe how we did what we did. They wanted to see how they might improve and enhance their own programs. This was a huge compliment to Bernard, but he would be the first to give all the credit to every member of our tennis staff. He was the leader with the vision who provided the guidance, and we were the ones who executed it on the tennis court every day.

The environment that Bernard created for us was extremely positive, and I looked forward to coming to work every day. He set a high standard for himself and for all of us to live up to, and he understood everything we were going through. Because we were at a school instead of a country club, the main focus was on the well-being of the students. He also attracted and put together one of the best tennis staff for the care and training of the students. He introduced "pro training" twice a year so that every staff member could share his or her best drills and games with one another. This kept things fresh and encouraged cooperation among our staff. He knew that each of us was a reflection of the others, and he wanted us to be the best we could be. He encouraged and supported every staff member to earn various tennis certifications and professional development. This added to each staff member's personal growth and also helped our team grow in the overall Punahou tennis program. Bernard knew all of our strengths and weaknesses and put us in the right roles to best help the students. He did not micromanage. He delegated and had confidence in us to get the job done.

There were many occasions when Bernard would get us together for a barbecue at his home or to sing karaoke, for instance, which added to the cohesiveness and togetherness of our staff. We each felt that we were truly part of a team. It was special, and it was fun. We all did our part to contribute to making Punahou tennis one of the best programs in the country. Our opinions and feedback mattered to Bernard. He cared about us. He had empathy. He paid attention to detail. He mentored us, which in turn helped us mentor younger or newer staff members. He created a healthy environment for everyone. Students loved to hang out at the tennis court area to do homework and socialize with their friends. Parents enjoyed coming to pick up their sons and daughters and then staying longer to socialize with other families. It was amazing to see how impactful one person can be in creating such a positive atmosphere and affecting so many in a positive way.

Bernard retired in 2016. In his retirement speech, he gave credit to his many staff members who'd helped and contributed to the success of Punahou tennis over the years. Today, his legacy extends far beyond Punahou School to the many children and adults who enjoy playing tennis in Hawaii. For these reasons, Bernard was the best Director of Tennis in the state of Hawaii and one of the best in the United States. He was a great leader we respected—but more importantly, he became my friend.

⏺ BERNARD GUSMAN

Chapter 23

KEY NO. 6
FIND YOUR PASSION

"The two most important days in your life
are the day you were born and the day you find out why."

—Mark Twain

PASSION CAN BE DEFINED as *working hard for something you really love*. Great leaders have love and passion for what they do. It may be work, but it doesn't really feel like it because they simply love what they do and would probably do it for free. In turn, their team will feel this passion. Love and passion are necessary ingredients for inspiring and motivating team members. Inspiring others is the difference between a good leader and a great leader. Think about why you're in your current leadership position. Did you receive a company promotion that put you in a position to lead others? Were you an assistant coach who was promoted to head coach? Whatever the case, it is imperative that you have passion for what you're doing in order to help others.

If you don't feel the passion, then find something else you can be passionate about and go do that. A leader needs to love and care about people. A leader needs to love interacting with people. A leader needs to love building relationships with people. You have to love what you do and genuinely love helping others. Passion leads to pursuing excellence, and excellence leads to inspiring belief in others to achieve goals they once thought impossible.

CHASING PERFECTION, CATCHING EXCELLENCE

Great leaders have high standards and constantly strive for excellence. You often hear the word *excellence*, but what does that really mean? Simply put, excellence can be defined as *being the very best at something.* I believe that before you start striving for excellence, you must start with the right mindset and attitude. In fact, I regularly challenge my teams to have not just a good attitude but a superior attitude and a superior state of mind. There are many teams that have a good attitude and a good focus on what they're doing. I consistently remind my teams that we need to do our very best because if better is possible, then good is not enough. Striving for excellence is trying to be the very best you can be in every possible way, every single day. There's a difference between excellence and perfection. Perfection is unattainable, but if we chase perfection, we can catch excellence.

When you chase perfection, you tend to focus on paying attention to little details. These details are part of the process that helps you achieve the results you want. Such details must be attended to daily, whether you feel like it or not. We're all human, and there are two situations we face multiple times every day. I refer to these as the "Two Daily Dilemmas."

- Dilemma #1: The first dilemma is you know you should do something that you need to do, but just don't feel like doing it—Can you *make* yourself do it?
- Dilemma #2: The second dilemma is you know you shouldn't do something, but you really want to do it—Can you *keep* yourself from doing it?

This is something I train my players to do on a daily basis. There's a difference between a champion and a finalist, I tell them. It's the difference between first place and second place—between winning and losing. Winners do things that losers don't like doing because it takes sacrifice and commitment if you want to achieve anything significant. If something is important to you, you make your decisions accordingly because you have a burning desire to accomplish it. Champions become champions because they settle for nothing less. They have a clear vision of what it takes to get there, and they focus and trust the process and do the right things all the time—whether they feel like it or not. They don't allow for distractions. If you believe it will work out, you'll see opportunities. If you believe it won't, you'll see obstacles. They have tunnel vision, and although they understand there will be roadblocks along the way, they consistently make good choices in overcoming any obstacle they face. This is excellence. These actions will become habits and lead to peak performance, which gives your team opportunities to achieve greatness and sustain success.

However, there are times when perfection *can* be achieved. A student can obtain a perfect score on a standardized test such as the SAT by getting all answers correct, thereby scoring the maximum 1600. In bowling, a 900 series is three consecutive perfect games bowled by an individual. A 300 is a perfect score in one game, so a player's maximum score would be 900, which is the typical number of games in a single session. That would entail a player bowling thirty-six consecutive strikes. So far, thirty-nine individuals have accomplished this perfection in bowling. In baseball, a perfect game occurs when a pitcher faces the minimum number of batters (twenty-seven) during the entire game and doesn't allow any opposing player to reach first base. This means no hits, no walks, no hit-by-pitches, and no errors committed by the defense. So far, twenty-four pitchers have thrown perfect games.

MAKE PEOPLE BELIEVE

A great leader can make a good person great. She can make a great person greater. She can make an ordinary person extraordinary. And she can make an extraordinary person even more so. Successful leaders do this by inspiring belief in their team members. They want them to not only have dreams and goals but also the belief in themselves to strive to achieve them. Records are made to be broken. A record performance shows you what was possible for someone else to achieve because he believed he could do it. I like it when the bar is raised higher and higher, as it is in sports or business. This challenges others, including your competitors, to better themselves to keep up with your success. Remember that a high tide raises all boats.

The four-minute mile eluded champion runners for many years. John Landy, a highly exceptional athlete from Australia, ran the mile in 4:02 on seven different occasions. In January 1954, Landy said, "Frankly, I think the four-minute mile is beyond my capabilities. Two seconds may not sound much, but to me, it's like trying to break through a brick wall. Someone may achieve the four-minute mile the world is wanting so desperately, but I don't think I can."

On May 6, 1954, on a windy, rainy day at Oxford University, Roger Bannister broke the four-minute mile with a time of 3:59.4. Bannister, an athlete from the United Kingdom, was contemplating not running that day because of unfavorable weather conditions. But his coach believed in Bannister and said to him, "I think you can run a 3:56 mile. If you have a chance and don't take it, you may regret it for the rest of your life." Then, forty-six days later, John Landy broke the four-minute mile with a time of 3:58. Since then, the mile record has been lowered by almost seventeen seconds. Once Bannister did it, Landy began to believe that it could be accomplished. Belief in yourself is so powerful and inspiring to others that it can turn dreams into reality. It can turn the impossible into the possible. The impossible is what nobody can do until somebody does it. Think of the many other nearly impossible things we see in life that could very well become possible.

Boxer Muhammad Ali famously said, "I am the greatest. I said that even before I knew I was." As a leader, I know that belief can be extremely powerful, but so is doubt. You need to consistently inspire belief in your team members to focus on what they want to achieve and on what you want the team to achieve together. But they must know you really mean it. You, as the leader, must believe it too.

The legendary San Francisco 49ers quarterback Joe Montana said, "Winners imagine their dreams first. They want it with all their heart and expect it to come true. There's no other way to live."

His coach, Bill Walsh, said, "Joe Montana came to the San Francisco 49ers believing he was extraordinary. My job was to convince him that he was beyond extraordinary."

And then there's Robert Kraft, owner of the New England Patriots, recalling the first time he met quarterback Tom Brady, during Brady's second season in the National Football League. "He came down to training camp and introduced himself," Kraft said. "Here was this skinny beanpole with this pizza under his arm. He says, 'I'm Tom Brady.'"

"I know who you are," Kraft told Brady. "You're our sixth-round pick."

"I'm the best decision this organization has ever made," Brady responded.

"Normally, that kind of bravado would be a turn-off," Kraft later recalled. "I don't know how to explain it, but with him, it resonated."

Most of us are aware of how Nike's Phil Knight revolutionized the athletic footwear industry. Geoff Hollister was a small-town Oregon farm boy who was a runner at the University of Oregon for coach Bill Bowerman and later became Nike's third employee. Geoff provided further insight into the Nike saga in his book, *Out of Nowhere: The Inside Story of How Nike Marketed the Culture of Running.* "I have thought often of what it all means," he wrote. "Life thrusts you into a competitive environment. How do you prepare for the realities and the unknown? Hopefully, you have a mentor, a Bowerman, who pushes you at that critical time. A time when someone has a belief in your future more than you do. It's not about how long you live but how you contribute. It's about doing your best and doing the right things. It's about recovering from your mistakes and not giving up. It's about the baton pass to a new generation. It's about the realization that you cannot go it alone. It takes a team. In the end, you are somewhere in the middle, part of a never-ending process. The future will never remember what was in your bank account or what kind of car you drove. The future will remember that wild ride of life where you believed in others and left a gift behind for someone else to dream the impossible. The gift was your own life. It does not matter whether it was long or short. What did you leave behind?"

RELENTLESS PURSUIT OF SUCCESS

All great leaders and successful teams are driven to succeed. If you're merely interested in something, you'll do what's convenient. If you have a major commitment, you'll do whatever it takes to succeed. You must have a relentless drive to achieve both small goals and big ones. It's true that if something is important to you, you will find a way. If it's not, you will find an excuse. Elon Musk, owner and CEO of Tesla, said, "If other people are putting in 40-hour work weeks and you're putting in 120-hour work weeks, you will accomplish in four months what will take others one year to do." Many things in life aren't fair or equal, but everyone gets the same twenty-four hours a day, seven days a week. The grass is not always greener on the other side. It's greener where you water it. We make time for what we really want.

In order to have this relentless drive to succeed, you must be comfortable in uncomfortable situations. You must be able to tolerate challenging and often unfavorable circumstances. For example, if you and I are in a swimming pool, what happens if I challenge you to see who can hold his breath longer underwater? Now, I assume that you are competitive and want to win. So, you accept the challenge, and we both go under. After forty-five seconds or so, what do you do when you begin to feel uncomfortable? Obviously, you come up for air. Now, I might be feeling just as uncomfortable as you at that moment, but I really want to win. So, I'll stay underwater a little longer and tolerate it. If you really want to win at something, you often must tolerate the discomfort. Leaders and team members who are driven to succeed will be determined to put up with a little extra when dealing with uncomfortable situations.

In a presentation I saw by actor and filmmaker Denzel Washington, he said, "Don't just aspire to make a living. Aspire to make a difference. Anything you want, you can have. So, claim it. Work hard to get it. When you get it, reach back. Pull someone else up. Each one, teach one. Just because you're doing a lot more doesn't mean you're getting a lot more done. Don't confuse movement with progress. So have dreams, but have goals. Life goals. Yearly goals. Monthly goals. Daily goals.

And understand that to achieve these goals, you must apply discipline and consistency. In order to accomplish your goals, you must apply discipline and consistency every day. Not just on Tuesday and miss a few days. You have to work at it. Every day, you have to plan. You've heard the saying, 'We don't plan to fail; we fail to plan.' Hard work works. Working really hard is what successful people do."

THE IKAIKA JOBE STORY

I first met Ikaika Jobe when he was ten years old, and I began training him in our Rising Stars tennis program at Punahou. I immediately recognized that he was a talented athlete with a great passion for tennis. Ikaika loved the sport and loved to compete against his peers. His strengths were his footwork, strokes, understanding of the game, and instincts with his shots. His weakness was his attitude and lack of discipline. And by that, I mean he had a bad attitude and very little discipline, and it was clear to me that this would keep him from developing his full potential in tennis.

Far too often, when he lost points or games, he reacted by throwing his racket, slamming a tennis ball into the fence, or using unacceptable language. Yes, I know—he was violating my no racket, ball, or verbal abuse rule. I always looked forward to seeing and helping Ikaika in our group training, but I also needed to contain his actions. There were other nine, ten, and eleven-year-olds in the program, and I needed to do this quickly to help put him on the right path and also to maintain the respect and control of the others. So, I warned Ikaika in front of his peers that the next time he violated any one of the abuses, he would force me to give him a time-out. Not more than ten minutes later, he lost a game and slammed a ball into the back fence. True to my word, I announced, "Ikaika has given himself a time-out because of the abuse violation and will sit and watch in the shaded area and will not participate in the next two games." He was shocked. It appeared to me that I was the first coach to ever give him any real discipline or consequences for his actions. Keep in mind that Ikaika has a great passion for tennis, and it was killing him to have to sit and watch while the others continued having fun in our training. After fifteen minutes, I had him rejoin the group, and his attitude was much improved.

In fact, he was fine for the rest of our session. He had been embarrassed but also, I hoped, impacted in a positive way.

But in our next training session, the outbursts happened again, and so the fifteen-minute time-outs continued. I knew Ikaika was trying not to react inappropriately, but he just couldn't help himself. He had been this way for so long. I really liked that he was trying, but a violation is a violation, and he needed this type of discipline to help him in tennis and as a person. Slowly, he learned to control himself better until one training session when he was having a really bad day. He lost a game within the first ten minutes of training and threw his racket, nearly hitting another player.

"Ikaika, get out!" I yelled. "You can get off the court, close the gate, and watch the rest of our training from outside." He looked frightened, but I knew I needed to shake him up.

I continued to help Ikaika for two years in Rising Stars, and slowly, his self-discipline improved, which also greatly helped his tennis. Soon after, his father hired a private coach to train his son, and this coach convinced his father to discontinue training at Punahou and train only with him. I would see Ikaika at junior tournaments because many of my players were competing as well. Ikaika is an extremely likable person, and his tennis game was improving mainly because of his talent. But how much could he improve? Could he develop correctly and reach his full potential—physically, mentally, and emotionally? As I observed him in tournaments over the next few years, I noticed that the improvement we had made with his discipline was fading away.

Then, when he was in the ninth grade, Ikaika tried out for Punahou boys' varsity and made the team with no problem at all. It was as if he was yearning for the discipline he knew our team stressed, and he began absorbing everything like a sponge. Ikaika was a strong freshman player, and I knew he would make an impact at the state championship. I missed being able to help him in his development during the past few years, and I felt he had missed me, too. He really loved being on the varsity team and was a great team player. As a singles player, he finished number three in the state championship.

The following year, he won the state singles championship as a sophomore, but even more importantly, his attitude and discipline improved tremendously, which gave him better results with his tennis. Before tryouts during his junior year, his father requested a meeting with me. The meeting also included my assistant coach, Ikaika's new private coach, and Ikaika himself. It was clear to me that his father had Ikaika's best interest at heart and was trying to make the best decisions for his son. It was also clear that his new private coach had only a vague basic understanding of tennis yet was representing himself as someone with advanced intelligence in the sport. The problem was that

Ikaika's father believed everything he said—for example, that Ikaika was going to be the next Andre Agassi.

In our meeting, the private coach asked me if I'd allow him to observe Ikaika in our team practices. "Absolutely not," I told him. Now, I began to understand what this meeting was really about. Because Ikaika was going to be "the next Agassi," they were debating whether he should even be playing on our team. I asked Ikaika what he wanted, and he said he wanted to play varsity tennis. But apparently, his father and private coach had already decided that he would instead train for the professional tour. I could see the huge disappointment in his eyes because he knew how much varsity tennis helped him. He knew how much he needed us and loved playing on varsity with his friends.

Throughout that year, the private coach overtrained and overworked him, apparently without any understanding of the importance of rest and recovery. Needless to say, Ikaika was injured. It was a bad shoulder injury that kept him from making serves or overheads. Of course, this was a major setback, and soon after, his father terminated the arrangement with the private coach. But the damage had been done. Ikaika then asked me for private lessons during his senior year and told me he was returning to play varsity tennis. The problem was that he was broken—the shoulder injury was still an issue, and I was supposed to help put the pieces back together. So, we trained and practiced shots that he could make while avoiding others that caused him pain.

During the regular season, I let him play in matches only if he served underhand and didn't hit any overhead shots so that his shoulder could continue to heal. He agreed. Everyone expected Ikaika to win the state singles championship as a senior, especially because he had already won as a sophomore. But no one outside of our team really understood his true condition. For his part, Ikaika didn't expect to win state—he just wanted to be healthy and play tennis with no pain. I knew this was a good mindset for him because he wasn't putting pressure on himself to win (although everyone else was). I felt some pressure myself, as everyone knew I was training Ikaika privately. If he didn't win, some would undoubtedly lay the blame at my feet. But in fact, that would be fine with me; all I wanted was to focus and give my best to every player on my team.

Ikaika did play his way into the state singles championship final. By this time, he could serve with regular form again, although he couldn't serve hard or with much power. His serves were actually quite soft and would definitely favor the other finalist. During the first set, his opponent played very well and made Ikaika look like his punching bag. I fully understood what Ikaika was feeling and thinking. I could see he was letting all the pressure and high expectations get to him, and this was affecting his performance. He wasn't even hitting his forehand as he usually did. He lost the first set, and I walked onto the court during the coaching break.

"Ikaika, you look like a punching bag out there!" I said. "You need to start throwing your own punches. You have the best and biggest forehand in the state, but you haven't hit it once. If you're going down, if you're going to lose, then at least hit all the shots that you have in your arsenal. Hit all the shots we've practiced and hit that forehand as many times as possible."

Ikaika went out for the second set and did just as we'd discussed. He looked like a different person out there. He looked like a champion. He won the second set, and we talked again during the coaching break before the third and deciding set. I told him how proud I was of him. I told him I was most proud of his attitude and discipline, and I reminded him about the time I'd kicked him out of Rising Stars and made him watch the rest of the training from outside the gate. We both laughed. I told Ikaika to continue hitting and trusting his forehand, and I reminded him to attack the net when his opponent was on defense. Well, he went out there and did exactly that. (I do love it when my players actually listen and do the things we talk about!) Ikaika won that third set and earned his second state singles championship. He represented our team and our school with class. Everyone could see the passion that he had for tennis, and I was happy to have helped guide him in the right direction.

After graduating from high school in 2001, Ikaika played college tennis at Saint Louis University for three years and at Boise State University in his senior year. He went on to play professionally and achieved a world ranking that placed him in the top fifty in the country. I strongly believe that if Ikaika had continued training at Punahou instead of leaving after Rising Stars and had the right private coach to mentor him, he could have fully developed his potential and reached an even higher level—much higher. Instead, he was virtually undisciplined for four years before coming back under the Punahou umbrella for varsity and then suffered that serious injury during his junior year. Still, all things considered, Ikaika had a pretty good tennis career.

But the story isn't finished yet. He also went to law school, and while he was a practicing attorney, he served for three years as head coach for Punahou's girls' varsity tennis team. And when

I retired as head coach of the boys' varsity, I recommended Ikaika to succeed me. He has now held this position since 2016. (He tells me that he likes law, but he loves tennis!) Even better, Ikaika was also named Punahou School's Director of Tennis and left his law firm for this new and exciting challenge.

Building other great leaders is so very rewarding. I'm so proud to have helped develop and mentor Ikaika Jobe. I'm confident that he will do the same in sharing his passion for tennis with all the students and staff at Punahou and that he will ultimately build and mentor other future leaders.

IKAIKA JOBE

Chapter 24

KEY NO. 7
WELCOME ADVERSITY

"Life is not about waiting for the storm to pass.
It's about learning to dance in the rain."

—Vivian Greene

WE ALL EXPERIENCE STRESS and adversity in our lives. Let me predict the future for you right now. You will continue to experience stress and adversity in your life. Your team will experience these challenges, and so will your children. Of course, stress and adversity are inevitable. However, we shouldn't be trying to protect either our team or our children from such challenges. Instead, we should be teaching them how to face them. We need to have the right perspective in viewing adversity as a challenge to overcome rather than a problem to worry about. Life doesn't get easier. You need to get stronger. In order to be stronger, we need to know that when stress and tough situations happen, we're prepared to deal with them properly. A great leader expects the unexpected and teaches and prepares his or her team accordingly.

When you and your team experience adversity, you become stronger and tougher because you dealt with it and got through it. You were tested, and you're a better person for having gone through that test. Being fearful or trying to avoid adversity won't prepare you for when it inevitably happens. This is one of the reasons why some people crack and choke under pressure. They aren't prepared for the bad times and are hoping they won't happen to them. But inevitably, they will. The best leaders in sports and business have trained their teams to be prepared and to expect and even welcome these challenging situations. They can look forward to new challenges, knowing they'll be stronger for the experience.

BE RESILIENT

Did you know that Abraham Lincoln lost eight elections, failed twice in business ventures, and had a nervous breakdown before he became president of the United States? Each of us has lost at something and has failed at one time or another. We've all heard the saying that when you get knocked down, you need to get right back up. It's called resiliency, and all great teams have it. All great leaders have it. They are able to consistently bounce back from disappointment. This is why they succeed. There are always highs and lows in life, and you have the choice to get back up from every "low," from being knocked down, from losing, from being disappointed or you can choose to stay down. This choice is critical and completely in your control.

Defeat is a temporary condition. Giving up is what makes it permanent. Bruce Lee said, "Defeat is a state of mind. No one is ever defeated until defeat has been accepted as a reality." He also said, "Do not pray for an easy life. Pray for the strength to endure a difficult one."

Being resilient is a choice. It's easy to punch, but can you also take punches? In one of his Rocky movies, I liked hearing Sylvester Stallone say, "Life isn't about how hard you can hit, but how much you can get hit and still keep moving forward." Challenges are going to happen to you and your team. I guarantee it. You'll win some, and you'll lose some. One of my favorite quotes, which I like to use when my players get beaten in a match, is from Confucius, who said, "Our greatest glory is not in never falling, but in rising every time we fall."

Let me share Bethany Hamilton's story with you. Bethany was born in Kauai, showed a deep love of the ocean, and had a natural talent for surfing. At eight years old, she began competing in surf competitions. However, on October 31, 2003, tragedy struck when she was thirteen years old. Bethany was attacked by a fourteen-foot tiger shark while surfing off the coast of Kauai. The attack resulted in the loss of her left arm just below the shoulder. Despite the trauma and physical challenges she faced, Bethany's determination to continue surfing and living her life remained unwavering. Just twenty-six days after the attack, she was back in the water, learning to balance on her surfboard with just one arm. It was remarkable to see how she adapted to her new reality—having to relearn how to paddle, catch waves, and maintain her balance.

Bethany's resilience caught the media's and the public's attention, and her story began to inspire people worldwide. She was determined to pursue her passion for surfing professionally, and just two years after the attack, she won the National Scholastic Surfing Association (NSSA) National Championships in the Women's Open division. Bethany's story reached an even wider audience when her autobiography, *Soul Surfer: A True Story of Faith, Family, and Fighting to Get Back on the Board,* was published and later adapted into a feature film titled *Soul Surfer.* She subsequently became a motivational speaker, sharing her story of resilience with audiences around the world. Bethany also launched the Friends of Bethany Foundation, which supports shark attack survivors and amputees and advocates for youth empowerment. Her courage, determination, and positive outlook serve as a testament to the strength of the human spirit in the face of life-altering challenges.

Jon Mauer

Leading an organization is often very challenging, and it's imperative to have the mindset to welcome adversity. Our company started in 2016 as a business carved out from a top Fortune 15 corporation. We took on many of the same challenges that you would expect to find in any start-up organization. Because of various circumstances, team members were faced with difficult decisions that were necessary for our company to survive. However, overcoming these difficult situations began to strengthen our organization's "muscles" and mental toughness.

I believe open communication and transparency are key skills for successful leaders. Of course, there are situations where circumstances dictate high confidentiality and utmost discretion, but those situations are relatively rare. I believe that when you can openly share the situation and adversities you are facing, it becomes much healthier for your team. Every team member wants to be informed and engaged so they can be a part of the efforts and solutions to help the business. Over time, our organization began to accept the challenges, gain more confidence, and resolve that we could overcome difficult situations. And then came COVID!

Like nearly all organizations, we were forced to take immediate and aggressive actions to preserve the financial capacity of the business. Our organization was quick to respond in a proactive manner despite losing over sixty percent of our sales revenues in the initial months of COVID. Working through those adversities and challenges only prepared our organization for what would be an even more difficult period the following year, with extreme volatility in the commodity markets that further stressed the financial capacity of our company. Our team readily took on these challenges, making adjustments to our business plans and strategies. Our organization became much stronger and more resilient as an outcome of those adversities. Moreover, our organizational attitude and mindset of welcoming adversity and overcoming tough challenges have helped us with business growth opportunities. Our organization is now successfully executing a very challenging and transformative project under an extremely aggressive schedule. I am confident that dealing with our prior adversities has prepared our company to take on this project and future challenges ahead.

Jon Mauer
President & CEO, Island Energy Services, LLC

PERFORM UNDER PRESSURE

Stress and adversity definitely build character. They are also a test of character. We shouldn't protect our team members from challenging and uncomfortable situations. We need to teach them how to deal with them and explain why that's important. It's how you respond with resiliency that makes all the difference. How you respond impacts everyone around you. I love watching players and teams in competition when their backs are up against the wall; seeing how they respond truly reveals their character. I like watching a team that's a huge underdog compete and rise to the occasion. I like watching a team that's heavily favored and under major pressure to win and witnessing their great attitude, poise, and discipline shine through, regardless of the score or whatever struggle they're dealing with.

The 2017 Super Bowl was a great example of this. The Atlanta Falcons were way ahead of the New England Patriots by a score of 28–3. But then millions of people witnessed an unprecedented comeback by Tom Brady and his teammates that resulted in a 34–28 overtime victory. What I found most impressive when the Patriots were losing was that they never appeared to turn against one another. Nobody placed any blame on anyone else because of the hole they found themselves in. Not one Patriot player looked negative or dejected. They just kept competing, one play at a time. If you have discipline, that's all you can do, and that's what you expect from your teammates as well. Head coach Bill Belichick, as their leader, has instilled this discipline in his team. They can handle adversity. In fact, it challenges them. It brings out the very best in them. They seem to expect it and thrive on it. This is what champions do.

Every person experiences setbacks, disappointments, and losses. Team members need to view these situations as opportunities to better themselves rather than feeling frustrated and discouraged. Frustration is the easy response. It's what average people do. Champions don't do this. Champions know they have a choice in how they respond to adversity. It's all about having the right perspective. You need to remember that stress and adversity are like a rainstorm. The skies might be dark and gloomy, and it might rain buckets today and tomorrow, but it won't rain every day for the rest of your life. The sun will eventually come out again, and you'll see blue skies. Champions always have the right perspective to motivate themselves to be better for the next challenge. It's an opportunity for them to make themselves stronger and tougher, which not only helps them in sports but also prepares them for life's greater challenges.

EXCITED VS. NERVOUS

In sports, every athlete experiences pressure during competition. Some athletes thrive on pressure, and others don't. But pressure in competition is inevitable, and coaches must prepare their players for it. There are basically two responses to pressure. One is when players allow fear to consume them, become overly nervous, and choke. The other is what we will focus on. I make my players understand they should be excited when they feel pressure because it means they're doing something significant. They're doing something special. They have a real opportunity in front of them. A coach must train players to have the correct perspective on pressure. When players are asked how they feel before a competition, they often reply that they're nervous.

But the coach must convince them that they're excited, not nervous. Feeling excited is clearly the better response. They must look at it as a challenge to overcome rather than a problem to worry about. Pressure can be a test of your players' toughness, an excellent indicator of where they stand in their overall development. The more pressure situations they experience, the tougher and stronger they become. It ultimately becomes a test of their character. Many coaches build physical skills in their athletes, but they also need to build internal mental skills. In order to win a championship or consecutive championships, players need to have mental toughness—a positive perspective in dealing with, and even looking forward to, pressure.

And then there's stress. Stress is a good thing. It helps you grow to be a stronger person. Great leaders train their teams to get comfortable in uncomfortable situations. I coach my players by identifying two types of stress: necessary and unnecessary. Necessary stress is fine; unnecessary stress is not. This is very simple for me to explain, and it's very important to keep things as simple as possible when communicating with your players. Players who worry about things they cannot control experience unnecessary stress. At the middle or high school level, they might be worried about an upcoming math test while they're in the middle of soccer practice. During a basketball game, they might be preoccupied with a science project that's due in two days. Nevertheless, they need to focus on the task at hand and not worry about something that they can't do anything about at that moment.

Necessary stress involves dealing with situations that players can control. An athlete might have a deadline for submitting college applications, and the stress might be related to their time management. Another athlete might experience stress in studying for multiple final exams. These stressful situations are necessary, and we've all experienced them. As coaches, we need to ensure that our players focus only on things they can control. Otherwise, they can become mentally and physically fatigued, stressing out unnecessarily over things they can't control.

THE WILL GROSSWENDT STORY

The fact is, most athletes do put pressure on themselves unnecessarily. A player's view of a pressure situation can often be magnified, which leads to performance below capability. In 2005, a senior named Will Grosswendt played third doubles on my team. He was a talented athlete and a good tennis player. He had delightful parents and was a very nice boy himself. As we finished our regular season and our qualifying tournament for the state championship, I received a phone call from Will's mom. She informed me that Will was feeling so much pressure to win that he was underperforming in matches, even though he and his partner Andrew Mau had qualified to participate in the state tournament. It was true. Will looked great in practice and even in practice matches. But when he played in the qualifying tournament, he seemed really shaky and uncertain with his shots. His play was inconsistent. Will's mom believed he felt so much pressure to win because of our long championship streak and that he didn't want to let his teammates or me down. I told her I'd talk with him privately.

The next day, as I prepared the courts for practice, Will arrived with his rackets in hand. I took him aside and said, "I got a phone call from your mom, Will. She says you're feeling lots of pressure, and it's affecting your performance in the matches."

"I feel tons of pressure to win, Coach," he replied, "so much pressure. My shoulders feel tight all the time, and I don't play nearly as good in matches as I do in practice."

"But why is that?" I asked. "The only player who should feel that kind of pressure is a number one ranked player or a defending singles or doubles champion. Are you ranked number one in the state? Are you the defending state singles champion? Or the defending state doubles champion?"

"No," he said.

"So you really shouldn't feel any pressure," I pointed out, "because you really haven't achieved anything significant yet!"

He thought about that for a moment and then said, "Coach, you're right!"

For some reason, I began bouncing up and down and said, "You don't have any pressure because you haven't done anything yet!"

Will responded, bouncing up and down in unison, saying, "Coach, I don't have any pressure. I haven't done anything yet!" We repeated this back and forth to each other five times while still bouncing up and down. (People watching us must have thought we were nuts!). I could almost see the tightness in his shoulders melt away and his head become clearer. Now, he could relax and play tennis with the correct mindset he needed to win matches rather than obsessing about what he had to lose. He now understood that he had nothing to lose and everything to gain.

When the state championship doubles tournament began a week later, I could see from the first match that Will had something to prove to himself. He was having fun, finally playing up to the potential he had shown in practice. After winning their first two matches, he and his partner competed in the quarterfinals against their teammates, a pair that was our number-one doubles team and also the number-one seed in the tournament. When our team members play each other in a tournament, I don't coach either team during the match. It's the fairest way to do it. Instead, I give all four players feedback when the match is over. It avoids misperceptions and keeps things clean.

Will and his partner Andrew had a focus and a drive that was getting stronger with every set they played. They defeated their teammates and found themselves in the semifinals, which they dominated. Their consistency and confidence continued to grow, and they soon found themselves on stadium court playing for the state doubles championship. Win or lose, I felt so proud of Will. He had exhibited good character from the first time I met him, and he continued to develop this character throughout high school. Our team's discipline and pursuit of excellence helped Will flourish even more as an individual. He was a great guy who was representing his school, team, and family at the highest level. And now he was unlocking his true potential in tennis with an opportunity to earn a state doubles title.

There was no denying him that day. He and Andrew won the match, and Will finished his senior year and his high school tennis career as a state doubles champion. He had definitely overcome the odds—as a freshman, he had barely made the junior varsity team and was ranked last on the JV roster. Then he went from being a varsity senior playing third doubles in the regular season to winning the state championship. Pressure can clearly play some weird tricks on people's minds. Accordingly, we must consistently help our team members *welcome* necessary pressure, viewing it as a challenge to overcome and making sure they don't put unnecessary stress upon themselves.

Chapter 25

KEY NO. 8
REAL WINNING
OCCURS WITHIN

"You never really play an opponent.
You are playing yourself and your own highest standards."

—Arthur Ashe

WHAT DOES SUCCESS REALLY MEAN? When does someone become successful? What is success versus winning? Is there a difference between losing and getting beaten? These are all important questions. Every great leader needs to have his team strive for real winning and real success. A great example of "real" winning is when my team keeps playing as hard as they can, even when they realize they might lose the match. This shows the character of the individuals and the team collectively.

Another example is always exhibiting a superior attitude and giving superior effort, even when you might be feeling less than one hundred percent. Sometimes, you may not be feeling your best because of a sickness, sore muscles, or a minor injury, but you might still be in a competition. If you truly give it your best, you will not feel regret if you get beat. The key is representing yourself with the highest level of class all the time—regardless of the circumstances.

LITTLE VICTORIES LEAD TO BIG VICTORIES

It's crucial to strive for little victories. Small wins lead to big successes. The little things matter. As an example, one little change that can make a huge difference is attitude—positive or negative. A bad attitude is like a flat tire. You can't go anywhere until you change it. The same thing applies to your mood. A bad mood is a reflection of your attitude. Change your attitude, and you'll change your mood.

You, as the leader, should give hope to your team. In tennis, some players only see the clouds and stormy skies of a match. Champions always see the sun peeking through. Getting through this match and focusing on the positives might give your team a little victory that could very well lead to a bigger one. Having hope and envisioning what might be possible is a powerful thing. Martin Luther King Jr. said, "If I cannot do great things, I can do small things in a great way."

Getting through a little challenge can help your team deal with bigger challenges later. Make your team understand that one small crack doesn't mean that you are broken. It just means you were put to the test and didn't fall apart. Life doesn't get easier. You just get stronger. Never be ashamed of the scars that life inflicts. A scar means the hurt is over, the wound is closed, you endured the pain, and you've moved on as a stronger person.

How can you have a little victory if you don't try? Don't worry about failure. Worry about the chances and opportunities you miss when you don't try. Tony Robbins said, "No matter how many mistakes you make or how slow you progress, you're still way ahead of everyone who isn't trying." Great leaders encourage their teams to strive for goals beyond their reach. They want them to try for things the team originally thought were impossible. No matter what level your team may be, always encourage them to strive for those little victories.

LOSING VS. GETTING BEATEN

There's an enormous difference between losing and getting beaten. Losing is what happens when you have a poor attitude or give poor effort that leads to a loss. Getting beaten is when you have a great attitude and give a great effort but still come out on the short end just because your opponent was better that day. There have been times when my tennis players won their matches with a poor attitude and maybe a seventy percent effort that was just enough to win. Needless to say, this is when I would gather them together for some honest communication. I would share with the team how disappointed and embarrassed I was watching their performance. That singles player or doubles pair was representing our team, our school, me, and their parents, and they should have exhibited their best attitude and their best effort. It's not a switch that you turn on and off. If anything, the switch should be on all the time. It's about giving your best from the first point until match point. It's about competing and playing with class all the time.

There have been many times when a player on my team had a great attitude and gave it everything and still got beaten. Again, I'd gather the team together for a talk. I'd share with them how proud I was watching that player's performance and how he represented our team, our school, myself, and his parents in the best possible way—with ultimate class. One benefit of these little post-match talks was that my team really understood what I was about and what we should be striving for. It definitely wasn't about winning. It was how we competed. It was about our attitude and effort. It was about having good character and giving our best. It was about having fun and enjoying the experience. This is real winning.

Most, if not all, of my players told me in one way or another that they appreciated my effort and dedication as their coach. Some of our athletes may have taken the things we did for granted because they hadn't previously had team experiences with any other coaches. But many of my players who went on to play college tennis expected their new coaches to be equal, if not better. The fact is, I believe the majority of them were extremely frustrated with their college tennis experiences because their new coaches were nowhere close to the standards they expected. Maybe the new coach didn't care as much, didn't have enough expertise, or simply treated his players unfairly.

This is when our players recognize and truly appreciate the priceless experience they had in high school varsity tennis. And this is when I received phone calls from many of them, thanking me for teaching them important life lessons while they were learning to play better tennis. I love when those players tell me how valuable and enjoyable their experience was, years and even decades after they graduated. I continue to have regular reunions with many of my alumni players, who reminisce about what they believe to be priceless experiences.

THE BRANDON LEE STORY

A ninth-grader named Brandon Lee signed up for tryouts with my team. Ultimately, Brandon would become one of our best stories because he exemplified what I believe real winning and real success are, which in turn reinforced our whole team's superior standard of excellence.

Before tryouts began, I kept hearing about Brandon's attitude and behavior in tournaments from numerous players and parents, which was the opposite of what our team was striving for. They all said that he was a very talented tennis player, but his attitude and behavior were very bad. So they were very curious about whether Brandon would actually make the team. I told all of them that I hadn't seen Brandon play and that I wouldn't prejudge anyone. He would go through tryouts like every other player, and I would observe him the same as anyone else.

In fact, I was very impressed with Brandon because he was so talented and because his attitude and behavior in tryouts were so good. Brandon made the team as a freshman. I believed he could help our team best that year by playing doubles, and he had a very good regular season. I saw no signs of any bad behavior during the season, and it appeared that Brandon really enjoyed being part of a team—rather than playing individually as he had before.

In our postseason qualifying tournament, Brandon and his partner William Chen were up against a very good doubles team from Iolani School, competing for third and fourth place. The match was very exciting because all four players competed well, and it went to a third-set tiebreaker. The tiebreaker was also very thrilling, but the other team beat us. After losing match point, Brandon walked toward the net to shake hands with his opponents. On his way to the net, he threw his racket to the side of the court near his tennis bag. It wasn't a hard, angry throw, but it was a throw nonetheless. As he and his partner exited the court in obvious disappointment, I took Brandon aside. I told him I was very proud of how he competed during the match, but throwing his racket was unacceptable. It was his only flaw, but it violated our team rules. He acknowledged this and did his one hundred push-ups right there on the walkway, just outside of the tennis court, in front of all the spectators and competitors. Some of these onlookers thought Brandon was doing push-ups because he'd lost the match! I set them straight. It was the first time I saw him exhibit behavior that was unacceptable, and it needed to be addressed immediately.

When the season was over, Brandon continued to play for his personal ranking. But I saw a different Brandon in these tournaments, exhibiting behavior that included racket, ball, and verbal abuse, visible frustrations, and strong negativity. It wasn't a pleasant sight, and it definitely didn't help him compete to the best of his ability. I began working with him in private and group tennis lessons, challenging him to only do things that would help him win. Once we identified and isolated the counterproductive behavior, he truly began to realize how high my standards were for him and for our team. Brandon began to understand that he needed to control his hands and mouth in order to control his thoughts and his destiny in tennis matches. Because he'd had a serious lack of discipline in his training prior to joining our team, I told him that it would be a process that would take time and lots of consistent reinforcement. I warned him that we would have some flare-ups along the way. But this was the only way he could change those bad habits into good ones and truly unlock his athletic potential in tennis and add to his fun and fulfillment when competing. Brandon worked really hard and was committed to achieving this high standard for himself during his high school career.

Brandon was team captain—a senior playing singles and seeded number one at the state singles championship tournament. Seeded second was an extremely talented eleventh grader from Kamehameha Schools whom Brandon had beaten twice during the season. Now, they found each other on opposite ends of the tennis court again, this time playing for the state singles title. Brandon was well-prepared and confident going into the match, which took place in front of a huge crowd of spectators, many of whom hadn't seen Brandon play in years.

Brandon executed his shots and strategy very well and won the first set. I coached him during the two-minute break between sets. I told him he needed to continue to execute this strategy but also to realize that his opponent was a great competitor and was definitely going to raise his level of play in the next set. He needed to do the same. During the second set, they each won many grueling points, and the level of play was very high. His opponent took that set with incredible shot-making skills to force a third and deciding set.

As Brandon and I reviewed our match strategy during the set break, I told him how proud I was of him and that he should be very proud of himself as well.

"Now, isn't this fun?" I asked.

He agreed and was excited to play the final set of his high school career. In the third set, both players exhibited brilliant play and extreme toughness, and spectators told me they hardly recognized Brandon—his attitude and behavior were exceptional, a truly remarkable turnaround from the way they remembered him. Both players exhibited respect for the game and each other, which was evident in the match. They both wanted badly to win, but Brandon was beaten, 7–5. As he walked toward the net to shake hands, I had that scary vision of Brandon throwing his racket at his bag as a freshman. I watched him closely as he shook hands, hugged, and congratulated his opponent. I breathed a huge sigh of relief. Then Brandon walked to his tennis bag, sat down, and began to cry. His teammates entered the court, congratulated the winner, and then sat next to Brandon, watching their captain and not knowing what to say to him. I congratulated his opponent myself, walked over to Brandon, and put my hand on his shoulder, crying myself.

"Coach," Brandon said, "I'm so sorry I let you down."

"Brandon, you didn't let me down in any way," I told him. "In fact, I'm prouder of you right now than ever because you represented me, the team, and our school with such class. We win a lot, but to get beat in that situation, under that kind of adversity, and to demonstrate the character you did—that speaks louder than any victory. This is what our team is all about."

Then, I took a walk around the tennis complex, reflecting on Brandon's high school career. I felt so fulfilled that we were able to help him go from the bad end of the spectrum during his freshman year to the good end as he neared graduation. It was also clear to me that if Brandon had better discipline when he was younger, rather than working on it for the first time in high school, he would have been playing at a much higher level now. But better late than never.

I received so many compliments from spectators who watched that championship final about the way Brandon represented himself and our team. What's more, he set a great example in leadership for our younger players, who saw firsthand the importance of attitude and behavior, especially in defeat. Seeing Brandon's character in action is something his teammates could strive for. And that would influence not only how they performed on the court but, more importantly, how they represented themselves, their team, their school, and their families. This is real winning. This is real success.

SUCCESS TO SIGNIFICANCE

Success can only be measured after a long period of time. You don't achieve success tomorrow or next week. It's not a short-term thing. It takes time to know whether or not you were truly successful. You might "win" by gaining a new client, making a sale, or winning a game, but does this one victory make you successful? The answer is no. Achieving success is done day by day. You need to better yourself every day. You need to learn something every day. After all, you don't go to the gym and work out for ten hours in one day to get in shape. You get in shape and improve your fitness by working on it every day. It's something you need to do consistently.

A river cuts through rock not because of its power but because of its persistence. Champions do things every day to make sure they are moving in the right direction. Franklin D. Roosevelt said, "There are many ways of going forward, but only one way of standing still." Hoping and praying for victory is fine, but deserving it is what really matters. Great leaders and great teams persevere and eventually achieve success. A great leader never says she'll do it tomorrow because she knows that tomorrow she'll wish she'd started it today. Babe Ruth said, "It's hard to beat someone who never gives up." Persistence becomes a habit and part of your identity if you have a burning desire for success.

Once you attain success, I want to inspire you to achieve *significance*. Going from success to significance often involves a shift in focus and priorities. While success is usually associated with personal achievements and reaching individual goals, significance is about making a lasting and meaningful impact on others and the world around you. Let me share with you some ideas that can help you transition from success to significance.

First, consider what you are truly passionate about by reflecting on your core values and issues that matter most to you. Second, determine your purpose beyond personal success. Think about how you can use your talents, skills, and resources to make a positive difference in the lives of others or to address a specific challenge. Third, cultivate a servant leadership mindset by embracing service and humility by focusing on how you can contribute to the well-being and success of others. The following are some examples of people who achieved significance.

Malala Yousafzai is a Pakistani activist who gained global recognition for her advocacy of girls' education because the Taliban began banning television, music, girls' education, and women from going shopping. She was born in Swat Valley in Pakistan, and when the Islamic Taliban took control of the valley, they burned down all the girls' schools. Malala recorded the events in her diary where she spoke out against the Taliban's terrorist regime, and an American documentary film made her globally famous.

At the age of fifteen, a Taliban gunman found Yousafzai and her friends as she was on a bus going home. The masked gunman shouted, "Which one of you is Malala? Speak up! Otherwise, I will shoot you all!" When she was identified, Malala was shot with one bullet, which traveled eighteen inches from the side of her left eye, through her neck, and landed in her shoulder. After being airlifted to a military hospital, the doctors performed a five-hour operation and successfully removed the bullet.

She survived the assassination attempt by the Taliban and continued speaking out about the importance of education for girls. On her sixteenth birthday, Malala spoke at the United Nations, calling for girls all over the world to have equal rights to education. Since then, she has become a symbol of courage and resilience, continuing her activism and fighting for girl's rights. She became the youngest Nobel Peace Prize laureate because of her fight for the right of every child to receive an education. Malala went on to graduate from Oxford University, and her inspiring story and ongoing efforts have shed light on the challenges faced by millions of girls and have motivated change on a global scale.

In 2013, *TIME* magazine named her one of "The 100 Most Influential People in the World." When you align your actions with your purpose by prioritizing the well-being of others, you can achieve significance and create a lasting legacy.

Billie Jean King is one of the greatest tennis players of all time, winning a total of thirty-nine Grand Slam titles. Although she is renowned for her exceptional achievements on the tennis court, King seamlessly transitioned from a life of personal success to one of profound significance. In 1972, she won the women's singles championship at the U.S. Open and received $15,000 less than the winner of the men's singles. Recognizing the glaring disparity in prize money between male and female athletes, she boldly fought for equal pay. This eventually led to the establishment of equal prize money in major tennis tournaments and became a watershed moment that catalyzed progress far beyond the sports world.

In 1973, she faced off against Bobby Riggs in the legendary "Battle of the Sexes" tennis match (watched by over ninety million people), which became a pivotal moment, not just in sports history but in the larger fight for gender parity. King's victory in that match symbolized a triumph of skill and determination over gender stereotypes, sparking a global conversation about women's rights and reshaping societal perceptions of women in sports. Her relentless pursuit of justice transcended tennis, inspiring individuals from all walks of life to challenge systemic inequalities. King also founded the Women's Tennis Association (WTA) on the principle of equal opportunity, which is the global leader in women's professional sports. The WTA currently consists of more than 1,650 players representing approximately eighty-five nations.

Billie Jean King's journey from athletic excellence to profound significance is a testament to the transformative power of using one's platform for the greater good. Her pioneering spirit and resolute dedication to gender equality and social change solidified her legacy as a true icon.

Another legendary tennis professional is the great Arthur Ashe, who won the 1968 U.S. Open, the 1970 Australian Open, and the 1975 Wimbledon Championships. Ashe was the first black man to win a Grand Slam singles title, which was a significant milestone in the history of tennis and sports in general. His success helped break down racial barriers and paved the way for more diversity and inclusivity in tennis. Ashe's victories on the court not only established him as one of the greatest tennis players of his time but also inspired countless aspiring athletes, particularly those from underrepresented communities, to pursue their dreams with determination and resilience. Ashe was known for his exceptional character and sportsmanship on and off the tennis court and was a role model who emphasized the importance of fair play, integrity, and humility in sports.

Because of his popularity and success in tennis, Ashe used his platform to advocate for civil rights, social justice, and equality. He fearlessly spoke out against racial discrimination and apartheid in South Africa. Ashe's efforts were instrumental in raising awareness and funds for these causes, demonstrating that athletes could be agents of change to make a profound impact on society. He also authored several books, including his memoir *Days of Grace*, in which he shared his life experiences and insights on sports, race, and society.

In 1988, Arthur Ashe was diagnosed with HIV/AIDS, which he likely contracted from a blood transfusion during heart surgery, during a time when there was limited understanding and rampant stigma surrounding the disease. Instead of retreating from the public eye, Ashe chose to become an advocate for AIDS awareness and education. His openness about his condition helped break down misconceptions and foster compassion, demonstrating his remarkable strength of character to make a positive difference in the world. The Arthur Ashe Courage Award, presented annually at the ESPY Awards, recognizes individuals who embody the spirit of Ashe by showing courage in the face of adversity. His legacy continues to inspire generations of people to strive for excellence, and his impact on the world of tennis and beyond is a testament to his enduring significance.

Section 5: The 8 Keys for Sustaining Success

Congratulations on completing all five sections! Again, please take ten minutes to honestly rank yourself and answer the questions to identify important action items that will help you with your journey to becoming a superior leader.

Rate your skill level at building character traits for your team members.

Elite teams have impeccable character traits. What can you specifically do to improve the character and identity of your team?

_____

_____

_____

How do you rate your ability to be self-disciplined?

Discipline leads to habits, and habits lead to success. What are some areas in your life where you need to be more disciplined?

_____

_____

_____

Accountability is everything. How would you rate your willingness to be held accountable?

Who can you identify to hold you accountable to achieve superior excellence? Aim high!

_____

_____

_____

Rate your ability to learn positive lessons from challenging experiences.

What is the most challenging experience you have faced recently, and what is your positive takeaway from it?

_____

_____

_____

How would you rate your ability to set aside issues that are beyond your control?

What are examples of situations that you have complete control of?

_____

_____

_____

How would you rate your current level of passion?

What are some examples of the Two Daily Dilemmas you face every day?

_____

_____

_____

How do you rate your ability to have the right mindset to welcome adversity?

What are the biggest adversities you are facing this quarter, and how can you improve your mindset toward them?

_____

_____

_____

Rate your skill level at inspiring hope in your team members.

What are various ways you can inspire hope in your team in unfavorable situations?

_____

_____

_____

How would you rate your ability to make high-integrity decisions for your team?

How do you define "success" for you at this moment in time?

_____

_____

_____

How would you rate your ability to transcend your current circumstances to significance?

What does "real winning" mean to you over the next twelve months?

_____

_____

_____

Which members of your team would benefit most from this playbook on superior excellence?

_____

_____

_____

Add up your total score for this assessment and enter your score here.

ABOUT THE AUTHOR

Rusty Komori was the Head Coach of the Punahou School Boys' Varsity Tennis Team for twenty-two years, winning twenty-two consecutive State Championships. He is a highly sought after inspirational Keynote Speaker, Executive Coach, and tennis professional based in Honolulu, Hawaii. Rusty was inducted into Creighton University's Hall of Fame in 2014.

www.rustykomori.com

Be Superior!